CRIME, CORRUPTION AND DEVELOPMENT

CRIME, CORRUPTION AND DEVELOPMENT

Edited by
D. NARASIMHA REDDY

DEEP & DEEP PUBLICATIONS PVT. LTD.
F-159, Rajouri Garden, New Delhi - 110 027

ISBN 81-7629-345-8

Typeset by THE COMPOSERS, 20/5, West Patel Nagar, Delhi - 110 064

Printed in India at ELEGANT PRINTERS,
A 38/2, Phase-I, Mayapuri, New Delhi - 110 064

Published by DEEP & DEEP PUBLICATIONS PVT. LTD.,
F-159, Rajouri Garden, New Delhi-110 027.
Phones : 5435369, 5440916

Contents

Foreword vii
Preface ix
Introduction x
List of Contributors xxi

1. *N.N. Vohra*
   Crime, Corruption and Development 1
2. *S. Iyyam Pillai*
   Socio-Economic and Political Dimensions of Corruption 12
3. *T. Lakshmanasamy*
   Economics of Corruption and Development 24
4. *Debes Mukherjee*
   Crime, Corruption and Development 35
5. *I.D. Gupta*
   Crime, Corruption and Development in Indian Economy 47
6. *Inderjeet Singh, Harvinder Kaur and Pramod Kumar*
   Socio-Economic Dynamics of Crime in India 63
7. *Ram Naresh Thakur*
   Crime and Corruption— Obstacles to Development 74
8. *S.C. Sharma, Shyam Sunder Singh Chauhan and Binay Kumar Singh*
   The Interface of Corruption and Development in the Third World 82
9. *Anil Kumar Jain*
   Tax Evasion and Corruption: The Indian Perspective 98

10. *Amita Kumari Choudhury and Nirmal Chandra Sahoo*
Economic Implications of Environmental Crimes 107

11. *N.B. Pradhan, B. Patro and S.K. Panigrahy*
Economic Analysis of Crime and Punishment 124

12. *Satya Pal Singh*
Economic Crimes: Key Issues 137

13. *Dipankar Sen and Sandip Mitra*
Socio-Economic Aspects of Organised Crime: A Case Study of Illegal Coal-Mining 155

14. *Santanu Ghosh*
Micro Theoretic Issues in Generation of Crime, with Reference to Mafia as an Oligopolistic Firm 166

15. *M. Zainul Abedin*
Corruption and Development: Bangladesh Perspective 190

16. *Pramod Kumar*
Globalisation of Economy and Conflicts in South Asia 200

17. *Gulab Mohite and S.P. Malapur*
Genesis of Crime and Corruption and their Impact on Development 212

18. *N.C. Ghosh*
Industrialisation, Environmental Pollution, Crime and Corruption: A Case Study 220

Appendix: Annoted Bibliography 230

Index 263

Foreword

The Indian Economic Association is a premier association having on it rolls the largest number of economists in any professional association. Over the years, the Association has extended its membership to economists working in colleges and universities in all parts of India. It is indeed a matter of great pride that several hundred scholars all over India responded to the invitation from the Association to contribute papers on selected themes for discussion in the ensuing Annual Conference of the Indian Economic Association.

But the receipt of a very large number of papers for each selected theme also poses its own problems. Since the Conference Volume of the Association can hardly accommodate more than 5-7 articles for a particular theme, many well researched articles fail to find a place in the Volume.

Keeping this in mind the Association under the leadership of the then presidents Dr. G.S. Monga and Prof. A.K. Sinha, initiated a scheme of bringing out separate books for each theme, containing 15 to 20 papers contributed by the members along with an editorial by the respective Editor(s). Besides accommodating more papers, the books are also expected to reach much larger audience.

The book entitled *Crime, Corruption and Development* edited by D. Narasimha Reddy is one in the series of books brought out by the Association. It contains a selection of articles contributed by members to one of the topics to be discussed at the 83rd Annual Conference of the Association being held at Jammu during 30.12.2000 to 1.1.2001.

In many developing countries, crime and corruption are quite rampant and impose a huge cost to society in terms of frittering away of large resources. Crime and corruption also adversely affect the efficiency of the various sectors of the economy thereby reducing potential domestic product. This results in diminished investment in essential physical or human capital and a consequent slowing down of growth of the economy. Furthermore, the development of a close nexus between crime and corruption has serious implications for the welfare of the society.

This book contains the contribution of various scholars to many aspects of this topic. I am confident that the book would be useful to both the scholars and the policy-makers.

New Delhi

PROF. G.S. BHALLA
President, Indian Economic Association

Preface

The Indian Economic Association (IEA) in its 80th year of academic activities, decided to publish theme-wise edited volumes out of papers contributed to IEA Annual Conferences during 1994-2000. As a result of sustained efforts, the IEA could publish in 1999 as many as five such volumes arising out of IEA Seminar/Conference papers of 1999 itself. A number of titles based on the themes of previous years' conferences including those related to the 2000 conference are being published this year. "Crime, Corruption and Development" is one such volume. This volume contains altogether 18 articles. The major contribution of these articles are available in a summarised form from the Introduction which follows. We sincerely hope that our readers will find the contents of this volume both light and fruit bearing.

We are thankful to Prof. G.S. Bhalla, IEA President for his Foreword and to Prof. D. Narasimha Reddy for his hard work as Editor of this volume and the Introduction. We also thank Prof. Reddy for his efforts to include in the Appendix an Annoted Bibliography on Corruption and Development which will be extremely helpful for the future researchers. We thank all the contributors of this volume without whose cooperation this volume could not be published. Last but not the least we thank Shri G.S. Bhatia of Deep and Deep Publications Pvt. Ltd. for the cooperation and help to publish this and other volumes in this series in record time and elegant manner. We also apologize to our members for any of the lapses that may remain in these volumes for reason beyond our control.

Calcutta

PROF. RAJ KUMAR SEN
Managing Editor and
Secretary and Treasurer, IEA

Introduction

Corruption has been a topic of sporadic interest among social scientists for over three decades. But there has been a renewed analytical interest since mid-1980s and the decade of 1990s witnessed a flood of literature on the concept, causes and consequences of corruption and on the reforms to check it. This upsurge, often referred to as "corruption eruption" (*Williams*, 1999) reflects the emergence of concern about the complex interwining of corruption as one of the central problems of development. It is not surprising that the growing focus of recent studies in on the developing countries.

DEFINITION

The use of the word "corruption" has been highly contextual. Williams (1999) sets out with a detailed discussion of the evolution of the concept of corruption. Before social scientists looked for rigorous analysis, corruption was used primarily as a term of moral condemnation. Later, in 1960s to the 1980s, a legally derived approach, 'the public office definition'—which denotes corruption as theft of the State by State officials, was dominant. As the economists entered the arena, the definition of corruption is recast into terms, which are more familiar and congenial to economists, but the 'public office' notion remains with an emphasis on the market for the powers of public office. Economists see government through economic prism and interpret its workings as akin to private business monopolies. Rent-seeking emerges as the key concept and with the principal-agent framework. Following Becker and Stigler (1974)—the two prime exponents—the new approach to corruption (*Rose-Ackerman,* 1975 and 1978), Klitgaard (1988 and 1991) focus on principal-agent model of corruption. It is premised on the assumption of maximization of self-interest as the motivation. The principal-agent model focuses on the relationship between the principal, i.e. the top level of government, and the agent, i.e. an official, who takes bribes from the private individuals interested in some government produced good or service. Corruption gets defined as "the sale by government officials of government property for personal gain." Obversely, 'payments are corrupt when they are illegally made to public agents with the goal of obtaining a benefit or avoiding a cost" (*Rose-Ackerman,* 1997, p. 36). Williams (1999) looks upon this narrow economic definition as misleading because the "public office notion of corruption is derived from western-style liberal democracies and are wholly inappropriate in non-democratic settings. . ." (p. 510). He looks forward to cross-fertilization of a range of concepts to capture corruption comprehensively. This "coincides with the notion that . . . corruption is one of a constellation of international development problems endogenous to societies and the changes they experience" (*Johnston,* 1997, p. 70). Thus, entrenched corruption is seen as a symptom of deeper difficulties. The choice of narrow economic approach for analyzing corruption may not be entirely free from ideology. . . " when economics was underlying ideological theme to reform (through marketization, privatization and economic liberalization) in the 1980s, corruption began to be defined and modelled through economic methods (for example, in the rent-seeking or principal-agent models where corruption is about office-income maximization within a context of exercise of monopoly or discretionary powers" (*Doig and Mclvor,* 1999).

CAUSES OF CORRUPTION

One of the central aspects of the narrow approach to corruption is the explanation of the causes for corruption. As it is obvious, substantive part of the explanation of causes for corruption in these models are foreclosed by the definition of corruption as the use of public office for private gain. The result is the explanation that it is the regulatory state with its elaborate system of permits and licenses that generates corruption. Trying to suggest that any norm-based culture-dependent explanations are not scientific, economists have come out with a series of models of multiple-equilibria of the incidence of corruption. Most of these, as reviewed by Bardhan (1977, pp. 1331-34) are exotic in nature and do not add much to our understanding of the problem as such. For instance, in these models, corruption represents frequency-dependent equilibria and the expected gain from corruption depends upon crucially on the number of other people expected to be corrupt. Some of the explanations, hold on to the public office definition to elaborate on the factors generating corruption. Rose-Ackerman (1997, pp. 36-37) discusses six structural features that create incentives for corruption. These include rules and regulation, low salaries of civil servants, tax evasion, government contracts, and room for substituting bribes for political influence.

Much to the chagrin of most of the narrow economic models of explanation, which depict State intervention as the cause of corruption and liberalization as the solution, there is new evidence to show that liberalization itself can cause more corruption (*Barbara Harris-White and Gordon White,* 1996). The roll back of the state in India and in China has sparked off increase in corruption and the transition to liberal democratic regimes in Korea and Philippines has not brought about any substantial reduction in corruption. IDS Bulletin (Vol. 27, No. 2, 1999) focuses on the political economy of 'new corruption' as a consequence of economic liberalization and the process of transition from authoritarian to democratization.

EFFECTS OF CORRUPTION

Interestingly, some of the early economic models explaining the impact of corruption have acquired the notoriety of rigorously demonstrating corruption as an efficiency improving mechanism. It would suffice to summarize some of the studies reviewed by Bardhan (1997). Leaf (1964) is credited with the corruption as efficiency-improving process since he argued that "if the government has erred in its decision, the course made possible by corruption may well be the better one." He was in the distinguished company of non-economist Huntington (1968), who also saw corruption as a facilitator of efficiency. He observed "In terms of economic growth, the only thing worse than the society with a rigid, over-centralized, dishonest bureaucracy is one with a rigid, over-centralized, honest burdancracy." Then come the arguments in defence of corruption as an efficiency-augmenting mechanism. Bribery in the coarse framework could be seen as a 'game theoretic' situation with competitive bidding where the least cost-firm will be in a position to offer the most high bribe and bag the contract. Since the contract has gone to the least-cost firm, corruption only adds to efficiency. Yet another efficiency argument is the 'speed money' reducing waiting time. The queueing models used here show that bribing minimizes waiting time for individual client and thereby reduce inefficiency in public administration. There are other studies, which draw from history to present the positive effect of corruption and try to console that there is nothing to be alarmed about corruption.

It is sought to be shown that Europian history of the growth of a class of sales monopoly rights, tax farms and other privileged access to public resources through bribes or political influence served as the basis for accumulation and growth of investment. Similarly, in the US, during the so called 'gilded age' of 1960s and 1870s, extensive corruption of state legislatures and city governments in franchising public utilities for private business, is also seen as stimulating accumulation, investment and growth (*Theobald*, 1990). Yet another favourable impact of corruption cited from history refers to the undermining of the sway of collective passions that meant internecine group warfare. "For two hundred and fifty years before 1688, Englishmen had been killing each other to obtain power. . ."

The settlements of 1660 and 1688 inaugurated the Age of Reason and substituted a system of patronage, bribery, and corruption for the previous method of blood letting (*Wraith and Simkins*, 1963). But it should be reminded that it took considerable time for reforms in governance to get rid of corruption that got entrenched in the process. Moreover, as Bardhan (1977, p. 1329) points out, it is impossible to confine corruption to areas, if any, of relative beneficial effects.

Quite contrary to the benefits, the recent research findings have provided ample evidence on the devastating effects not only on efficiency, investment and growth but also on the political and social fabric of affected nations. Perhaps in one of the first systematic/cross-coventory empirical analysis, Paolo Mauro (1995) relates indicators of bureaucratic honesty and efficiency to economic growth. Using the *Business International* data of 1980-83 for 68 countries on 56 'country-risk' factors, he confines to nine indicators of institutional efficiency of which corruption is one. His results show that corruption lowers private investment, thereby reducing economic growth, even in sub-samples of countries in which bureaucratic regulations are very cumbersome. "The negative association between corruption and investment, as well as growth, is significant, both in a statistical and in an economic sense". (*Mauro* 1995, p. 683). Corruption is found to be strongly negatively associated with the investment rate, regardless of the amount of redtape. Shleifer and Vishny (1963) focus on the resource allocation and came out with the conclusion that corruption distorts resource allocation and development process. Rose-Ackerman (1978) was one of the earliest to study the impact of corruption and arrive at the conclusion that it adversely effects economic development. It is shown how bribes distort the political fabric by buying political influence, votes and even judicial decisions (*Rose-Ackerman* 1997, pp. 38-42). Corruption distorts allocation choices. It is not beneficial because of high distributive costs. Corruption involves heavy costs to the nation by way of lost taxes and inefficient investment projects.

The above overview on the concept, causes and consequences of corruption based largely on the studies of economic analysis of the problem does lead to certain broad inferences. First, any single definition of corruption is elusive. Some differentiation between contemporary context of developing countries and the historical context for developed countries may be necessary. In any case the 'public office' definition of corruption as "... sale by government officials of government property for personal gain" is too narrow to be of any significance particularly in the context of developing countries some of which seem to be still under neo-patrimonial political structures. Even at the risk of making it too broad for any rigorous uni-causal analysis, it may be helpful to see corruption as "one of a constellation of interrelated development problems endogenous to societies and changes they experience" (*Johnston,* 1997, p. 70). It is indeed not simply a development problem. It is also a problem of governance, of trade of morals and ethics, and of a weak and emotive system of public order (*Ruzindana* 1977, p. 95).

In spite of the limitations of the narrow definition used, an heartening feature of some of the recent academic studies on corruption is that these ". . . see corruption as a negative force, rejecting the 'revisionist' stand of corruption (in helping capital formation, speeding up development, and 'humanising' politics) outweigh the costs (*Nye,* 1967; *Leff,* 1964, *Doig and Mclvor,* 1999, p. 659)." Recent studies accept that corruption has damaging public and social consequences: "It undermines the development capacities of state, distorts priorities, and is in essence a form of redistribution from those in poverty to the office-holding rich" (*Doig and Mechoor,* 1999, p. 659). In these empirical studies,". . . corruption is associated with slow economic growth (*Mauro,* 1997), reduced investment, feeble property and contract rights, ineffective institutions (*Knack and Keeper,* 1995), limited social interaction and weak rule of law (*Cooter,* 1997), poor economic competitiveness (*Ados and Di Tella,* 1994), deep ethnic divisions and conflicts (*Easterly and Levine,* 1996), low popular participation in politics and weak protection of civil liberties (*Isham, Kaufmamn, and Pritchett,* 1995, 1996), low educational attainment (*Mauro,* 1997), and closed economic and political systems" (*Elliott,* 1997, *Johnston,* 1997, p. 70).

REFORMING CORRUPTION

A large number of studies on corruption have paid substantial attention to the problem of combating corruption. Though it is true that the strategy proposed is often based on the distinct viewpoint over causes and character of corruption, the reform proposals include a wide array of measures. Rose-Ackerman (1977, pp. 45-53) suggests four broad categories of reforms: (i) reducing discretionary power of government officials, (ii) enforcing anti-corruption laws, (iii) reforming civil-service, and (iv) increasing the accountability of government to citizens. The first set of reforms of reducing the power of government officials is based on the premise that, in general, "any reform that increases competitiveness of the economy will reduce incentives for corrupt behaviour (*Rose-Ackerman* 1997). And these coincide with the Structural Adjustment Programme (SAP) commended to all the developing countries and include policies to loosen controls on foreign trade, to remove entry barriers for private industries and to privatise state firms. Yet another measure in this regard is establishment of multiple-officials with overlapping jurisdiction (*Rose-Ackerman,* 1994) like the FBI and local police investigating a local crime separately. Strategies of enforcing anti-corruption laws include establishment of agencies like Hong Kong's Independent Commission Against Corruption (ICAC). Reforming civil service includes higher salaries and other benefits for civil servants. Bardhan (1997, pp. 1335-41) discusses at length some of the reform measures referred to above.

There are others who feel the need for the development of vigorous civil society, involving a plurality of independently organised groups, while some suggest the need to examine the corrupt activities of Western business (*Doig and Mclvor,* 1999, pp. 661-62). That competition will kill corruption is questioned. An empirical study by Bliss and Di Tella (1997) concludes that

". . . we cannot say that increases in competition lead to lower levels of corruption". This is corroborated by the fact of 'new corruption' that is sparked-off by economic reforms in the name of promoting competition. (*Harris-White and White,* 1996). The studies on liberalisation-sparked 'new corruption' emphasise that the role of human agency is crucial in combating corruption. "Countries of similar levels of political, social and economic maturity may be characterized by varying levels of corruption. For example, Italy and the UK, Japan and Germany or Singapore and South Korea have similar levels of maturity but varying levels of corruption. The task of combating corruption has its own 'autonomous' political status and needs a protracted battle over political space . . ." (*Harris-White and White,* 1999, p. 5). A significant aspect of many of the new studies on corruption is that these are premised on the belief: "Many countries have overcome serious corruption in the past; those experiencing entrenched corruption today can do much to alleviate it. . ." (*Johnston,* 1997, p. 88).

QUESTIONS OF METHODOLOGY

An overview based on the corruption studies, especially those extending the economic analysis, cannot avoid at least a brief reference to the methodology underlying these studies. The extension of economic analysis to corruption, by and large, has been in the tradition of economic methodological imperialism of Becker, Buchanan and the public choice kind, a kind where rational self-interest maximisation behaviour is extended to political and bureaucratic behaviour as well. Not disregarding some of the valuable results of these studies, the methodology imposes serious limitations. First, subjecting a complex phenomenon like corruption to methodological individualism denudes the analysis of any nuances of the intricate political processes, historical contexts and culturally rooted institutional complexities. Second, an "over-adherence to economic modelling is akin to knowing why corruption takes place but offers little in the way of practical guidance on prevention" (*Doig and McIvor,* 1999, p. 659). Preventive measures do not go beyond breaking up the context—say deregulation—since it fails to take cognizance of specific political processes, political actors and political institutions. Third, ". . . given the modellers' belief in the shrinking of the state as a macro-means of reducing levels of corruption, such measures deny the role that the state could provide for developing countries and tend to ignore the wider constituency—the public—and widen developmental issues concerning democratization, social provision, human rights and sustainable economic growth". (*Doig and Mclvor*, 1999, p. 660). What needs to be remembered is that morally and ethically disturbing social issues need a teleological concern in the social science approaches. It would be foolhardy to expect that: "If the study of corruption is to extend the mainstream of social science, an empirically testable paradigm that can explain the causes of all types of corruption is required" (*Buscaglia*, 1997, p. 64). Methodologically, what is needed is an infusion of more of the political economy approach which pays as much attrition to historical, class, cultural and institutional factors as to private and public agency. The accomplishments of such an approach, among many, could be seen in terms of contributions in the *IDS Bulletin* (Vol. 27, No. 2, April, 1996).

In combating corruption the World Bank has been trying to assume a self-appointed role of a savior. Some believe that "... there may be scope for organisations such as the World Bank to provide institutional support to reduce corruption and to help create an environment conducive to equal growth and poverty alleviation" (*Pleskovic and Stiglitz,* 1997). But the ability of reforming corruption by outside agencies like the World Bank is questioned (*Pope,* 1997). Given the growing evidence that the emerging 'new corruption' is sparked-off by the reforms initiated by the World Bank (*Harris-White and White,* 1996), the credibility of the latter to spearhead measures to check corruption is suspect. There is neither the inclination nor capability of the World Bank to use anti-corruption measures as conditionality. At the best, these agencies could disseminate information on anti-corruption strategies.

CRIME AND CORRUPTION

A surprising aspect of the studies on corruption is almost negligible attention paid to the link between corruption and crime. This seems to be coming to fore in the light of the experience of transitional countries. There has been reference to the links between corruption, large scale fraud, organised business crime and international theft. The absence of studies on the links between crime and corruption is rather intriguing for two reasons: one, there has been well known operations of various forms of Mafia activities linked to corruption and second, substantial sources of corruption in developing countries like India are related to operations of criminal gangs. One exception is Gambetta (1997) who refers to a number of ways in which organised crime and corruption feed on each other. Mafia like groups supply protection to illegal markets which trade in not only out-lawed commodities but also indulge in illegal practices in trade of legal commodities. Mafia fosters corruption in three ways: by enforcing trust, by stabilising corrupt cartels and by lowering the cost of corrupt services. One difference between mafiosi and other corruption is that the former enforce it by violence. The most pervasive threat that the mafia poses to economic development is not its ability to boost markets of illegal commodities such as narcotics but lies in its ability to make illegal practices more attractive to ordinary citizens and legal firms, enabling them to rely on collusion and corruption rather than on proper practices and market competition (*Gambetta,* 1977, pp. 60-61).

The relevance of these observations can hardly be exaggerated for developing countries like India where there has been gradual and steady entrenchment of Mafia like groups in the real estate, entertainment, sports-related betting and of course in political crimes.

THE PRESENT VOLUME

The present volume is an attempt to put together in a book form a select number of papers from among the ones received for presentation on the theme 'Crime, Corruption and Development' at the 83rd Conference of the Indian Economic Association. It may be necessary to caution that extension of economic analysis for the study of the interface between crime, economic analysis and development in India is still in a rudimentary form. The eighteen papers included here could only be seen as a modest attempt in this direction. The first four papers represent as an effort to introduce some of the economic approaches to the analysis of corruption. In the first paper N.N. Vohra gives a historical development of crime, corruption and development and deals with the present overall environment of crime and corruption. Pillai's paper is more of a summary of Bardhan (1997) and serves as an introduction to corruption studies literature for those who have missed Bardhan. While Pillai draws heavily on Bardhan, in the third paper, Lakshmanaṣamy dilates on the Rose-Ackerman's (1997) classification of the types of corruption. The fourth paper by Mukherjee focuses on the narrow economic rationale for corruption. Unintendedly, it turns out to be useful to see how rational economic analysis may end up in search for an 'Optimal Level' of corruption. The rest of the papers attempt to apply economic analysis of the experience of corruption in the developing country context. In the fifth paper, Gupta picks up the classification of corruption and uses Kleptocracy prism to look at the interventionist state as the source of corruption, brigandage and violence. Indrajit Singh and others analyse levels of crime in India and try to relate it to levels of development using inter-state comparison. Thakur relates the level of crime and corruption, based on impressionistic observations, to the situation of a backward state. Sharma and others make an attempt to evaluate the limitations and the limited contribution that corruption makes to development. Jain presents an overview of tax evasion as a source of corruption in India. Chaudhary and Sahoo based on rich field data analyse the emerging environmental crimes in Orissa and its deleterious consequences for development. Pradhan and others make a valiant attempt to model crime and punishment within Becker's (1968) expected utility model. That the hopes raised are not held because there is no application of the model to Orissa. But there is interesting description of Orissa experience in crime and punishment.

Satya Pal Singh discusses economic crimes with particular reference to India. There are interesting and revealing accounts emanating from the enforcement and other agencies. Sen and Mitra attempt modelling of mafiosi in the coal belt with a case study of Giridih district in Chotanagpur plateau. Ghosh tries a micro-economic model of crime as a firm. Abedin provides a brief but succinct account of corruption in Bangladesh, which should be of interest to all analysts of the Indian situation. Pramod Kumar deals with globalisation and conflicts in South Asia. Mohite and Malapur give a brief account of crime and its adverse developmental consequences. The last paper by N.C. Ghosh is the analysis of how an industrial unit like a power plant with polluting by-products like fly-ash generates an atmosphere conducive for crime and how police records of crime are silent on the pollution which is the source of crime.

REFERENCES

Ades, Alberto and Rafael Di Tella (1997), "National Champions and Corruption: Some Unpleasant Interventionist Arithmetic", *Economic Journal*, 107 (July), 1023-42.

Alam, M.S. (1990), "Some Economic Costs of Corruption", *Journal of Development Studies,* 27, 1 (Oct.), 89-97.

Bardhan, Pranab (1997), "Corruption and Development: *A Review of Issues*", *Journal of Economic Literature,* Vol. XXXV (Sep.), 1320-46.

Becker, Gary S. (1968), "Crime and Punishment: An Economic Approach", *Journal of Political Economy*, 76, 2 (March-April), 167-217.

Bliss, Christopher and Rafael Di Tella (1997), "Does Competition Kill Corruption?" *Journal of Political Economy,* 105, 51 (Oct.), 1001-1023.

Buscaglia, Edgardo, (1997), "Comment on 'Corruption and Development' by Susan Rose-Ackerman", *Annual World Bank Conference on Development Economics,* 1997.

Doig, Alan and Stephanic Mclvor (1999), "Corruption and Its Control in the Development Context: An Analysis and Selective Review of Literature", *Third World Quarterly*, Vol. 20, No. 3, 357-76.

Gambetta, Diego (1997), "Comment on 'Corruption and Development' by Susan Rose-Ackerman", *Annual World Bank Conference on Development Economics,* 1997.

Harris-White, B. and Gordon White (1996), "Educational Introduction: Corruption, Liberalization and Democracy", *IDS Bulletin*, Vol. 27, No. 2 (Apl.), 1-5.

Johnston, Michael (1997), "What Can be done about Entrenched Corruption?" *Annual World Bank Conference on Development Economics*, 1997, 69-90.

Mauro, Paolo (1995) "Corruption and Growth", *Quarterly Journal of Economics,* (August), 681-711.

Mookerjee, Dilip and IPL Png (1995), "Corruptible Law Enforcers: How Should they be Compensated?" *Economic Journal* (105), Jan., 145-56.

Pleskovic, B. and J.E. Stiglitz., "Introduction", *Annual World Bank Conference on Development Economics,* 1997.

Pope, Jeremy (1997), "Comment on What can be done about Entrenched Corruption? by Michael Johnston", *Annual World Bank Conference on Development Economics,* 1997.

Rose-Ackerman, Susan (1978), "Corruption: A Study in Political Economy," Academic Press, New York.

Rose-Ackerman, Susan (1996), "Democracy and Grand Corruption", *International Social Science Journal*, 149 (Sept.).

Rose-Ackerman, Susan (1997), "Corruption and Development", *Annual World Bank Conference on Development Economics,* 1997, 35-57.

Ruzirdana, Augustine (1997), "Comment on What can be done about Entrenched Corruption?' by Michael Johnston", *Annual World Bank Conference on Development Economics,* 1997.

Shleifer, Andrei and Robert W. Vishny (1993), "Corruption", *Quarterly Journal of Economics* (Aug.), 598-617.

Theobald, R. (1990), *Corruption, Development and Underdevelopment,* Duke University Press, Durham, WC.

Williams, Robert (1999), "New Concepts for Old?", *Third World Quarterly,* Vol. 20, No. 3, 503-13.

Note: Besides books, reports and several articles on corruption, a separate international journal, *Corruption and Reform* was launched in 1986. *The International Social Science Journal,* 149, (Sept.) (1996), *IDS Bulletin* (Vol. 27, No. 2, 1996) and *Third World Quarterly* (Vol. 20, No. 3, 1999) have brought out special issues on the subject of corruption. The World Bank has established an *Anti-corruption Knowledge Centre.*

List of Contributors

1. **Prof. G.S. Bhalla**, President, Indian Economic Association.
2. **Prof. Raj Kumar Sen**, Secretary of Treasurer, Indian Economic Association.
3. **Prof. D. Narasimha Reddy,** (Editor), University of Hyderabad, Hyderabad.
4. **Dr. N.N. Vohra,** IAS (Retd.), India International Centre, New Delhi.
5. **Dr. S. Iyyam Pillai,** Bharatidasan University, Tiruchirapalli.
6. **Dr. T. Lakshmanasamy,** University of Madras, Chennai.
7. **Shri Debes Mukherjee,** St. Paul's College, Calcutta.
8. **Prof. I.D. Gupta,** Lucknow University, Lucknow, U.P.
9. **Dr. Inderjeet Singh,** Punjabi University, Patiala, Punjab.
10. **Dr. Harvinder Kaur,** Punjabi University, Patiala, Punjab.
11. **Shri Pramod Kumar,** Punjabi University, Patiala, Punjab.
12. **Shri Ram Naresh Thakur,** Samastipur College, Samastipur, Bihar.
13. **Dr. S.C. Sharma,** P.C. Bagla P.G. College, Hathras, U.P.
14. **Dr. Shyam Sunder Singh Chauhan,** Government College, Aligarh, U.P.
15. **Dr. Binay Kumar Singh,** P.D.U. Govt. College, Shahjahanpur, U.P.
16. **Prof. Anil Kumar Jain,** Banaras Hindu University, Varanasi, U.P.
17. **Dr. Amita Kumari Choudhury,** Berhampur University, Orissa.
18. **Dr. Nirmal Chandra Sahoo,** Berhampur University, Orissa.
19. **Prof. N.B. Pradhan,** Berhampur University, Orissa.
20. **Dr. B. Patro,** Berhampur University, Orissa.
21. **Shri S.K. Panigrahy,** Khemundi College, Digapahandi, Orissa.
22. **Dr. Satya Pal Singh,** Maharashtra Police Academy, Nasik, Maharashtra.
23. **Shri Dipankar Sen,** SRU, Indian Statistical Institute, Calcutta.

24. **Shri Sandip Mitra,** ERU, Indian Statistical Institute, Calcutta.
25. **Shri Santanu Ghosh,** Presidency College, Calcutta.
26. **Prof. M. Zainul Abedin,** IBS, Rajsahi University, Bangladesh.
27. **Prof. Gulab Mohite,** Lala Lajpat Rai Institute of Management Studies, Mumbai.
28. **Shri S.P. Malapur,** Sydenhan Institute of Management, Mumbai.
29. **Dr. N.C. Ghosh,** S.N. Bose School of Mathematics and Mathematical Sciences, Calcutta.

1

Crime, Corruption and Development

N.N. VOHRA

There is, *per se*, no inherent relationship between crime, corruption and development. However, corruption (which is a crime by itself) may, in certain cases, also involve the commission of other crimes. Likewise, the commission of certain crimes may also involve resort to corruption. And very little development can take place in an environment which is permeated by crime and corruption.

People all over the world, to whichever country they may belong, eternally aspire to improve their lot and lead better lives. As historical experience has shown, such aspirations do not get dimmed or diluted merely with the passage of time or change in circumstance. They sustain from generation to generation with added strength and provide the unceasing motive force for continuing human growth and development.

In the centuries past, powerful nations were able to freely pursue their hegemonistic designs, annex territories and establish colonies. Thus, among the colonial powers Britain's imperial sway extended to many countries, including the entire Indian subcontinent. However, the period after the end of the second World War ushered in winds of change which have led to the liberation of erstwhile colonies, a general decline of totalitarian regimes and the emergence of democracies.

Since the 1980s more than 100 countries have been liberated from military dictatorship of single party rule. While military juntas and non-democratic governments continue to exist in many parts of the world, the struggles for liberty and the yearning of people to lead free and unfettered lives have become more intense in the recent years.

In the decades past the essential focus was on achieving progressive economic growth even if, in its wake, this led to the fruits of development being inequitably shared among the various segments of the society and sharper disparities appearing between the rich and the poor. In the post-Cold War period there has been growing realisation that the goal of meaningful and sustaining development is not merely to reduce income poverty and achieve higher per capita incomes but to secure civil, cultural, social, political and economic rights for all people. This has led to a universal recognition that all possible policy initiatives must be undertaken to establish a firm relationship between human rights and human development if the latter is to proceed in the right direction. Nonetheless, discriminations by gender, race, caste, ethnicity, age and domicile continue and are still a very long way from being eradicated. Experience, specially in the past five decades, has shown that such discriminations contribute to tensions, clashes and confrontations which vitiate governance, disrupt the normalcy of functioning and thwart the pace of growth and progress.

Despite the continuation of an exploitative international world order and the failures of nation states to deliver good governance progress has been achieved in improving the standard of life of people all over the world: malnutrition has been progressively reduced, access to safe drinking water is now available to larger numbers and income poverty has also been reducing. However, 1.2 billion people are still living on less than $1 a day (1993 PPP US$), a billion and more in the developing countries do not have access to safe water and more than 2.4 billion suffer from the lack of adequate sanitation. People in a larger number of developing countries continue to suffer from unacceptably high rates of infant mortality, low life expectancy, large scale illiteracy and widespread poverty. In such a scenario it would be irrelevant to comment on the varied human rights abuses to which the deprived people of the world are subjected—exploitation and injustice, lack of employment, shelter and health care, denial of freedom of participation, speech and association, bonded and child labour, etc. Poverty is a grave impediment to the attainment of harmonious human growth and development. Consequently, almost every developing country devotes high priority to the execution of poverty alleviation programmes. In the past two decades (1980-99) the developing countries have been able to secure mentionable headway on several fronts:

- percentage of underweight children has declined from 37% to 27%;
- percentage of stunted children has fallen from 47% to 33%;
- child mortality rate has decreased from 168 per 1,000 live births to 93;
- enrolment at the primary and secondary levels has increased to 86% and 60%, respectively.

However, in both developing and developed countries about a third of all children under the age of 5 years still suffer from malnutrition.

The safety and security of people all over the world continues to remain threatened by exploitation, oppression and conflicts. 5 million people were killed in civil wars in the past decade and wars and conflicts forced 50 million to flee their homes. The virtually unthwarted circulation of over half a billion "small arms" which include the most sophisticated weapons and devices to cause death and destruction—all over the world poses a variety of threats from non-state actors, specially terrorist and militant groups and mafia networks. Nearly 7 million such weapons are estimated to be in circulation in South Asia.

Among the more threatened segments of society are women and children. About a quarter million people, mostly women and children, are estimated to be trafficked every year and about 100 million children live or work on the streets.

The volume and spread of narco-trade has continued to increase. The street value of the drug trafficking operations is reported to be in trillions of dollars. Among others, the enormous gains from the illicit drug trade support the activities of militant and terrorist organisations which operate in several countries and have been spreading their activities. The parallel growth of fanatic religious fundamentalist groups has led to the emergence of narco-terrorist networks whose activities endanger the peace and stability of countries all over the world. In our region, Pakistan has been systematically promoting narco-trade to fund terrorism and militancy in India, and carrying on its proxy-war in J&K for over a decade now, with its proclaimed objective of "dis-membering" the country.

India waged a prolonged struggle for gaining freedom. The first generation of political leaders, to whichever party they may have belonged, were highly educated persons who were imbued with deep commitment to the national cause. For their involvement in the freedom struggle most of them had undergone long periods of imprisonment in the British jails and made large sacrifices. When India became free these tall personalities, many of whom were inducted to serve the Central and State cabinets, commanded the respect and trust of the common man because of their established reputations, high integrity and unblemished records of public service.

The innumerable problems which faced the country in 1947 were resolutely faced and tackled with strong political will and determined implementation. Despite varied serious constraints the country achieved steady progress in the first two decades and more after independence. Though much berated today, the centralised planning system succeeded in establishing priorities and providing a strong impetus to the launching of vital community and rural development programmes; consolidation of land holdings; execution of minor irrigation schemes; construction of village roads, wells, primary schools and rural dispensaries; afforestation; distribution of improved seeds and plants, fertilizers and agricultural implements to the farmers; improvement of live-stock and arrangements for veterinary care; promotion of cottage and rural industries; establishment of village level cooperative societies to provide credit and services to the farmers; immunisation against communicable diseases and varied other developmental programmes.

Side by side, attention was devoted to establishing Universities and enlarging the facilities for technical and medical education; science and technology, business management, and agricultural education; research and extension institutions; expansion of highways, railways and public transport systems, etc. Initiatives were launched to expanding capacities for thermal, hydro-electric and nuclear power generation, increasing the production of coal, steel and cement and development of infrastructure. Industrial production proceeded apace, to satisfy the requirements of the manufacturing and consumer goods sectors. Among the areas which received special attention were the establishment of facilities to produce drugs and pharmaceuticals, chemicals and fertilizers. Considerable progress was also achieved in implementing agrarian reforms, construction of large dams and expansion of irrigation systems, all of which contributed to the success of the Green Revolution. The achievement of self-sufficiency in food-grains production within a democratic framework has perhaps been the most outstanding success story of the last century, anywhere in the world.

During this period the country faced foreign aggression on four occasions. Except for the humilitation faced in the 1962 Sino-Indian conflict, our defence forces acquitted themselves with honour on all occasions, safeguarding the country's territorial integrity. Overall, while serious challenges continued to face us on varied fronts, the nation seemed well set to achieve the targeted goals of a welfare state, providing opportunities for equitable socio-economic development.

Unfortunately, around the end of 1960s, the country's political stability suffered a serious setback from internal feuds and the emergence of a new brand of power politics. The decline was highlighted by the imposition of Emergency (1975-77), negation of the Constitution and the abrogation of the Rule of Law. The emergence of "committed" coteries and extra-constitutional power structures had a serious adverse effect on the functioning of the organs of governance, specially the constitutional working of the cabinet system. Nepotism, corruption and maladministration, not unknown in the earlier decades, gained ascendancy and adversely affected the pace and direction of the nation-building programmes and processes.

Irrespective of which political parties have been in power in the States in the past two decades, there has been a progressive decline of governance. The credibility of the political parties in power, both at the Centre and in the States, has been seriously impaired by the continuing series of scandals of bribery and corruption at the highest levels which have created a growing impression among the public that the elected representatives of the people are concerned only with seizing and retaining power at any cost. The pursuit of such short-term objectives has resulted in continuing failures to devote timely and effective attention to the efficient implementation of nation-building programmes, specially to contain and stabilise the population growth, reduce infant and maternal mortality, provide universal primary education, implement equitable human and economic development programmes, generate employment opportunities and reduce poverty.

The serious damage arising from misgovernance would perhaps have not been so severe if the political executive had left the public services relatively undisturbed in discharging their mandated role and responsibility. Most unfortunately, the public service cadres at all levels have been subjected to continued politicisation. This has contributed to indiscipline, inefficiency and unaccountability in the functioning of the administrative apparatus. As if this were not enough, this decline has been accompanied by increasing dishonesty and corruption in the functioning of the bureaucracy, upto the highest echelons. The indifference which has permeated governance has led to another grave consequence: the development of linkages between corrupt politicians, unprincipled public servants and known criminals.

The abovesaid triangular relationship, often referred to as the criminal-nexus, poses a most serious threat to national security. Such networks have the resources and capacity not merely to kill and destroy at will but, in conjunction with adversary external agencies like the Pak ISI, to also subvert and sabotage the most sensitive arenas of governmental functioning. The unthwarted activities of such elements pose a grave risk to the very unity and integrity of the country.

Despite continued public criticism, the electoral process remains vitiated by the role played by those who wield money and muscle power. Persons of questionable antecedents or those facing charges for serious offences and even known criminal background have been finding their way into the State legislatures and the central parliament. Notwithstanding the incessant debates and discussions for the past two decades, within and outside parliament, the much needed reform of the election law and procedures to prevent criminals and unseemly elements from gaining entry into the representative framework has still to materialise.

The executive and the parliament have not yet gathered the necessary will to evolve and enforce the various measures required to tackle the serious aberrations which plague our polity and society. It has become fashionable to repeatedly bemoan that maladministration arises from "our polity being criminalised and our society being brutalised" and then close the debate by attributing the entire mess to the failures only of an unaccountable and corrupt bureaucracy!

In the emerging political environment it does not appear any longer necessary for a party to be founded on a given ideology or a known agenda. This has led to the mushrooming of political parties at the local and regional levels and, presently, the State legislatures and the parliament are comprised by varied political parties and groupings. The inescapable consequence of this phenomenon has been the emergence of coalition governments at the Centre. The continuing environment of political instability has generated uncertainties and further decline in the effective functioning of the executive. The country has had to face three general elections in the past 5 years; the present is the fourth coalition government at the Centre since 1996.

With each of the cabinet ministers representing sharply diverse and disparate regional interests, it is not possible for the Central Government to evolve and implement well considered policies to deal with vital national issues. In such a scenario, the Prime Minister faces perpetual threats to the survival of his government and is left with little choice except to devote almost all his time and energy merely to working out compromises and appeasing members of his flock who serve him notice on day-to-day basis.

In the aforesaid environment the functioning of both the executive and the parliament has been most adversely impaired. Among the many grave ramifications, the obtaining situation has led to prolonged delays in the parliament enacting even such legislation as is most urgently required to meet existing and emerging national objectives and the executive failing to timely and efficiently execute vital developmental programmes. This has led to the governments of the day losing their credibility and the trust of the people, comprising several hundred million, still continue to subsist below the poverty line. Virtually half our population is illiterate and about two thirds of our people live in the rural areas, some of which are unconnected and inaccessible and, besides, suffer from acute disadvantages arising from difficult terrains and extreme weather conditions. The prolonged neglect of such deprived segments of our population has inescapably generated feelings of disgust, anger, resentment and cynicism.

The despair of the disadvantaged and neglected rural population and the growingly large numbers who dwell in urban slums has contributed to a feeling of alienation which is accentuated by the varied exploitations to which they continue to be subjected. Feudal systems and archaic structures continue to operate in many parts of the country in which agrarian and other crucial reforms have still to be implemented. Besides their acute economic sufferings certain segments of the society are also subjected to harassments and contrived confrontations which arise from almost every political party exploiting religious, caste and ethnic factors for electoral gains.

Besides the failures of governance to deliver social and economic justice, the sufferings of various ethnic and tribal groups also arise from the indifference of the State administrations to respond sensitively and timely to their felt needs and political aspirations. It is indeed unfortunate that the responses to such demands have invariably related to viewing them in terms only of the likely gains and losses to the political parties in power. The deprivations of the neglected people in many States is further accentuated by the fact that even the financial assistance provided by the Centre for the implementation of poverty alleviation schemes and welfare programmes is embezzled or diverted to non-productive areas. Such pilferages arise from the continuing corruption among the public servants and their political masters.

Among the various serious consequences of the failures of governance is the virtual break-down of the entire apparatus for the administration of the criminal justice system. Besides being inadequately educated, improperly recruited and deficiently trained and equipped the functioning of the State Police organisations has been vitiated by the endless interference and politicisation to which they have been subjected. No longer in a position to enjoy the trust of the people they serve, the Police have acquired an image of inefficiency, brutality and corruption. The public at large has, understandably, little interest in seeking to know the essential reasons for the decline of the Police which is no longer viewed as an agency which enforces the law and brings the offenders to book. On the contrary, an impression has gained ground that the Police is involved with and supports the activities of crooked elements. This has also led to the belief that the rich, powerful and unscruplous elements are beyond the pale of law and can procure "justice" at a price.

The functioning of the subordinate judiciary presents an equally worrying picture. Cases before the courts remain pending for years, under-trial prisoners remain in jails for periods far longer than the sentences they would have had to undergo if found guilty and convicted. The advocates, public prosecutors and the presiding officers of the courts are not held accountable for the prolonged delays in the conclusion of trials or for the miscarriages of justice. Corruption, inefficiency and unaccountability have permeated the judicial system as much as the other areas of governmental functioning. It is reported that over 22 million cases are pending disposal by courts at various levels in the country. According to the *Crime in India* (1998), in 1998—over 2.3 million cases under the I.P.C. were awaiting disposal/investigation by Police;

- over 5 million cases under the Special and Local Laws (SLL) were pending disposal/investigation by the Police;
- over 5.6 million IPC cases were pending trial in the courts;
- over 7.9 million SLL cases were awaiting trial in the courts;
- there was 40.1% increase in sexual harassment incidents, over 1997;
- there was 18.1% increase in juvenile crimes, over 1997;
- there was 8.3% increase in crimes against women, over 1997.

Side by side with the above picture and a progressive decline in the conviction rate in respect of heinous crimes; there is growing evidence that mafia and organised criminal groups are spreading their networks to carry out extortions, kidnappings for ransom, contract killings, illicit drug trafficking, smuggling, hawala operations and money laundering, circulation of fake currency etc. Some of these networks enjoy the support of the criminal-nexus, earlier referred to, wield enormous power in influencing, co-ercing, black mailing and, as necessary, even eliminating those who may be seen to be thwarting their objectives. When such groups operate in tandem with the Pak. ISI (as happened when serial bomb blasts rocked Bombay in 1993, leading to the killing of thousands in the ensuring communal rioting and economic losses running into thousands of crores) they pose a most serious threat to the national economy and the maintenance of internal security in the country.

The UNDP have, over the years, evolved criteria for assessing the growth and development of countries all over the world. The Human Development Report 2000 reveals that, in 1998, India was placed at the 128th position (among 174 countries which were studied) in the Human Development Index. Under the Human Poverty Index it was at serial number 58, among the 85 developing countries which were assessed against the poverty reduction criteria. Under the Gender Related Development Index, India was 108th among 143 countries under examination. The per capita income (at 1995 US $) had, in 1998, grown to US $ 444 (against US $ 222 in 1975). The progress achieved in other crucial areas has also been far below the envisaged targets:

Life Expectancy at Birth (years)		*Infant Mortality Rate (per 1000 Live Births)*	
1970-75	*1995-2000*	*1970*	*1998*
50.3	62.6	130	69

The adult literacy rate (%age, 15 and above) was 55.7 (1998) and the rural population (% of total) stood at 72.3 (1998).

India has miles and miles to go before it can be ensured that all our people are literate, gainfully employed, provided with the basic amenities and enabled to lead free, secure and useful lives. We have vast physical and manpower resources. Our people are hard working, enterprising and possess high potential for acquiring skills. To engender the required momentum and pace of sustained socio-economic development of the country, it would be inescapably necessary to have a committed political leadership, at all levels, whch is totally devoted to maintaining peace and harmony and securing growth and progress on all fronts through speedy, honest and efficient execution of all schemes and programmes which promote the welfare of our people. Once such political will obtains not much time will be required to cure the organs of governance and public services of the malaise from which they are suffering—inefficiency, corruption and unaccountability—and proceed on the path of delivering fair and just administration to every segment of our vast population.

The honest execution of prioritised goals through the close involvement of those who are sought to be benefitted will enable our numberless communities to take the requisite interest and accept the responsibility for acting as watchdogs to secure timely and honest implementation of all works and developmental programmes relating to their areas.

Corruption and crime can perhaps never be altogether eliminated. However, they can be controlled and contained. And this can happen only if those who carry the responsibility of governing the country work with a singular mission of securing the greatest good of all our people in an accountable manner. Such a goal is achievable if the political parties at all levels keep politics strictly where it belongs; immunise the functioning of public institutions, as well as those who run them, from politicisation and day-to-day interference; and not allow any kind of compromise in ensuring that every corrupt act is met with prompt and severe punishment irrespective of the power, influence or status of the offender. If such a path is followed, we can look forward to our country achieving speedy progress and development and eradicating poverty, discrimination and exploitation. If, however, there is failure to cure our polity and governance of their existing ills, there is every danger that the growing dissatisfaction and anger of our people may soon engender a situation which imperils the very unity and integrity of our country.

2

Socio-Economic and Political Dimensions of Corruption

S. Iyyam Pillai

INTRODUCTION

Received literature on corruption shows that (a) it is neither a new phenomenon nor found only in developing countries, and (b) its levels and effects influence and get influenced by the existing socio-economic and political conditions of the country in question. Though increasing trends and harmful effects are generally felt, ups and downs in the levels over a period and positive effects on development are also reported. These varying situations would definitely make any curious researcher to look into as to how it happens? What are the conditions under which these differences are observed? Can the variations be explained by the anti-corruption measures undertaken? What are the anti-corruption methods available and used? Why and how the effectiveness of these measures vary across the countries and in a country over a period? Can we suggest a package of measures suitable to all possible situations? Can liberalisation and privatisation be an answer to this problem? Would the emerging, trends in behaviour—earn as much as possible and as early as possible—lead the people to be more and more corrupt? This paper is an attempt to answer some of the above questions. However, no claim is being made for originality since the basic ideas have been developed by several writers earlier. This aim has been, rather, to put together information that is now widely scattered.

THE CONCEPT

Corruption is defined as the illegal use of public office for private gains. In other words, it refers to a transaction between two individuals or parties, in which a person with accumulated political and/or bureaucratic power demands and accepts cash or some favour in return for rendering a service or showing a favour to another. The payment made for such favour or discrimination is called bribe, speed money, spoils, rent, kick-backs, grease payment, side payment, graft payment and so on. If money is not directly involved in the abuse of public office for private gain, that may be called discrimination, patronage, favouritism, nepotism, etc. Corruption could be collusive or non-collusive (*Bardhan,* 1997). In the collusive corruption, neither the briber nor the bribee has an incentive to report or protest. Corruption is also classified into two types, namely, primary and secondary. Primary corruption is the class misappropriation of the surplus value created by the labouring majority (*Theobald,* 1990), while the secondary corruption, which is discussed in this paper, refers to the everyday abuse of public office for substantial personal gain. Other crimes (*Sinha,* 2000) are out of the scope of this paper.

ORIGIN

Corruption in one form or another has existed for ages. It has had variegated incidence in different times at different places, with varying degrees of damaging consequences. Dating back to the fourth century B.C. in India, Kautilya writes in Arthasastra, "Just as it is impossible not to taste the honey that finds itself at the tip of the tongue, so it is impossible for a government assistant not to eat up, at least a bit of the King's revenue" (*Kangle,* 1972). In ancient Egypt, problems of bribery and nepotism were clearly recognised. But, in recent times, it is reported to have taken a quantum jump.

REASONS

Corrupt public officials would thrive in the states which cannot enforce the laws and property rights (*Bardhan,* 1997). Corruption would be rampant and pervasive where rules and procedures are inadequately articulated and lines of authority are unclear and where, above all accounting techniques are primitive. Under such conditions it will be extra-ordinarily difficult to determine where or when serious corruption has occurred. Hence, when corruption is favourably paying to the policy-makers, the policy-makers would certainly find it a disincentive to make any improvement in the articulation of rules and procedures, definition of lines of authority and in the accounting techniques. If at all there is any reduction in the corruption in response to an anti-corruption measure initiated by any policy-maker, then it can be considered as something extra-ordinary in the history of the country in question.

Corruption is expected to worsen under three circumstances. First, changes in life style demanding command over more of goods and services (emergence of consumerism) leading to scarcity, rise in prices and crisis, decline in values, low level of morality and ethics in professions. Two, the war time controls, regulations and red-tapism in public administration. Three, wages perceived to be low for public servants, lower expected punishment for corrupt persons, middlemen's vested interest in spreading disinformation that 'nothing gets done without bribing the officials', and rapid commercial and entrepreneurial expansion. These are observed to be the order of the day. Hence, corrupt practices are more likely to expand.

DIFFERENCES IN LEVELS OF CORRUPTION

Why the incidence of corruption is so palpably different in different countries and why in some cases it is so persistent? Liberal economists say that different countries with different degrees of insertion of the regulatory state in the economy give rise to varying amounts of corruption. This explanation is largely valid but inadequate. For instance, in South Korea and Taiwan the state intervention was not much less as compared to that in Mexico, but as per the Business International Survey data for the early 1980s, corruption was supposed to be much more in Mexico than in South Korea or Taiwan. Sociologists cite differences in social norms across the countries as an explanation for differences in the levels of corruption.

WHY CORRUPTION IS MORE APPARENT IN UDCs?

As the underdeveloped countries (UDCs) exhibit a marked tendency towards overdeveloped state and as the governments there typically engage in a range of activities (which in industrial capitalist societies would be left to private business and market forces), the bureaucrats are vested with abundant opportunities to get bribe. The nature of politics, badly underinstitutionalised administration, process of class formation, caste-related patronages and the inter-relationship between the state and the emerging bourgeoisie in UDCs play supportive role.

TREND AND LEVEL OF CORRUPTION

In the absence of official data it would be hard to estimate the level of corruption. However, some available evidences show a rough idea about this problem. For instances, New York Congressman Mario Biaggi received three Florida vacations worth $3000 (*Bardhan,* 1997, p. 1326). In South India, an Executive Engineer in-charge of irrigation is reported to have bribed upto 14 times of his annual salary in order to obtain a two-year tenure at a particular location; and this is the lower bound of how much he expects to earn in bribe in two years (*Bardhan,* 1997, p. 1338). In UK, many Metropolitan officers were found to have accepted bribes. In the former USSR, General Nikolai Shchlolokov used ministry appropriations to purchase Mercedes cars for the personal use of himself, his son, his daughter and daughter-in-law; he kept private apartments in different parts of Moscow, one for his personal tailor, his personal dentist and so on. Cement scandal in Nigeria was very much in the news in 1975. The other notorious instances are: in 1976, a deal between President Mobutu of Zaire and the German Rocket Corporation, ORTAG; a $22 million kickback on the sale of jet fighters by a British aircraft manufacturer to Nigeria's Shagari regime (1978-83); in 1981, Oscar Flores Tapia, Governor of the Mexican state of Coahulia amassing a fortune of about $30 million, when his official salary was $1600 per month; in July 1987, in India, kickbacks for the supply of military equipment from the Swedish firm, Bofors and German submarine deal (*Theobald,* 1990, p. 103). This list which has not come to mention even Macros of Philippines or Suharto of Indonesia can not be considered nowhere near being exhaustive.

Some evidences on patronages are also available. One estimate claims that about half of the eight million local government employees in USA are appointed on a patronages basis. There, substantial federal aid such as the award of government contracts to local industry, the siting of military bases of public utilities such as airports and dams, will be granted to states to which the president owes a political debt (*Theobald,* 1990, p. 56). Thus, the appropriation of public resources for private ends, appears to be normal among dominant groups in industrial societies, both capitalist and socialist.

The size of a bribe that an individual pays to another individual is linked to the opportunity cost of time for the individual clientele, urgency, bribees' and bribers' socio-economic status and reputation, size of fine if he/she is caught, the cost of hiring hoodlums to discipline the bribee, number of bribers and bribees involved, and the need to keep the corruption secret (*Bardhan,* 1997).

Although the requisite time-series evidence in terms of hard data is absent, circumstantial evidence suggests that over the last 100 years or so, corruption has generally declined with economic growth in most rich countries and in some developing countries like, Singapore, it is reported to have declined quite fast in recent decades (*Bardhan,* 1997). It is, however, not true in all the countries. As the economy expands and becomes more complex, public officials see more opportunities for making money from their decisions, hence corruption may also grow with the economy. For instance, in the process of transition from controlled to market economy in Eastern Europe, China and Vietnam, it has often been observed that corruption has increased as income grew. But definitely after some time, the corruption will stall the growth due to its adverse effects on productive and allocative efficiency (*Bardhan,* 1997 and *Theobald,* 1990).

EFFECTS OF CORRUPTION

Positive as well as negative effects of corruption have been identified and discussed, though some of the positive effects have been later on refuted by others. Also it is found that whatever be the net positive effects, they may not be substantial and sustainable and it may not be possible to contain it within a sector.

NEGATIVE EFFECTS

While moralists maintain that corruption is definitely detrimental, the reformists argue that corruption provides some benefits to developing nations, which in some cases may exceed the costs. Reformists argue that corruption helps attain allocative efficiency through competitive bribery procedures. Since the corrupt official determines the winner by the amount of bribe, also since the lowest cost firm can afford the largest bribe, it is the very firm that will be ultimately awarded. This however, is refuted by Lien (1976, p. 1) and many others. Under many situations the above may not be correct. For instance, firstly, a firm efficient in manipulating the quality of the goods/services would manage to bribe more while the others may not be able to achieve their goals. The cost of kickbacks will invariably be recouped by charging higher prices or by delivering an inferior product. For instance, Nigerian building contractors during the Shagari era put up numerous public buildings, many of which rapidly collapsed altogether (*Theobald*, p. 127).

Secondly, in real world, the corrupt official determines the winner, not only by the amount of bribe, but by some other considerations, such as friendship or caste relations. Thus, the possibility of inefficient allocations increases as the degree of discrimination increases (*Lien*, 1976).

When inefficient projects are accepted, the rate of return and hence the growth rate would be lower. Large spending on inefficient projects would reduce the resources available for other developmental aspects. The corrupt officials would be more interested in taking up larger and new projects. So, small projects, however important, will not attract due attention. And, the existing projects which are inefficiently executed may require more maintenance works but, would not be properly maintained in order to generate chance for newer projects and new chance for bribe seeking. This will spoil the tax payers' confidence and they may also hide the income sources, leading to generation of black money. Using cross-country data and regression analysis, the IMF Survey (1997, p. 376) finds that higher corruption is associated with: (a) higher public investments, (b) lower government revenues, (c) lower operation and maintenance expenditures, and (d) reduced productivity of public investment.

Under this situation, higher public sector investment need not always result in higher growth rate (*IMF*, 1997).

Also, corrupt bureaucrats would opt for imports of complex technology or goods in preference to more standardised and more appropriate technology or goods.

Other than these allocative inefficiencies caused by corrupt practices, the corruption engenders a climate of greed, selfishness, cynicism and total loss of faith in efficiency (when inefficient ones are accepted on the basis of personal relations), which would hamper the hard work and efficiency. The loss of faith in merit particularly among the youth may cause suicides, terrorism and other socio-psychological crises and crimes. When stupendous fortunes can be made out of corrupt government office, it would be a major disincentive to embarking on a career in legitimate business activity.

When public resources meant for building productivity enhancing infrastructure are diverted for politicians' private conspicuous consumption (it is hardly possible to see that the amount is invested on productive ventures by the corrupt bureaucrats/politicians), growth rates obviously will be affected adversely (*Bardhan*, 1997, p. 1328).

On the basis of corruption rankings data assembled from the Business International Correspondents in 70 countries in the early 1980s, Mauro (1995) finds a significant negative association between the corruption index and the investment rate or growth rate.

There seems to be strong inverse relationship between the level of corruption and respect for human rights. Extensive opportunities for self-enrichment through control of the state apparatus places a fantastic premium on actually being in power. Hence, those with vested interests would join together to get themselves into power; once in power, the victors do everything they can to stay there. They will do ballot-rigging, imprison political opponents or cause mortal harm the political rivals. If they lose in the elections, they will carpet-cross to the government side, resort to unconstitutional means; economic sabotage, conspiracy, fomenting communal tension, riot and even armed rebellion. The corrupt politicians would not have mass patronage but maintain maximum clientele with minimum pay-off—a meal or a temporary job (*Theobald*, p. 129).

POSITIVE EFFECTS

Corruption may be helpful as grease for the squeaking wheels of a rigid administration. Oiling the wheels of the administration can result in considerable savings of time, effort and money. Nepotism, bribery and spoils may be the only means of making a remote and rigid administration responsive to the needs of politically weaker groups in society. Many a time innocent voters are looking for a politician who can broker the remote and anonymous government departments to them; who can intervene personally to 'fix' things for them; or get their children registered for school. Thus, corruption in the forms of bribe, nepotism and favouritism humanises an impersonal and inimical state apparatus and so helps to assimilate newly enfranchised masses to national politics and to national life. Bribery provides a means of interest articulation for those who lack the organisational base for expressing their needs through more formal and unknown channels (*Theobald*, p. 124).

It is also stated that if corruption is centralized and effectively monitored, it will have less adverse consequences for efficiency than the decentralised bribe-taking. For explaining this, Bardhan (1997, p. 1325) gives the following example. Corruption in Indonesia was perceived to be much worse than in India in the early 1980s, yet the economic performance by most accounts has been much better in Indonesia, because, in Indonesia corruption was much more centralised and hence more predictable, but in India, it is more fragmented.

In the US, "gilded age" of 1860s and 1870s widespread corruption of state legislatures and city governments by business interest and those seeking for franchises for public utilities is reported to have helped rather than hindered economic growth.

Wraith and Simpkins write that before 1688, Englishmen were killing each other to obtain power; the settlements of 1660 and 1688 inaugurated the Age of Reason, and substituted a system of bribe, corruption and patronage for the previous method of blood letting to get power.

Uganda with corrupt practices could get a TV station that too more quickly and more cheaply than was the case in neighbouring Kenya where an administratively less corrupt policy had been pursued. When there was inflation in 1960s stagnation in food production was exacerbated by a non-corrupt Chile bureaucracy who behaved correctly to enforce price controls. By contrast, in Brazil, a corrupt bureaucracy allowed the controls to be undermined with the result that food producers received higher prices, which in turn stimulated agricultural production (*Theobald,* p. 111).

In many cases, where the volume of private wealth was too small, the public resources, offices, pension and sinecures have been better used to build party organisations. England in the 18th and the USA in the 19th centuries provide clear cut examples for this. In Europe, the prospect of spoils played a key role in binding together the factions out of which were to emerge political parties. In the USA, graft played pivotal role in galvanising nascent parties into action. In the 1920 and 1930s, Ataturk used the resources of the Turkish state to promote the development of the Republican People's party. In Mexico government, patronage played a vital role in the emergence and institutionalisation of the National Revolutionary Party. In Korea, the Democratic Republican Party, in India Congress and in Israel Mapai were all launched down a ramp of official patronage. Communist parties also subordinated the state apparatus to their own needs (*Theobald,* 1990, p. 115).

SUGGESTIONS

Suggestions for eliminating corruption cannot be discussed without involving the larger question of the nature of the state that is supposed to carry out the policies. Such examples as Hong Kong Police Department and Singapore Customs and Excise Department are stated to be the most successful cases in controlling corruption in the recent history. In the following paragraphs some of the suggestions and their effects wherein they were adopted are discussed:

(a) *Emphasis on moral character of the individuals:* In Philippines in the 1970s, a tax commissioner fought pervasive corruption in the Bureau of Internal Revenue and he made substantial impact.

(b) *Strengthening the functional aspects of institutions like Lokayukta and establishing multi-membered Vigilance Commissions with uncorrupt officials:* In India, since 1964 a Central Vigilance Commission with branches in each ministry has been the principal watchdog over the civil service, but that did not arrest the situation in any meaningful manner. The Santhanam Committee recommended that political parties should be asked to give details of accounts of their receipts and expenditure and that these should be published annually and audited, but, the lack of political will on the part of all political parties resulted in non-acceptance of this recommendation (*Vijayakumar,* 1998). Suharto in Indonesia in 1965, after seizing power, set up a Corruption Eradication Team, but some of his most corrupt friends were shielded from investigation at all.

(c) *Legalising the activities that were formerly prohibited or controlled:* When Hong Kong legalised off-track betting, police corruption fell significantly (*Bardhan,* p. 1325). When Singapore allowed more imported products duty free, corruption in customs went down. In the US, the overlapping involvement of local, state and federal agencies in controlling legal drugs has reduced police corruption. In US again, the 1977 Foreign Corrupt Practices Act forbids American companies from making payments to foreign officials. However, 'grease payments' to speed up transactions are not ruled out; the 1988 amendments to the Act expanded the range of such payments allowed.

(d) *Incentive payments for civil servants:* In Imperial China under the C'hing Dynasty, district magistrates were paid an extra allowance called yang-lien yin—money to nourish honesty. In recent times both Singapore and Hong Kong have followed an incentive wage policy for public officials with a great deal of success. In Singapore a wage premium above private sector salaries has been found useful.

(e) *Bringing military regimes:* In Brazil during 1964 and in Indonesia after 1965, military or at least highly authoritarian regime, by restricting entirely competitive politics, reduced significantly political pressure on the administration and with it the abuse of public office. But strengthening the restraints on the exercise of power has not played any significant role in limiting the abuse of office by the politically powerful in Brazil, Mexico, Egypt, Libya, Syria, Iraq, Mali, South Korea, etc.. There is, however, no logic why the soldiers in power, while others are corrupt, are less likely to use their position for self-aggrandisement than civilians.

(f) *Announcing anti-corruption campaigns:* Many times in the recent history (of Africa and China) these campaigns were usually *ad hoc* and targeted at political enemies. The effectiveness of these measures have varied from situation to situation (*Bardhan,* 1997, p. 1337).

The other measures suggested are: (a) reducing the role of the State and encouraging the privatisation, but at the same time it should be seen that will not result in monopoly exploitation; (b) ensuring greater transparency and accountability by decentralising the decision-making process; (c) strengthening the people's voice by giving them the right to information; (d) attractive rewards for honest and severe punishment for indulging in corrupt practices; (e) attacking the monopoly of the rent-seekers by introducing competition in the system; preventing the nexus between politics and corruption; (f) giving competing jurisdictions to the officials so that a clientele, who is not well served by one official, can go to another (it must be seen that there is no collusion among the officials); (g) authorising periodic probing of ostensible but unexplainable assets; (h) making the officials to work in team (in Singapore the customs agents were asked to do so); and (i) periodic job rotation, without giving scope to maximise the looting.

CONCLUSION

The above discussion shows that: (i) corruption is generally harmful to the society, though it could bring some favourable effects in some corner for time, (ii) it is extraordinarily difficult to do away with the misuse of power for personal gains so long as government offices exist, (iii) though some efforts have brought some favourable results in the history, they cannot be relied upon for all situations, and (iv) the present kind of development pattern—ever raising the demand for exhaustible and competitive resources leading to deficit supply, conflicts, crises and crimes—would enhance opportunities for the public officials to be more corruptive in one form or another. However, a controlled corrupt administered system may be preferable to the tyrant market forces, where the valued social objectives (like rationing of basic necessities like food, water etc.) exist. (*Bardhan*, 1997, p. 1335).

REFERENCES

Bardhan, Pranab (1997), "Corruption and Development: A Review of Issues", *Journal of Economic Literature*, Vol. XXXV, September, pp. 1320-46.

IMF (1997), "Corruption Linked to Capital Spending Can Slow Growth", *IMF Survey*, Vol. 26, No. 22, Dec.1, pp. 375-77.

Kangle, R.P. (1972), *The Kautilya Arthasastra, Part II*, University of Bombay, Bombay, p. 91.

Lien, Donald (1976), Corruption and Allocative Efficiency", *Kyklos*,.

Mauro, Paolo (1995), "Corruption and Growth", *Quarterly Journal of Economics*, August, pp. 681-7122.

Sinha, Ajit Kumar (2000), "Organised Crime and Political Economy of Development—The Indian Panorama," *The Indian Economic Journal*, Vol. 47, No. 3, January-March, pp. 1-10.

Theobald, Robin (1990), *Corruption, Development and Underdevelopment*, Macmillan, London.

Vijayakumar, V. (1998), "Corruption in Public Life and Legal Responses". *Southern Economist*, Vol. 36, No. 18, January 15, pp. 11-14.

Wraith, Ronald and Simpkins, Edgar (1963), *Corruption in Developing Countries*, London, Allen and Unwin.

3

Economics of Corruption and Development

T. LAKSHMANASAMY

I

INTRODUCTION

Corruption is generally defined as 'the abuse of public office for private gain'. Payments are corrupt when they are illegally made to public agents with the goal to obtain a benefit or avoid a cost. Evidently public officials abuse their power to extract or accept bribes from the private persons for personal benefit. Whenever a public office is abused, a public function or objective is set aside or compromised.

This paper is a summary account of the various aspects of corruption and development. It doesn't claim to make any analytical contribution but to highlight different aspects of the problem. The second section briefly examines the two views on the interaction between corruption and development. The third section examines the causes and consequences of corruption. The fourth section refers to the problem of measurement of corruption. The fifth is an account of control and the last section closes with concluding observations.

II

Two contrasting aspects of corruption and their role in economic development have been observed in the literature. One is that 'corruption is like cancer, retarding economic development'. There are several channels through which corruption hinders economic development, including reduced domestic investment, reduced foreign direct investment, overblown government expenditure and distorted expenditure on education, health and infrastructure. No region has escaped the negative impact of corruption. Even East Asia's 'miracle' economies were not immune.

The other view is that 'corruption can be like grease, speeding up the wheels of commerce'. In countries with bad and heavy regulations, the opportunity to offer bribes to circumvent bad government control and official harassment is like deregulation, and hence can be good. However, when the official machinery is so highly corrupted, even the bribes may not be a beneficial 'grease'. Using data on a survey of nearly 2400 firms in 58 countries, Kaufmann and Wei (1998) show that managers of the firms that pay more bribes on an average spend more rather than less time negotiating with government officials. Moreover, bribing is not a one-time gesture and it will be perpetuated by both the parties. Hence, bribing supports the view of 'tailored harassment', 'extortion' and 'endogenous obstacles', rather than exogenous obstacles and beneficial 'grease'.

III

CAUSES AND CONSEQUENCES OF CORRUPTION

A country's level of corruption depends not merely on the potential for economic rent, but also on the political structure. It depends largely on the organization of the government. On the basis of whether corruption is centralized or decentralized, Rose-Ackerman (1997) identifies four types of corrupt states:

(i) *Kleptocracy:* In a pure kleptocracy the head of the government organizes the political system to maximize the possibilities for extracting rents and reallocates these rents for personal use. He might act like a private monopolist as he faces a large number of potential bribers.

(ii) *Bilateral Monopoly State:* In this case the corrupt ruler faces a single major briber. In some cases the briber may be a mafia group—an organized crime group that provides protective services. The possibilities for rent extraction are shared by briber and ruler, depending on their relative strength and the size of the pie.

(iii) *Mafia-dominated State:* In this case the state is very weak and disorganized, with many officials engaged in freelance bribery. These officials face a monopolist briber in the private sector, a domestic mafia or a large corporation.

(iv) *Competitive-bribery State:* In this case many corrupt officials deal with large numbers of ordinary citizens and firms. The corruption of some officials encourages others to accept bribes, thus creating the potential for an upward spiral of corruption.

In many mafia dominated states, for illegal markets for outlawed commodities or illegal practices in the trade of otherwise legal commodities corruption is the payment for providing protection by organized crime groups. Mafia protection provides enforcement of corrupt charges and it promotes illicit cartel agreements.

Rose-Ackerman (1977) identifies six structural features of an economy that create incentives for corrupt behaviour:

(i) Bribes clear the market.
(ii) Bribes act as incentive payments to bureaucrats.
(iii) Bribes lower the costs for those who pay them.
(iv) Bribes affect the level of monopoly rents and their allocation between private investors and public officials.
(v) Bribes buy influence and votes for politicians.
(vi) Bribes can override legal norms and buy judicial decisions.

Besides, the benefits and costs under the discretionary control of bureaucrats, the laws on corruption and the mobility of the enforcement machinery, service and incentive conditions of civil service, auditing and monitoring systems, freedom of citizens to scrutinize the public decisions and the effectiveness of political opposition also influence the level of corruption (*Rose-Ackerman*, 1997).

According to Buscaglia (1997), the capacity of public officials to extract illicit rents will be enhanced by:

(i) Uncertainty about prevailing doctrines, laws, and regulations.
(ii) Numerous and complex procedural steps, coupled with a lack of procedural transparency, in a public agency supplying the service.
(iii) A high concentration of internal organizational roles overseen by a few decision-makers in a public agency.
(iv) The absence of alternative sources for the good or service provided by the public agency.
(v) Limited collusion among the parties demanding a service from the public agency.

Some of the consequences of corruption on economic development are discussed here.

Corruption and Domestic Investment: Mauro (1975) obtains a point estimate of the slope of 0.012 in a regression of total investment/GDP ratio on the corruption index. This implies that if India could reduce its corruption level to the Singapore level it would have been able to raise its investment/GDP ratio by about 6 percentage points. Higher the level of corruption, lower is the domestic investment.

Corruption and Foreign Investment: Wei (1997), for a data set of bilateral foreign direct investment from 14 major source countries to 41 host countries has obtained the coefficients on corruption and host country marginal tax rate as –0.09 and –1.92. This implies that if India could reduce its corruption level to the Singapore level, its effect on attracting foreign investment would be the same as reducing its marginal corporate tax rate by about 22 percentage points. Corruption discourages foreign investment.

Corruption increases the size and composition of public expenditure, because many items in public expenditure lend themselves to manipulations and extractions by officials to demand bribes. Corruption tends to skew public expenditure away from needed and welfare-oriented programmes and increases expenditure on unproductive and popular programmes wherein it is easy for officials to extract rent from.

Corruption would reduce the economic growth rate, as the growth rate is conditioned by the level of investment (*Mauro,*

1995). This implies that if India could reduce its corruption level to the Singapore level its average annual per capita growth rate would have been higher by .375 percentage points.

Corruption is not only prevalent at the bureaucratic level and its unhealthy consequences are not mere restricted to the economy level. Corruption between private parties is also widespread with serious consequences. Corruption in any form reduces the quality of the services provided and induces the parties to involve unfair and unlawful activities. In most developing countries corruption is rampant within political parties, trade unions, organizations, trusts and societies.

Corruption at high levels may alter average citizen's perception of social equity and efficiency. Under corruption, the macro-social environment is adversely affected by diminishing economic productivity over time caused by the general perception that the allocation of resources is determined by corrupt practices and so inherently inequitable. In such an environment productive activities take a back seat to rent seeking.

Thus, corruption leads to wrong policies and programmes. Corruption-induced policy bias may worsen the income distribution and divert the needed resources away from the needy. Particularly the poor are hurt much by corruption: (1) the poor receives a lower level of social services, (2) infrastructure investments are biased against projects that aid the poor, (3) the poor faces higher taxes and fewer services, (4) the poor are disadvantaged in selling their products, and (5) their ability to escape poverty is very weak and diminishes with growing corruption. High and rising corruption thus perpetuates increasing income inequality and poverty.

Corruption is one of the constellation of inter-related development problems endogenous to societies and the changes they experience. Corruption is associated with slow economic growth, reduced investment, feeble property and contract rights, ineffective institutions, limited social interaction and weak rule of law, poor economic competitiveness, deep ethnic divisions and conflicts, low popular participation in politics and weak protection of civil liberties, low educational attainment, and closed economic and political systems (*Johnston*, 1997).

IV

MEASUREMENT OF CORRUPTION

Corruption is very difficult to quantify. However, one can gauge the level of corruption in an economy from the 'corruption perception' of the citizens. At the internationally comparable level, there are a few attempts to construct indices of corruption level. They are listed below:

Business International Index (BI): The BI is based on surveys conducted by Business International. It ranks countries from 1-10, according to 'the degree to which business transactions involve corruption or questionable payment'.

International Country Risk Guide Index (ICRG): The ICRG is produced by a private international investment risk service viz., Political Risk Services. It is also based on the opinion of experts on the extent to which 'high government officials are likely to demand special payments' and to which 'illegal payments are generally expected throughout lower levels of government' in the form of 'bribes connected with import and export licenses, exchange controls, tax assessments, police protection, or loans'.

Global Competitiveness Report Index (GCR): The GCR of the World Economic Forum is based on a 1996 survey of firm managers about various aspects of 'competitiveness' of investment. It ranks corruption on a 1-7 scale according to the extent of 'irregular, additional payments connected with import and export permits, business licenses, exchange controls, tax assessments, police protection or loan application'.

Transparency International Index (TI): The TI produced annually since 1995 by Transparency International is based on a weighted average of approximately 10 surveys and ranks countries on a 1-10 scale.

Table 1 presents some measures of corruption for some countries. Most indices show that the level of corruption is very low in industrialized and developed countries and very high in Asian and African and less developed countries. In these poor countries the bureaucratic and administrative regulations perpetuate the scope for corruption.

TABLE 1

Corruption Ratings for Selected Countries

Country	*BI*	*TI97*	*GCR97*
Asian Countries			
Singapore	1	2.34	1.77
Hong Kong	3	3.72	2.17
Japan	2.25	4.43	2.96
Taiwan	4.25	5.98	4.60
Malaysia	5	5.99	5.67
South Korea	5.25	6.71	6.20
Thailand	9.5	7.94	7.93
Philippines	6.5	7.95	7.94
China	n.a.	8.12	8.86
India	5.75	8.25	7.30
Indonesia	9.5	8.28	7.94
Pakistan	7	8.47	n.a.
Bangladesh	7	9.20	n.a.
Non-Asian Countries			
Canada	1	1.90	2.37
United Kingdom	1.75	2.72	1.93
Germany	1.5	2.77	1.93
United States	1	3.39	2.41
France	1	4.34	3.51
Mexico	7.75	8.34	6.24
Kenya	6.5	8.70	n.a.
Columbia	6.5	8.77	7.41
Russia	n.a.	8.75	7.61
Nigeria	8	9.24	n.a.

Note: All the indices have been rescaled so that large numbers imply more corruption, though the originals are the other way. The GCR ratings are rescaled from 1-7 range to 1-10 range.

Source: Wei (1999).

V

CONTROL OF CORRUPTION

Corruption being a crime in many countries, it is common to strengthen the role of law enforcement in the fight against corruption. Recent cross-country studies indicate that strong legal and government institutions and low levels of corruption help foster foreign investment and economic growth (*Mauro*, 1995). In situations of entrenched corruption, some even suggest that some widely accepted illegal payoffs should be legalized. The public sector may as well accept the widespread corruption induced by low pay and inadequate incentive mechanisms. In certain institutional settings many commonly perceived ills of public bureaucracies are actually in the public interest; they merely manifest underlying problems of information and dissonance of objectives.

However, recant literature on corruption also emphasized the need for non-legal mechanisms such as the performance-linked incentive schemes to combat corruption, because in high corruption situations even the law and judicial system are more corrupt. Improvements in performance of bureaucrats through incentive mechanisms may not entirely eliminate corruption; optimal government mechanisms may simultaneously involve corruption, large rents to government officials, and the misallocation of talent between private and public sectors. But the effect of reform on achieving the original intent of the government intervention—raising revenue, regulating externalities, delivering public services—may be welfare increasing even though it induces greater corruption. A number of countries have recently introduced incentive reforms for tax auditors, as part of a comprehensive reform of tax administration (*Das-Gupta and Mookherjee*, 1998). Mexico adopted incentive measures during 1988-92 under which each office is awarded, as a bonus fund, about 60 percent of additional collections which is to be shared among members of the office in proportion to the proximity of the official to the discovery and collection process. Brazil implemented a similar reform in 1989, introducing a bonus program among tax officials that has amounted to 68 percent of fines collected. Peru instituted reforms beginning 1991 through performance based promotions and salaries. The reform represented a move toward paying efficiency wages. In less than a year staff strength shrank by two-thirds and salaries increased almost ten-fold. Thus, these evidences may be limited, but they do indicate that bold initiatives are possible. In spite of these successful attempts, most tax administrations are focussing on reforming information systems and tax legislation.

Given the political structure and organization of many third world countries, an outside organization such as the World Bank can help fight corruption only under certain political and economic conditions. The challenge for corruption reforms is to identify the level of corruption. Some states may experience corruption at the top political level and some at all levels of government. Then, the problems is where should the reform efforts be concentrated? The general consensus is that states should move from a high level to a low level of corruption and anti-corruption efforts should focus on lower-level corruption.

In fighting against corruption it is also important to look into the root causes of corruption, the institutional environment and the incentive structure under which corruption thrives.

One the causes for corruption is excessive government regulation. In the context of taxation laws, it is more complicated and difficult to comprehend by ordinary individuals and there is vast scope for tax administrators' discretion in matters relating to granting tax incentives, determining tax liabilities and selecting audits and litigations, and hence it is more likely to encourage corruption and bribery. The size of public spending and the procedures used in allocating the expenditure also influence the based of for corruption.

The moral character and quality of civil servants is another important determinant of the level of corruption. The bureaucratic quality and morality in turn depend on the nature of recruitment, payment, promotion and compensation aspects. When the civil servants are poorly paid and their recruitment is not meritorious, they are likely to be induced by corruption. There is also a view that civil servants are poorly paid in relation with their 'control' over the decision on illegal money and wealth, and hence they are more likely to apportion the confiscated wealth. It is being recognized increasingly that it is naive to give people power, pay them a pitiful wage, and expect them to be more virtuous and not to use their power for personal gain.

Thus, low compensation and weak monitoring are generally considered the main causes of corruption. Increasing the salaries of public enforcers based on their performance will improve the quality of law enforcement.

In addition to changing social attitudes and expectations, anti-corruption efforts should limit public officials' opportunities, for corruption and increase the benefits of being honest and the costs of being corrupt. In short, a corruption reform in a highly corrupt political setup should concentrate on:

reducing the incentives for payoffs, establishing credible law enforcement, reforming the civil service, increasing accountability to citizens and in facilitating the organization of independent watchdog groups and grass root citizens' groups.

Thus, basic institutional reforms which increase the transparency and accountability of the organization of government may be a precondition for corruption reforms in developing countries. To what extent the institutional setting be reformed in order to directly confront the root cause of the corruption problem—the excessive discretionary power and lack of accountability of bureaucrats? Mookherjee (1997) suggests that the incentive reform initiatives are more likely to succeed if they are widened to include organizational restructuring involving: enhanced supervision, improved personnel quality, limited discretionary authority, more functional specialization, computered information systems, established appropriate staffing policies, motivated high-level officers and improved appeal mechanism.

VI

CONCLUSION

The above analysis shows that the negative effects of corruption are more dominant than its positive aspects. Most of the corruption is associated with the political and bureaucratic structures of the economies. Corruption also induces policy bias, wasteful and excessive public expenditure on populist programmes. Excessive discretionary powers to the bureaucrats and poor salary compared to their authority over money matters, induce them to be more corrupt and accept bribes. Empirical evidence shows that higher the level of corruption, lower the levels of both domestic and foreign investments and poorer the benefits to the really disadvantaged groups and worsen the income distribution. Anti-corruption laws are necessary but not sufficient in fighting against corruption. Many advocates economic reforms and restructuring suggest that the excessive government regulation of economic activities and the discretionary powers to public agents must be restructured. They also suggest civil administration and judicial system reforms, as well as the increasing of government functioning more transparent and accountable, and strengthening of civil society. In addition to changing social attitudes and expectations, anti-corruption efforts should limit public officials' opportunities for corruption and increase the benefits of being honest and the costs of being corrupt. The recent literature on corruption also emphasizes the need for non-law mechanisms such as the performance linked incentive schemes to combat corruption, because in high corruption situations even the law and judicial systems are more corrupt. But the main problem for many corruption issues is where to start: whether at the higher levels or at the lower levels or at all levels of political and bureaucratic organization? Many believe that in fighting against corruption it is important to look into the root causes of corruption, the institutional environment and the incentive structure under which corruption thrives.

REFERENCES

Buscaglia, Edgardo (1997), "Corruption and Judicial Reform in Latin America", *Policy Studies Journal*, 17, pp. 273-86.

Das-Gupta, Arindam and Dilip Mookherjee (1998), *Incentive and Institutional Reform in Tax Enforcement: An Analysis of Developing Country Experience*, New Delhi, Oxford University Press.

Johnson, Michael (1997), "What Can Be Done About Entrenched Corruption?", *Annual World Bank Conference on Economic Development*, pp. 69-90.

Kaufmann, D. and Shang-Jin Wei (1998), "Does 'Grease Payment' Speed Up the Wheels of Commerce?", World Bank, unpublished.

Mauro, Paolo (1995), "Corruption and Growth", *Quarterly Journal of Economics*, 110, pp. 681-712.

Mookherjee, Dilip (1997), "Incentive Reforms in Developing Country Bureaucracies: Lessons from Tax Administration", *Annual World Bank Conference on Economic Development*, pp. 103-25.

Rose-Ackerman, Susan (1997), "Corruption and Development", *Annual World Bank Conference on Economic Development*, pp. 35-57.

Wei, Shang-Jin (1997), "How Taxing is Corruption on International Investors"?, NBER Working Paper 6030.

Wei, Shang-Jin (1999), "Corruption in Economic Development: Beneficial Grease, Minor Annoyance, or Major Obstacle?", The World Bank.

4

Crime, Corruption and Development

DEBES MUKHERJEE

I

INTRODUCTION

Corruption—a social malaise—is as old as civilization. Corruption in one form or another existed even in biblical and classical times in varying degrees. It is not peculiar to any economic system, nor it is culture-specific. Today, the entire globe is its territory. A World Bank study on corruption in 1998 reveals that India is ranked the sixth most corrupt nation of the world, though it is difficult to quantify the level of corruption of any country since perceptions relating to corruption are likely to be highly subjective in nature. Anyway, it is believed that corruption has become a part of Indian life. Desparate remedies are needed to enjoy greater fruits of national progress.

Crime and corruption are anathema to all honest people. Corruption may thus be defined as the 'abandonment of expected standards of behaviour by those in authority for the sake of unsanctioned personal advantage', (*Kuper, A. & Kuper, J.*, 1996). If some individuals enjoy special rights or power to 'overfish' others, then unsanctioned personal advantage appears. Thus, corruption is the outcome of a mutual exchange process (assuming no bribery by extortion) that sanctions some individuals more rights and powers than others (*Benson, L.*, 1981). It is because of asymmetrical power public officials are strongly motivated by illegal "rent-seeking" behaviour. Corruption or the so-called alternative pay system (APS) or incentive pay system (IPS) exemplifies misuse of power by civil servants. It is embedded in 'dysfunctional public and private institutions' (*Rose-Ackerman, Susan*, 1999).

Political and economic corruption is also defined as 'the violation of established rules for personal gain and profit' (*Sen, Amartya*, 1999), or 'use of public office for private gain' (*Bardhan, Pranab*, 1997), or 'abuse of public power for private gain' (*World Bank*, 1997). In addition, one experiences electoral corruption that is defined, as 'the abuse of process by which public office is won'. In recent time, this has assumed monstrous proportions in a large number of states in India. Match-fixing in the game of cricket or cyber crime are the latest innovation in corruption germane.

On the other hand, crime ordinarily refers to the violations of criminal laws. Whenever law-enforcing authorities are bribed to overlook criminal law violations, there occurs misuse of power. Thus, crime and corruption are not mutually exclusive social malaise. In fact, crime and corruption are the Siamese twins of any corrupt society. Corruption, in its ugly form generates criminal activities or Mafia-controlled cartels.

Crimes involving violence like murder, robbery, arson, kidnapping, rape, dowry death, etc. are kept outside our discussion. It is said that these crimes are high-risk but low-yield crimes committed by low-status citizens mainly out of economic necessity. However, crime involving violence is not necessarily a lower-class phenomenon. Even high-profile citizens resort to corrupt practices like fraud, graft, kickbacks in the form of call-girls, tips and cash. In course of their occupation, higher-ups of the society indulge themselves in low-risk but high-yield white-collar economic crimes which mostly go unreported as well as undetected. It is believed that "an immunity attaches to corruption in high places; it is an area of *non-liquet*, where no human law and justice may ever reach." (*Shah, Ghanashyam*, 1990).

II

ECONOMICS OF CORRUPTION

While exercising his power or right, an individual measures both personal gain and profit and private and social costs of corruption. As corruption is defined as the use of public office for private ill-gotten gains, the probability of (both bribers and bribees) being caught and punished is the economic cost of illegal pay-offs. In a country where such costs of violating laws are lower compared to personal benefits, people are tempted to resort to "rent-seeking" behaviour. Distrust and disrespect to country's laws, cynicism, and above all disintegration of social institutions consequent upon degeneration of moral values are the social costs of corruption and crime.

It is believed by some people that bribes and gifts act as a bulwark against endemic delay and red tapism in public business. Thus, corruption, in a bureaucratic regime, may be regarded as a non-Pareto superior policy. We are afraid to say that if such APS or IPS is allowed to perpetuate, it will 'tend to deligitimate government in the eyes of its citizens.' (Rose-Ackerman, Susan, 1999). Thus, social benefits of corruption are nil, if not negative.

If private benefits outweigh private and social costs of corruption, bribal cultures and shadowy dealings develop in the society. In the process, dishonest and corrupt people stand to gain while society suffers. This is after all bad economics.

Two hypotheses can be drawn, however, from the economics of corruption. First, gifts and bribes act as incentive payment. Second, it allocates scarce public good (such as, industrial licences, export-import licences) only to those who offer bribes and gifts. A scarce item is bought at a premium in a controlled or unfree imperfect markets. This premium removes shortages and scarcities and, hence, clears the market. Though this price mechanism serves an important economic function—allocation of scarce resources—it brings about a psuedo-equilibrium. It is so-called because although it meets all the mathematical requirements for an equilibrium, it is rather difficult to understand why should people pay an 'extra' when the good in question is a public good. The bribal-price mechanism has 'no advantage over prices.' It provides benefits only to bribers and bribees.

Relationship among Crime, Corruption and Development

Traditionally, economic development is defined as the GNP growth over time. Amartya Sen defines economic development as the process of introducing substantive freedoms of people. For instance, unequal distribution of voice is undesirable as unequal distribution of income in the functioning of a democracy. Human freedoms are vital for economic development. Since corruption refers to the denial of access of disadvantaged people, it means someone is *deprived* of something. Any denial of opportunities of transaction or absence of transparency and information in any business deal is a source of 'unfreedom' itself. The process of economic development should include the removal of this 'unfreedom' and 'deprivation'. Sen puts the issue thus: ". . . freedoms are part and parcel of enriching the process of development." (*Sen, Amartya*, 1999).

It is believed by a section of people that corruption may positively improve efficiency and growth. Bribes and gifts grease the wheels of rigid administration, business and trade. It enables entrepreneurs to cut through red tape. It has been observed from the surveys of business people of a number of countries that in 1996 business executives as well as the owners of the business spent on an average 30 p.c. of their time dealing with government bureaucrats. (*Rose-Akerman, Susan*, 1999). It is the 'time preference' that induces people to offer gifts and bribes. In the words of Nathaniel H. Leff, "If the government has erred in its decision, the course made possible by corruption may well be the better one." (*Bardhan, Pranab*, 1997). But unscrupulous civil servants, instead of speeding up the work, actually create delays in order to attract more special but illegal payment (*Bardhan, Pranab*, 1997).

This false notion of corruption as an indicator of bureaucratic efficiency destroys the basic premise of meritocracy. Efficiency and denial of merit cannot go hand in hand. Corruption then impinges adverse effects not just on static efficiency but also on investment, productivity and growth. Corruption has greatly damaged the prospects for economic growth especially in Africa and Latin America.

Paolo Mauro (*Mauro, Paoplo*, 1997) finds a significant negative correlation between the corruption index and the investment rate or the rate of economic growth. An improvement in the corruption index causes investment rate to rise by 4 p.c. and the per capita GDP to rise annually by half percentage point. An empirical result obtained by Alberto Ades and Rafael di Tella suggests than in the presence of corruption, the direct positive impact of industrial policies is halved. (*Rose-Ackerman, Susan*, 1999). Another study says that 'if corruption levels in India were reduced to those in Scandinavian countries, investment rate could increase by 10 to 12 per cent per annum and the GDP growth rate could increase by almost 1.5 per cent per annum.' (*Gandhi, Ram*, 1997).

Because of the high cost of doing business in a corrupt environment (as investors are required to pay a risk premium for the sanctioning of the project) cost of capital tends to rise, thereby dwarfing the size of actual amount of capital investment and hence growth.

Another disturbing element is that corruption not only reduces returns on investment but also distorts investment structure. Paolo Mauro observes that countries that rank high in the levels of corruption have the tendency to invest less on education as a ratio of GDP. Probably, education is the area where opportunities for corruption are few. Other components of government expenditure, such as transfer payments are also negatively and significantly associated with the corruption index. Mauro adds further that one does not find any significant relationship between corruption and government spending on defence or transportation. This does not mean that these areas are corrupt-free. In India, sarcastically, the Public Works Department, *i.e.* PWD and Military Engineering Service, *i.e.* MES, are called Plunder Without Danger and Money Earning Service. May be these are folklores about corruption, but people believe these through their experiences.

Investment in infrastructure projects (like road-dam construction) gets stimulated in a corrupt regime as the bribery potential of these projects tend to be high. But empirical evidence reveals that higher the level of corruption poor is the quality of infrastructure. "An important implication of the results is that the costs of corruption should be measured in terms of deterioration in the quality of existing infrastructure, since costs can severely inhibit economic growth." (*Tanzi V. and Davoodi H.*, 1998).

One cannot draw a significant correlation between corruption index and the foreign direct investment. The cleanest country may expect a high FDI inflow or a corrupt country may not attract high FDI inflow.

Other things being equal, high corruption is associated with low government revenue since tax evasion takes place on a large scale. Thus, corruption and black money are inseparable. A black economy lowers the savings rate and adversely affects the growth of an economy. Above all, the democratic system gets perverted in a corrupt regime. A psuedodemocratic government cannot be conducive to economic growth.

III

EXTENT OF CORRUPTION IN DIFFERENT COUNTRIES, INCLUDING INDIA

Although the requisite time-series evidence in terms of hard data is absent, an optimistic view prevails that corruption tends to decline as economic growth takes place. The experience of the UK, the USA, and other rich countries over the last 100 years or so support this view. This means corruption is benign to LDCs. Corruption is not rare in rich countries and even in communist countries of Europe, China and Vietnam. Pranab Bardan's explanation of corruption in these erstwhile socialist countries may be presented here: "For a considerable period of time the transition economy is on a dual-track system: a part of output is still under obligatory delivery at controlled prices, while the rest is allowed to be sold at market prices. This creates all kinds of new opportunities for corruption." (*Bardhan, Pranab*, 1997).

Here we will consider two different sets of data for estimating the extent of corruption. It is to be kept in mind that these are all guesstimates since white-collar economic crimes mostly remain either unreported or undetected. Anyway, a World Bank study on corruption of different countries is given in Table 1.

Another attempt to estimate corruption is made regularly by Transparency International (TI). It constructs every year Corruption Perceptions Index (CPI) on the basis of multiple surveys relating to perceptions of degree of corruption as seen by business analysts and the general public. CPI ranks countries in terms of the degree to which they are perceived to be the

TABLE 1
World Bank Study on Corruption

Countries	*Rank of Corruption*
South Africa, Mauritius, Colombia, Ecuador, Venezuela	1
Benin, Mali, Nigeria, Bolivia, Paraguay, Peru	1
Guinea, Guinea-Bissau, Senegal, Cameroon, Chad, Congo	1
Armenia, Azerbaijan, Georgia, Kazakhstan, Kyrgyz Republic	2
Uzbekistan, Jordan, Morocco, West Bank and Gaza Strip	2
Kenya, Tanzania, Uganda, Zambia	2
Czech Republic, Hungary, Poland, Slovak Republic	3
Estonia, Lativa, Lithuania, Madagascar, Malwai, Mozambique	3
Zimbabwe, Albania, Bulgaria, FYR Macedonia, Turkey	3
Cote d'lvoire, Ghana, Togo	3
Costa Rica, Jamaica, Mexico	4
Belarus, Moldova, Russia, Ukraine, Fiji, India, Malaysia	6
Italy, Portugal, Spain	6
Austria, France, Germany, Switzerland	9
Canada, United States	12
Ireland, United Kingdom	13

Source: How Business See Government, IFC Discussion Paper 33, 1998.

homes of the bribe-takers. To construct CPI, TI conducted survey over 52 countries in 1997, 85 in 1998 and 99 in 1999. A '10' CPI score indicates a completely clean country and a '0' CPI score indicates a completely corrupt country. Table 2 shows a country's rank and CPI score.

As far as this table is concerned, Denmark tops the list in CPI ranking with an essentially corrupt-free score of 10 as against Cameroon's 1.5. High income OECD's ranking is also high. Index of corruption for most of the CISs hovers around 2.3 and 2.6. India's CPI score in 1999 is 2.9 *vis-a-vis* China's 3.4. Thus, corruption in the communist systems or the so-called transition economies is widespread.

Truly speaking, there has been a structural change in the pattern of corruption in India. It has spread even to those levels of administration where it was conspicuously absent some 20 or 30 years ago. Political leaders with criminal records, bureaucrats, judges, police, and other high-profiles of the society are involved in nourishing and nurturing corruption in India. The decade of 1990s saw the high season of corruption in India when some of the Chief Ministers, Ex-Prime Ministers, more than 2 dozen Union

TABLE 2
The 1999 CPI

Country Rank	*Countries*	*1999 CPI Score*
1.	Denmark	10.0
3.	New Zealand, Sweden	9.4
7.	Singapore	9.1
13.	United Kingdom	8.6
18.	USA	7.5
19.	Chile	6.9
38.	Italy	4.7
50.	South Korea	3.8
58.	China	3.4
72.	India	2.9
75.	Vietnam	2.6
82.	Russia	2.4
90.	Paraguay	2.0
94.	Uzbekistan	1.8
99.	Cameroon	1.5

Source: Transparency International: 1999 Bribe Payers Index and 1999 Corruption Perceptions Index.
Website: www. Transparency./de/documents/cpi/index.html.

Ministers, bureaucrats, technocrats, police and even judges were implicated in corruption charges. How sinister linkages between the underworld dons and political leaders as well as bureaucrats have fostered crime syndicates/Mafia organisations in India has been succinctly put forward by the N.N. Vohra Committee in its 1993 report: "The linkages developed by Crime Syndicates get generally confirmed when pressure is mounted on the concerned agencies not to take action against the offenders or to go slow in the cases against them."

All these have led to criminalisation of politics to take a front seat. Roughly, one-fourth of our people's representatives have criminal records. Criminals are sheltered by politicians, and *vice versa*. Thus, crime and corruption are paying.

Causes

Corruption has its roots in power and discretion of the public officials and the opportunities generated by policy environment and outdated colonial laws. In a state-controlled mixed economy like India, civil servants apply their discretion and power and indulge themselves in interpreting laws and procedures that suit them most. All these causes delay or red tapism in administration. Speed money can remove this hurdle. An Indian is supposed to offer bribes to collect birth certificate, passport, driving licence, plan sanction and mutation of a building, tax assessment, ration card, pension order, death certificate and what not, to circumvent the rules and regulations. Bureaucrats indulge themselves in interpreting laws and rules and regulation according to their wishes and whims, particularly because of poor drafting of laws. Procedural wrangles encourage delay in decision-making. All these explain why corruption culture become strong when distortions in rules and regulations are cunningly created. Power, thus, absolutely corrupts people.

Indian bureaucracy is marked by notorious rigidity as far as rules and regulations, practices and procedures are concerned. Power and discretion stems from such regulations and control. The building construction in Mumbai city requires 47 different approvals. A small-scale entrepreneur has to face as much as 36 inspectors each month and 46 separate documents are required to be submitted for each export consignment (*Gandhi, Ram*, 1997). Clearance of such projects obviously demands illegal payments. In the process, the bribal markets thrive.

Secondly, we see a plethora of bureaucratic control over business and industry through licensing, quotas, foreign exchange, monopolistic and restrictive trade practices, company laws, etc. It is strongly argued that an over-controlled economy is an ideal breeding ground for corruption. "Any policy that creates an artificial gap between demand and supply creates a profitable opportunity for opportunistic middlemen." (*World Development Report*, 1997).

Thirdly, outdated colonial laws enforced by the 'soft' government are responsible for creating opportunities of corruption in India. Laws are full of loopholes and often contradictory. Judiciary takes unusually long time to punish the accused.

Fourthly, low wages in civil service relative to wages and perks in private sector and inflation are the source of low-level corruption.

Finally, the western culture of consumerism and bandwagonism has made deep inroads in India. Man's needs for more and more material goods or purchase beyond one's means necessarily requires dishonest means. The wave of consumerism is so strong in India that the typical 'middle class ethic of hard work' has been superseded by money that nourishes dishonesty.

For all these reasons, opportunities and the temptations for economic and political crimes are high. A data published by the Government of India in 1999 reveals that there was an increase in economic crimes by 7.4 p.c. over 1995 as against a decline of violent crimes by 0.7 p.c. and property crimes by 2.6 p.c. during the same time period. In India, one defends corruption behaviour by the argument that "others do the same". (*Sen, Amartya,* 1999). An author has elegantly described this argument in the following words: "Corruption is the hard core pornography of power; and has all its voyeuristic attractions." (*Shah, Ghanashyam,* 1990).

IV

COMBATING CORRUPTION

Whenever business and industry enter into 'sleazy' dealing or 'underhand' dealing, the businessmen add the price of red tapism on the cost of his product. In the process, common man is affected 'through higher prices, bad roads, and poor product quality'. Thus, the impact of crime and corruption on an economy is widespread.

A multi-pronged strategy is needed to combat corruption in India. What is recommended is the reforming of the civil service so that public officials do not enjoy any blanket discretionary power. A time-bound decision-making process should be devised to off-set bureaucratic delay. Some people suggest decontrol, deregulation, debureaucratisation and privatisation to root out corruption. But we are afraid that corruption relating to privatisation will inevitably perpetuate in a society where moral values are in shambles. What we suggest is the removal of unnecessary controls and regulations and unlimited as well as unjustified discretionary power. Amartya Sen says that "any system of governance cannot but give some power to the officers that is worth something to others who may try to offer inducements for corruption. The reach of such power can certainly be reduced, but many substantive executive power can be potentially open to abuse." (*Sen, Amartya,* 1999).

Outdated and ambiguous laws are to be streamlined and scrapped so that discretionary power enjoyed by civil servants can be reduced. Legal process dealing with corruption must not be a long-drawn affair. Above all, laws, regulations and procedures are to be made more transparent.

Sometimes, "corruption-preventing allowance" or "money to nourish honesty" is suggested to tackle corruption. Informers who pass on information relating to bribery may also be rewarded. But this will not work effectively in India because of criminalisation of politics as well as "there is also the complex issue of providing the right incentives for thief-catchers (so that they are not bought off)." (*Sen, Amartya*, 1999). What we suggest is adequate wages and salaries combined with merit-based recruitment and promotion schemes without any signs of favouritism and patronage.

We also recommend that people with criminal records must be disqualified for contesting any public office. Political leaders must declare their assets and liabilities to an appropriate quasi-judicial body. What is wrong if salary structure for ministers, legislators are introduced instead of providing perks to virtually in unlimited amount? Donations and gifts for electioneering purposes to political parties by industrialists, businessmen should be stopped immediately. Unfortunately, the proposal of state funding for meeting election expenses of the recognised political parties recently came to nought because of the resistance made by political parties themselves. Herein lies the importance of a strong and committed political will. So far as the political power equation in India is concerned, required political will and dedicated leadership are not forthcoming.

Finally, one of the most important anti-corruption strategies is the empowering of citizens. People should have easy and greater access to various government documents (except sensitive information) so as to propagate the 'right to information'. Greater access to information and transparency act as a strong bulwarks against crime and corruption. Thus, a paradigm shift is necessary.

CONCLUSION

Should not our goal be no or zero corruption? Ideally, we say 'yes' but total elimination is hardly conceivable since it is the power that corrupts people. It is the controlling and regulatory mechanism that spawns corruption. So, what is needed is the abatement rather than total elimination of corruption. Under the circumstances, one may argue for 'optimal level of corruption' (*Basu, Kaushik*, 1991), or break-even point or 'an efficient corruption abatement level'. To determine an optimal or efficient level of corruption economists can apply the marginal principle. The efficient or optimal level of corruption is determined at that point where marginal social benefit of reducing corruption equals marginal social costs of that reduction. However, economists may differ over this issue since unlike 'pollution rights', the concept of 'corruption rights' may not work. Further, differences of opinion relating to fixing of an exact optimal volume of corruption may be very strong. Anyway, corruption has the debilitating and destabilising impacts on the society, but "it may be a bad strategy to weed it out altogether."

REFERENCES

Bardhan, Pranab K., "Corruption and Development: A Review of Issues," *Journal of Economic Literature*, Vol. XXXV (September 1997).

Basu, Kaushik, "Economic Graffiti, Essays for Everyone," Oxford University Press (1991).

Benson, L., "A Note on Corruption by Public Officials:" The Black Market for Property Rights," *Journal of Libertarian Studies*, 5, No. 3 (Summer, 1981).

Grandhi, Ram, "*Combating Corruption: A National Agenda*," Forum of Free Enterprise (December, 1997).

Kuper, A. & Kuper, J., "*The Social Encyclopedia*," Routledge, London & New York, (1996).

Mauro, Paolo, "*Why Worry about Corruption?*" IMF, Washington, D.C. (1997).

Rose-Ackerman, Susan: "*Corruption and Government*," Cambridge University Press (1999).

Sen, Amartya, "*Development as Freedom*," Oxford University Press (1999).

Shah, Ghanashyam (ed.), "*Capitalist Development: Critical Essays*". Felicitation Volume in Honour of Prof. A.R. Desai, Bombay. Popular Prakashan Pvt. Ltd. (1990).

Tanzi Vitto & Davoodi Hamid, "*Roads to Nowhere: How Corruption in Public Investment Hurts Growth*," IMF, Washington, D.C. (1998).

World Bank, "*World Development Report, 1997*," Oxford University Press, (1997).

5

Crime, Corruption and Development in Indian Economy

I.D. GUPTA

I

INTRODUCTION

India is termed as one of most corrupt countries in the world. At the same time it is said India is set to be a super power in the Twenty-first Century. While Indian economy is recognised as one of the less developed countries whose prime characteristics are low per capita income, low living standard, lower productivity levels, its efficient manpower pool is recognised all over the world. She is one of the largest suppliers of engineers, doctors and other technical personnel. Now there is a rush for trained engineers in computers and information technology. So how do we reconcile these cross currents?

It is not only India but Transparency International has recognised China, Philippines and so many other countries of the world as highly corrupt. Is upsurge of crime and corruption a global tendency? Is it going to be discussed at par with inflation—which at one point of time was recognised as short-term local market disequilibrium phenomenon? Classicals never discussed it and even Keynes left it as one of the phenomena

The author thanks Prof. S.P. Dikshit, Dr. Rakesh Kumar, Dr. Arvind Awasthi, Department of Economics, Lucknow University, Lucknow and Dr. Rameshwar Tandon for motivating to write this paper and valuable discussions on the earlier draft of the paper.

after attainment of full-employment in his inflationary-gap analysis.

This paper attempts to analyse the setting and crystalization process of corruption *vis-à-vis* planned economic and social development in India in the past fifty years. It seeks to answer the basic questions of development for what and development for whom. It also seeks to analyse the degeneration that has set in the country and attempts to find its ideological background. The developments in development theory regarding corruption is one of the areas of search. Briefly in the last sections it puts its impact on economy and attempts to find out the "way-out" in its concluding section.

The agenda of corruption is being discussed since Plato and even before him while discussing "sins" of the citizens. We have to recognise it as part and parcel of life, an essential truth, which emerges and had been emerging in the "mind-set" of people since ages. The point of discussion ought to be the sustainable level of corruption that a country could bear.

II

VISION OF DEVELOPMENT: PAST AND PRESENT

Leaving aside corruption for the moment we may take up the concept and meaning of development itself, which is changing over time, as also the relevance of development for different classes of society. Development is a complex phenomenon that tends to resist analysis cast in simple and aggregate terms. Development economics, by and large, remains a "young" branch of economics, one which still grapples with the problem of finding a stable identity. As a result, the focus of study has shifted, time after time, and old "truths" have had to be re-examined.

The definition of development with changing emphasis from aggregates or rates of changes in national production, to quality of life, to human development, to attainment of human rights and civilized life, to poverty alleviation, to gender justice and gender empowerment, to sustainable development, to social sector development and human face of development, to maintenance of "core values" of society, it has been encompassing concrete to abstract levels of longings, hopes and aspirations of different nations and people. Still the agenda of arriving at a universally acceptable concept is unfinished.

Is development a tool for attaining certain ends? Then could we fall in line with Gandhi or Tilak in stressing or obviating purity of means and purity of end? This could only answer development for what and how. The third answer development for whom will automatically come then.

The development of a country depends on the ideology that she follows as also on the character of its people—the inner qualities and disqualifications of its citizens. These are two things. India had been looked upon as a country of high spiritual attainments in the past, and for its sages allegiance to God and His realization to them dominated their thought process in prescribing a path of development based on "simple living and high thinking" for centuries. It is reputed that the Indians least bothered for material acquisition and had given no weight to amassing wealth, for the higher thing to attain in life was His realization and the path suggested was that of sacrifice and service to humanity and relieving people of their sufferings. This had been in a true sense the philosophy of life. They believed in Karma philosophy—of cause and result, embodied in the Indian way of life.

With the advent of Moghuls and the English and their cultural cross currents and more so in the post-industrial revolution era the emphasis shifted towards material acquisition and "standards" of living based on material things of life. There was a changed prescription for alleviation of human sufferings. Our emphasis of development shifted from wantlessness and minimising wants to maximising wants and how to attain new peaks of material acquisition.

At the cross roads in the Indian history, after our political independence, we were confused over acceptance of value systems: whether Indian or western and students in universities and seats of higher learning were taught lessons in line with the western vision of development. Nehru's ideological predilections and his vision of India, however, put India on a path of mixed economy. The objectives of economic planning and policies being attainment of socialistic pattern of society. Nehru's socialist leaning was not out of context, in view of the excellent Soviet performance, in prescribing a mixed economy pattern which keeps at bay capitalist exploitation (of labour and consumers) as well as socialist regimentation which almost negates civilised values so avowedly fought and won through French Revolution and Lincoln's crusade against slavery.

Planning in India was intended, in the words of the Government Resolution of March 1950 "to promote a rapid rise in the standard of living of the people by efficient exploitation of resources of the country, increasing production, and offering opportunities to all for employment in the service of the community." In December 1954, Parliament adopted a resolution which contained the clauses: "the objective of economic policy should be a socialistic pattern of society; and, towards this end the tempo of economic activity in general and industrial development in particular should be stepped up to maximum possible extent." It also declared that "the basic criterion of determining lines of advance must not be private profit, but social gain". Article 39 of the Directive Principles of State Policy declared "that State's policies would ensure that operation of economic system does not result in the concentration of wealth and means of production to the common detriment." The intentions were clear (although we adopted a western vision of development).

III

DEVELOPMENT EXPERIENCE

Now it is time to review the progress. How we performed? And where we erred? The Indian economy was divided into public and private sectors; public sector was assigned commanding heights and economy started growing through planned efforts. The overall rate of growth of GDP had been 3.7 percent per annum uptill 1980s, thereafter it escalated above 5 percent. Despite severe set backs in the form of three wars of 1962, 1965 and 1971 and droughts in the late sixties the performance was not unsatisfactory, if not impressive.

However, due mainly to massive population growth, (which doubles the population in every generation according to Malthusian projection), in India most of our growth targets started belying hopes and a system of 'regulated economy' and shortages of food and foreign exchange which began after Second Five Year Plan contributed to a system of black money economy and degeneration of moral values started setting in the system.

It took some years uptill 1970s and then it got matured from an infancy stage of 1960s which was ridden with years of food crisis. The second element of development, the character and quality of the vehicles of growth, as mentioned earlier, now becomes important. We have to analyse as to what are the basic constituents of the character of people and in totality nation, and its driving force. And who constitute the functional part of the "people". The vocal among the people, the urban elite, the upper twenty percent segment of population, or who form important or functional part of people? Because it is those are vocal take away substantial (due or undue) share—the fruits of development. In this so-called free system (democratic), development share goes to those who form functional part of people; i.e., those who matter.

If we could define the basic traits of character we could get into its motive force and read the "mind-set" of the larger part of the people. We have to get into the facts which corrupt the psyche of the people. Defining "mind" or 'motivation' which drives one to work, we can say, it is an interplay of thoughts, emotions and intellect. Human beings are supposed to be superior to other living beings due to their development of mind. Hence, it is direction of mind in a particular way through intellect or reason which makes man superior to other animals. Reason contains emotional outbursts and that makes man superior and civilized. This is not to ignore the conditioning influence of the social environment.

Factors which made its people (most or few) corrupt over the years needs to be analysed. It is amply clear that economic events cannot be explained in isolation and we shall have to find its roots in social and political developments in the country as well, during this period.

In India particularly since the "food crisis" in the early sixties and beginning of rationing and control regime things started moving from bad to worse. With rationing and control emerged black market system which started growing under "Inspector raj". Officials in power—the empowered ones—started misusing their authority. Such was the allurement of black or 'easy money' in the form of bribe that forces employed to combat corruption fell prey to corruption itself. The lure to become rich quickly in a starved country like India has a 'demonstration effect'. We observe that while during the fifties only court clerks and octroi posts were recognised for accepting petty grafts, over the years almost all public institutions fell prey to earning easy money. Whether it is police, tax, municipal, public works, railways, electricity, telephones, forest departments or even it is judiciary everywhere corruption pervades. We cannot single out the government department where it is non-existent.

There was a change in ethos. Society over the years legitimised and accepted it. Those who were indicted earlier in society for getting through corrupt means were exonerated and being powerful with money power became respectable. This could not have been possible unless and until protection had been granted to the 'players' by the godfathers. Over the past three decades in every street and corner 'toughs' emerged protected by local mafias which again were protected by police and political godfathers. The local market of corruption later developed into state, national and international syndicates. We shall revisit the Indian scenario.

IV

Recent works in development theory brought to light that in the Third World countries of Africa and Asia the political system has started moving from democracy to Kleptocracy. Kleptocratic or predatory state has been defined as a political system where brigandage constitutes the predominant form of power and the ruler or elite are those who are specialists in violence. Economists like Douglas North even define the state as a praetorian entity with a comparative advantage in violence and it uses this advantage to specify property rights in a way which favours the ruler and the group supporting him, i.e., the state easily becomes predatory.[1] Margarate Levi argues that all states are predatory in principle. It is only the existence of a number of constraints on government behaviour that prevents predation from being practised in some cases.

With the criminalisation of politics and increasing influence of money (black money) the Indian political and economic scenario since seventies present a picture of the above described predatory character where the ruler or the ruling clique uses the state apparatus to maximise his or its private net revenue. One of the main problems of a ruler or a party in such a state is how to remain in power, for without power there in no income.

Douglas North[1] opines that one method of predation is the use of 'ideology'. Typically ideologies entail norms and values which run counter to self-interest, and what is more, ideologies are often created with this very purpose in mind: to make citizens of a country loyal to its rulers and their official proclaimed goals (seldom real ones). In this context ideology serves to make citizens do something contrary to what they actually want. A functioning ideology increases the legitimacy of the sitting regime in the eyes of the public. Framing the things in an ideological get-up can be easily done by the 'elite' which is subservient to the ruling class. The group of intelligentsia in and around the government machinery and administration can easily make the things 'presentable' and 'marketable'. The slogans of 'Garibi Hatao' in seventies, and Mandal divide in the name of 'social justice' in 1980s were all merely diplomacy of terms. The inner objective was clinging to the seat of power.

We observe changes in the politico-economic scenario of the country in subsequent decades after the attainment of independence; forties and fifties—in the *Gandhi-Nehru period*—reflected a value system embodying Gandhian philosophy of sacrifice and selflessness. Obviously the freedom struggle was fresh in the mind set of the people. The policies were tuned in the direction of attainment of a 'socialistic pattern of society' and nation's well-being superseded individual's well-being.

By the seventies many of the premises had changed and as a result of rationing and control regime developed a parallel system in the economy vitiating the value system of fifties and in politics during *Indira Gandhi-Sanjaya era* criminalisation of politics started setting in. Disappearance of work culture in public sector and in permanent government jobs made the system sick. The country was swiftly moving from Gandhian selflessness norm to a materialistic and 'self' before nation philosophy. The rat race for becoming rich by any means became preponderant. Obviously, the distributive justice was at a jeopardy and income and wealth inequalities began to widen. It was observed that despite the four Five Year Plans around 40 percent of the population were below the poverty line. Equations started changing and society found neo-rich classes of industrialists, bureaucrats and a few others flourishing with 'easy money'. Uptill now as stated earlier those with acquired riches by corrupt means were regarded condemned in the society. Later on society started accepting it and money and muscle power started dominating every scene. This was the time when old generation of people was replaced by next-generation who were born and brought-up in peace time free India.

Narasimha Rao period 1990's was marked with political corruption and scams. The very forces which started setting in during the earlier period were crystalised and plundering of nations' wealth became systematic. Many of the ministers, bureaucrats and those in power and position left no stone unturned in fulfilling the duties of their inner self (Kleptocracy). In one of the discussions during a seminar, one of the famous historians estimated that plundering of nation's wealth during free India and that kept in Swiss Bank accounts, far exceeds the wealth plundered by Mahmud Gazanavi, and the British rule. Had this not happened, the country would not have been as poor as it is.

By now criminal-police-politician nexus has come of age and the infant is grown up. Black money pervades this nexus and, as said earlier, lubricates the system to keep going. It feeds corruption and corruption feeds it. Long back, it was estimated in 1953-54 by Nicholas Kaldor while talking of Indian Tax Reform that the size of unaccounted income was six percent of GDP or Rs. 600 crore. Wanchoo Committee's final report in 1979 put it at 4.2 percent. Rangnekar estimated in at 7 to 9 percent. Recently, NIPFP has estimated the size of black money economy at Rs. 40,000 crores. Some opine that the amount involved is as much as 20 percent of the GDP of the economy. Suraj Bhan Gupta put the size of black money at over 50 percent of GDP in 1987-88 (1,49,297 crores). It is stated that the annual rate of growth of black money is higher than the annual growth rate of GDP.

Direct Taxes Enquiry Committee in its final report (1971) had recognised, "black money and tax evasion, which go hand in hand, have also the effect of seriously undermining the equity concept of taxation and warping its progressiveness. Together they throw a greater burden on the honest tax payer and lead to economic inequality and concentration of wealth in the hands of the unscrupulous few in the country".

Now we may look into the system that has developed over the years. As stated earlier, crime, corruption and black income requires for its protection, proliferation and expansion, the service of organisation composed of musclemen, toughs, touts and brokers to combat the forces of law and order, on the one hand and on the other hand there are tax advisers, consultants and chartered accountants in the pay role of black money operators. Then there are contactmen who negotiate favours from top bureaucracy and political bosses through bribes of black money.

We may also look into this process from another angle. The politics of black money has eroded the moral fibre of Indian polity and society. Musclemen and criminals are fed by political parties to capture booths and thus elections are becoming more and more of a farce. National policies are, therefore, being bent in favour of the big business under the pressure of black money. Big subscriptions to party funds during elections is an example. Thus, it is the parallel economy which does back seat driving (remote controlled driving), while the political leadership only acts as a mouthpiece of big business to justify the abolition of controls or introduction of dual system of price in the name of productivity or national interest.

As stated earlier too, the malignant growth of corruption in India is eroding the value system of society. Virtues such as honesty, hardwork and sincerity are undermined. This has serious consequences for economy, political system and society. This virus has multiplied at a tremendous rate. In a recently concluded press meet one of the DGP's in U.P. remarked candidly about increasing political interference and corruption in the IPS cadre. "Honest police officers are being systematically sidelined while the corrupt are getting crushy postings", said the Director-General. "When I joined the cadre, only five officers out of 175 were known to be dishonest. They were singled out and ostracised. But now there is a dramatic rise of this tribe and this is cause of concern" lamented he. "Law and order in U.P. is deteriorating over the last one decade and this can be attributed to social and political changes. The nexus between student leaders and criminals has contributed to this and politicians are also responsible for the phenomenon". He diagnosed.[2]

Police patronizing criminals (and criminal activities) and then political leaders patronizing police and criminal through political interference in the working of combative machinery has become common practice. Researches have shown that many of the criminals themselves have become politicians. And many elected leaders and ministers have criminal cases pending against them.

Divided on caste lines since Mandal divide in 1980s the things have become more complicated. Parties for getting majority in elections have invited and given party tickets to dacoits and there is a competition to outnumber the rival party by any means. For, in a democracy it is the number and weight of personality that counts. Persons with higher degree of nuisance value have high rating of eligibility in the matter. Recurrent violence in council houses of many states (whether it is U.P., Bihar, Andhra or Maharashtra) speaks volumes about the quality of encumbents and their culture.

The situation has reached to such proportions that every lucrative police post is auctioned, every lucrative seat in almost all the government departments are auctioned to highest bidders. There are rates of appointment from peon to the higher posts. Every public department have developed percentage system. The contractor passes on the premium and gets the payment. System is smooth with 'honesty of thieves' in dividing the loot.

Even educational institutions are now not free from the menace. There are operating rackets from admissions to the award of degree. This is not to touch upon the fake universities and colleges running on donations. So-called student leaders and corrupt officials and clerks of Universities and Colleges in remote areas are live demonstration of admission to copying to degree rackets. Even Vice-Chancellors—the god of local academia—of many reputed universities have been indicted for being involved in money rackets and appointments scandals. They have either been arrested or vigilance enquiries are pending against them.[3]

Politics is the best refuge of scoundrels, said a thinker. It makes one 'above law' and immune to punishment. This explains why politics has become so lucrative a pastime.

Crime and corruption have insurmountable impact on the economy and society. First and foremost it makes correct estimate of the size and volume of economic activities difficult and therefore policy formulations may be, in most of the cases, misdirected. Then, the scarce national resources being put in for poverty removal go waste in the 'leaking bottles'. The huge public fund diversion for the purpose in Plans is being usurped by bureaucrats, *netas, mafias* and middlemen flourishing on the corrupt system. Again, this heavily hampers the equitable distribution of income and wealth. Inequitable income distribution again leads to social tensions besides economic tensions. Growth of crime too is partly attributed to unjust income distribution. This also explains why the lots of the landless, small and marginal farmers and those identified below the poverty line have not improved despite sustained planned efforts for fifty years. Was the planning meant for 'trickle-down' or 'trickle-up'? We can easily identify which classes have gained over successive decades and through what means. Hence, there is a need for a cogent income policy and tax system based not on recorded incomes only but on expenditure levels. The exercise has to be worked out by the government and ways and means could be suggested by the economists.

V

As the "way-out", there may be three dimensions to the solution. One pertains to the ideological clarity, second relates to strengthening the institutions which inculcate value system and prepare civilized and responsible citizenry for the future and the third concerns with the combative machinery and evolving systems which eliminate opportunities for corruption.

The paper has mentioned in the earlier parts about the ideological confusion in defining goal of economic policies. One important aspect is the lack of direction, mainly after the acceptance of globalisation, privatisation and marketisation as the economic reform measures since 1991. India may not avoid the pressure of international forces but at least it can find out our own solutions to protect our national identity and people of the country, particularly the common man and those below the poverty-line. Again, the question to be answered is, development for what and for whom. Our economic policies cannot afford for ever to subserve the interests of only the 'elite' and upper twenty percent segment of the population.

Since the problem has emerged from the 'mind-set' of the people in India (due mainly to disregarding real Indian character and philosophy of life) hence the solution has to be searched there. We are living with the Western ideology in formulating our economic system which will never suit the psyche of the people in true sense and is bound to derail.

India is a home of some major religions of the world. She has also democratic form of government. Both, people's involvement with religion and democratic polity, are major constraints on speedier growth. However, the rate of economic growth cannot be a true measure of well-being in the Indian setting. Development of non-material resources has also to be viewed as a vital component of social advancement. This implies that India does not have to be in the market for full scale liberalization.[4]

Just as our planned mixed economy was unique we will have to look for an alternative path within. 'Leaders of great nations cannot afford to be puppets'. Affirming faith in Socialism on the occasion of the recently held celebrations of the 50th anniversary of the founding of Communist China President Jiang Zemin spoke of "socialist modernization" emphatically repudiating *laissez-faire*. In view of India's large cultural diversity and involvement of her people with religion and a value system bequeathed by an ancient civilization, her development strategy cannot avoid "explicit dealings with values".

Solution to to-day's problems does not lie in either capitalism or socialism. Changes in the past fifty years and particularly growth in technology has recently led to a drastic redefining of the relative role of State and Market and such a re-definition need not be a uni-directional retreat on an across-the-board expansion. World has seen the futility of either of the two systems and hence even in market economy countries national leaders are talking about the "Third-way". To quote Tony Blair, the British Prime Minister, "I have always believed that polities is first and foremost about ideas. Without a powerful commitment to goals and values, governments are rudderless and ineffective, however large their majorities. Furthermore, ideas need labels if they are to become popular and widely understood. The "Third-way" "is to my mind, the best label for the new polities which the progressive centre-left is forging in Britain and beyond".[5]

"The Third-way stands for a modernised social democracy, passionate in the commitment to social justice and the goals of the centre-left, but flexible, innovative and forward-looking in the mean to achieve them."

It is opportune time for India, whose democracy is matured one, to rethink about the so-called reforms and decide what policies would best conserve the contents of welfare state. What would be best way in the interest of masses. Obviously we will have to go back to the middle path of mixed-economy in its new form. Redefining the role of market and state and a new mix of the mixed economy is the need of time.[6] The discussions in academia should be on this point.

And here again we will have to discuss the path of "rationalising wants". Our scarce resources should decidedly go into the production of those goods which are "needed most" by "most people". In deciding and re-directing the consumption pattern of Indian economy we will have to distinguish between "legitimate consumption" and otherwise.[7]

The next step in dealing with corruption and development issue would be strengthening the institutions: where family comes first and next to it the schools (upto universities) where our young generation is prepared to face the world and make it an ideal place to live and grow. Many of degeneration that we find in society to-day is due to the weakening of these institutions. There was an old saying: "as the king so the people". Now it is "as the people so the king" for it is a democracy—the people's government.

The point here is what are the forces which are responsible for degeneration of these institutions. We may mention one among them the massive growth of population over the years. One of the Swedish Economists was of such an opinion that he had not awarded the university degree unless students believed that source of all the problems is population growth.

We visualise crowd and crowd everywhere in schools, in colleges, in universities, on roads, on railways, on buses, in hospitals. How can we compare Indian living standards with those of Switzerland and Sweden and compare with them in Human Poverty Index ranking

Correct the atmosphere of homes and schools, the school of thought will automatically develop in right direction. We talk about student leader-criminal nexus and politicians patronizing them. Why we allow student unions in colleges and universities at all? May be they are the democratic institutions. But is it the right place where they have set in? Most of the student leaders are indisciplined, ruffians and toughs. The more one excels in breaking glass-panes, furnitures, burning buses, pelting stones on vehicles, intimidating and beating teachers, the best suited he is for student cause. The students cause—to allow their admissions by obviating rules, not to attend classes, freely copy in the examination halls and if failed in the examination get a pass degree in connivance with corrupt clerks and officials of universities. Time has come when not only we have to discuss Electoral Reforms we will have to discuss the legitimacy of allowing student unions in Universities. They are the degenerating force (in society) under preparation. Why not reform begin there and salvage the universities and colleges to breath in free and fresh air?

Assess the role of electronic media in deciding their role in our cultural degeneration by invading our home frontiers. We may use and develop this institution in expressing mature public opinion and starting debate over complex issues. This has started showing signs in analysing budgets, elections and other things.

Of the institutions, we may explore the role of media in responsible investigative journalism and the institution of public interest litigations (PIL). It is a new invention of the past few years which expresses maturity of the public opinion. Hope in true sense lies with it and there seems to be light in the dark tunnel in these forms. It is necessary to address the issue of judicial reforms in weaning out corruption from there and in particular evolving quick punishment system in cases involving corruption.

On the issue of political corruption, there is no point in harping on improving the moral fibre of our leaders or exhorting our voters not to elect corrupt leaders. It may help to legislate that persons with a criminal record or an established record of corruption should not be eligible to stand for any public office. But beyond that, the moral fibre of a nation or a group or a class hardly changes over the short-run, and if it does, it is only if our families became more principled and our so-called saints less opportunistic and more gifted at persuasion.[8]

The next dimension of the 'way-out' would be strengthening the combative machinery dealing with cases of corruption and reducing tax rates. We have come out of the phase of high marginal income tax rate. Three four years back they have been moderated. Still it needs to be reduced so that the allurement to tax evasion is reduced. People should not be burdened to the level where they revolt to become dishonest. To my humble suggestion income tax rates should be streamlined to 10, 15 and 25 percent for the existing slabs. What is required is to bring in more and more people in the tax net and as stated in the text earlier we should replace taxation on income with a suitable expenditure tax. So is the case with commodity taxation. This will go far in containing black money generation.

One of the basic psychological points in mind is that people with equal status are not taxed equally. It is only the salaried class whose income is reported pays tax rightly. The others equal to and above his income status in other profession either pay no tax or pay a meagre amount not disclosing their real incomes. Another point is why pay taxes at all, on hard earned income, when government machinery is corrupt and inefficient in catering the results and huge sums are wasted on un-economic ceremonial pomp and show, wastages on politicians' security and their useless foreign visits. Can a poor country afford for long their ministers, MPs and MLAs flaunting in luxurious air-conditioned class when most of the townships and villages are reeling in darkness? The question is, how the combative machinery of vigilance and police be given more teeth in fighting with gangs, and *mafia* syndicates.

In the concluding lines we may suggest that we will have to develop a transparent system everywhere in administration and to remove corruption from offices we may take the help of technological advancement and put the data and record on internet so that it could be available to all and "babu-raj" be given farewell. We could think in the direction of getting younger ministers, Chief Ministers and administrators replacing those tired ones living in the past. We may introduce a bar of 65 (or 70 years) as it is in all public institutions and judiciary.

Our young generation finding no jobs here flee to USA and other countries of Europe. Why can't we stop this brain drain of trained personnel? This enormous flow of human capital is not being utilized by us. If they can convert waste into gold elsewhere, why can't they do it here? Ultimately the responsibility comes on the shoulder of matured public opinion and persons in academia. This could not be done by only newspaper columnists. Universities have to come out in directing the countries on vital issues. I conclude by quoting that "Battle of Waterloo was won on the playfields of Eton".

NOTES AND REFERENCES

1. Douglas North, The Economics of Kleptocracy, Some Reflections on Underdevelopment and the Predatory States," in *Development That Lasts,* Kartik Roy *et. al* (Ed.), New Age International (1997).
2. *Times of India,* July 31, 2000.
3. *India Today,* July 31, 2000, Chancellors of Vice, p. 57.
4. Manmohan Singh, H.K., "Rethinking Reforms, Back to the Middle Path," *Indian Economic Journal,* Vol. 47, No. 3, Jan.-March 2000, pp. 19-30.
5. Blair, Tony, "New Politics for a New Century", *Indian Fiscal Journal,* Vol. IX, Nos. 1-3, Jan.-March, 2000, p. 11.
6. Reddy, Y.V., "State and Market, Altering the Boundaries and Emerging New Balances", *The Asian Economic Review,* Vol. 41, No. 3, Dec. 1999.
7. Gupta, I.D. "Development and Environmental Imperatives of Sustainable Development, India's Options", in Satyanarayan, B(Ed) *Social Sciences and Planning for Sustainable Development,* Himalaya Publishing House (1998).
8. Patel, I.G., *Economic Reforms and Global Change,* McMillan India Ltd. (1998).

6

Socio-Economic Dynamics of Crime in India

INDERJEET SINGH, HARVINDER KAUR AND PRAMOD KUMAR

I

INTRODUCTION

During the post-Second World War period, growth theory highlighted limited market size and vicious cumulation of market-oriented processes as the basic causes for underdevelopment of the third world, warranting balanced growth with industrialisation at its centre stage (*Myrdal,* 1955, *Nurkse,* 1973). Balanced growth thesis relied on the sectoral interdependence as the base of the equilibrium growth of economy (*Hirschman,* 1969). Empirical researches and the theoretical explorations have, however, highlighted the inadequacy of the conventional growth accounting in terms of expansion of homogeneous capital stock and undifferentiated labour, leaving an extremely large residual temporal rises of income unaccounted (*Leontief,* 1953). The residual has subsequently been explained by contributions of human capital to growth of income by its productivity effects (*Schultz,* 1959, *Dennison,* 1962, *Prakash, S.,* 1970, *Singh, I.* and *Singh, R.,* 1999). Presently the concept of development is seen in a broader sense, encompassing all types of economic, social and political change leading to human welfare.

For the emerging problems, our theory is much less complete and so is the database. The problem is associated with two hard and uncomfortable facts. First, the economy does not operate on abstraction relations. Second, the old, convenient assumption that the economy operates at a state of Pareto optimality in which marginal private cost is always equal to marginal social cost. In reality, the deviations between private and social costs are frequently significant. The socio-economic system, alongwith its products, produces many by-products. This causes a serious harm in terms of environmental destruction, crime, stress, etc. Thus, crime is partly an outcome of the socio-economic system of the economy. This paper is an attempt to analyse the crime in relation to socio-economic development experience of the country. The paper after relating the crime to different types of deprivation at state level attempts to analyse the pattern and structure of crime that has emerged in the 1990s decade.

II

THE MODEL

In its broad sense crime may be defined as an act of commission or omission which is baneful to the society in general. But all acts tending to the prejudice of the community are not crime, unless they are punishable under the law. Hence, crime includes such offences being acts of or defaults which have been made punishable by the Penal Code. Hence our analysis is limited to those crimes only which are punishable under Indian Penal Code (IPC).

Why does crime occur? There are many theories which explain the process. Some theories relate crime to psychological factors, while others relate it to the environment. Thus, in addition to psychological factors, crime is a function of the pace, nature and structure of socio-economic development. The nature and quantum of crime is a function of human development level, i.e., access to education, health and resources explain the level of crime to a good extent. In addition to this, poverty, unequal distribution of wealth and unemployment also contribute a lot to it.

Crime: For the inter-state analysis of crime, absolute quantum of crime (TOTCRIM) is of little use because there are wider differences in the state populations. There are two options: first it can be normalised by population (SPOP) as:

$CRIM_j = TOTCRIM_j/SPOP_j$

Second, it can be normalised by the State Domestic Product (SDP) as:

$CRIM_j = TOTCRIM_j/SDP_j$

Most of the studies have proved that the normalisation by population, i.e., crime per capita gives better results.

Deprivation: For measuring the deprivation, the methodology of HDI can be used. The best way to measure the human development is the UNDP's Human Development Index (HDI). HDI combines three indicators, i.e., life expectancy, educational attainment (defined as adult literacy mean years of schooling) and per capita income. HDI defines a measure of deprivation for each of these variables. For calculation of deprivation the maximum and minimum values have to be identified for actual values of these variables. The deprivation measure places a country in the zero to one range defined by the difference of maximum and minimum. The deprivation indicator, I_{ij}, showing deprivation for j^{th} state with respect to i^{th} variable is defined as:

$$I_{ij} = \frac{(\max X_{ij} - X_{ij})}{(\max X_{ij} - \min X_{ij})}$$

Average deprivation indicator I_j is computed by taking a simple average of the three indicators:

$$I_j = 1/3 \sum_{i=1}^{3} I_{ij}$$

Human Development Index is defined as one minus average deprivation indicator as:

$$HDI = (1 - I_j)$$

So, the crime per capita and the deprivation indicators can be used for inter-state comparative analysis.

III

THE ANALYSIS

There are two theories of crime, viz. the Lambrosian theory and the environmental theory. The Lambrosian theory of crime lays emphasis on psychological characteristics and heredity. The environmental theory, however, stresses on factors like association, educational background, geographical factors, economic and financial factors, etc. which play a dominant role in the creation of an environment leading to crime. Poverty or deprivation is one of the reasons of crime. A family entering a state of pauperism loses self-respect that is invariably found in every human being. And once the self-respect has been lost, the very instinct that distinguishes right from wrong, virtue from vice, no longer prevents the pauper from committing a crime. Necessity, on the other hand impels him to resort to it. Inequality in distribution of wealth and poverty means a denial of opportunities of access to resources, education and health. A renowned French author, Quetelet, in his famous book "*Social Physics*" has aptly described it: "Society contains within itself the germs of all crimes that are about to be committed, and the criminal is only the instrument which executes them."

State-wise composition (Table 1) of incidence of crime in India is indicative of the fact that states differ marginally as far as different heads of crime are concerned under the IPC. Major proportion of crimes fall in the "other crimes" category which includes crimes against women and juveniles. Next to it, theft is the most popular crime in the states of India. In Uttar Pradesh, murder and burglary together account for more than 26 percent of the total crimes. Hence, crime is not evenly distributed across the states.

Generally, deprivation is thought to be the root cause or crime-level of a region. Table 2 gives the crime in relation to deprivation indicators and Table 3 cross-classifies the crime according to different levels of deprivations. Experience of the Indian states shows an interesting behaviour. In terms of socio-economic development, Kerala, Punjab, Maharashtra and Haryana are the least deprived states. Punjab depicts a very low crime rate. Haryana and Maharashtra show a medium crime rate, whereas

TABLE 1

Structure of Incidence of Crime under Indian Penal Code by Crime Heads for Indian States, 1995

Year	*Murder* %	*Dacoity* %	*Robbery* %	*Burglary* %	*Theft* %	*Riots* %	*Others* %	*Total IPC Crime*
Andhra Pradesh	2.35	0.53	0.81	6.15	14.34	4.47	71.36	100.00
Assam	3.49	2.12	2.95	9.52	20.16	11.30	50.47	100.00
Bihar	0.05	2.32	2.42	6.08	15.59	11.18	62.36	100.00
Gujarat	1.16	0.25	0.90	5.21	16.15	1.83	74.50	100.00
Haryana	2.12	0.21	0.79	9.07	13.92	1.88	72.02	100.00
Karnataka	1.45	0.25	0.90	8.51	15.83	7.97	65.08	100.00
Kerala	0.56	0.11	0.27	5.06	3.75	7.73	82.51	100.00
Madhya Pradesh	1.73	0.08	0.96	9.15	15.50	1.98	70.59	100.00
Maharashtra	1.49	0.36	1.61	8.40	25.40	3.18	59.55	100.00
Orissa	1.80	0.56	1.89	8.78	15.88	3.82	67.27	100.00
Punjab	6.09	0.11	0.42	9.13	12.33	0.05	71.87	100.00
Rajasthan	0.93	0.06	0.78	5.63	10.89	13.75	67.97	100.00
Tamil Nadu	1.55	0.11	0.42	4.73	14.91	5.86	72.43	100.00
Uttar Pradesh	10.52	1.59	6.41	16.03	43.37	9.48	12.60	100.00
West Bengal	2.58	0.69	1.24	1.19	30.40	8.80	55.10	100.00

Source: National Crime Records Bureau, Ministry of Home Affairs, *Crime in India.*

TABLE 2

Crime in Relation to Deprivation Indices and Human Development Index in Indian States

State	*Crime per Thousand Population*	*Level of Deprivation*			*Average Deprivation Level*	*HDI*
		Life Expectancy	*Adult Lit. Level*	*Real Per Capita Income*		
A.P.	1.464 (5)	0.338 (7)	0.617 (10)	0.719 (8)	0.559	0.441 (7)
Assam	1.483 (6)	0.459 (14)	0.580 (9)	0.804 (12)	0.614	0.386 (6)
Bihar	1.218 (4)	0.407 (11)	0.743 (14)	0.866 (15)	0.672	0.328 (2)
Gujarat	2.769 (13)	0.369 (9)	0.509 (5)	0.678 (5)	0.519	0.481 (9)
Haryana	1.871 (8)	0.287 (4)	0.533 (6)	0.487 (2)	0.436	0.564 (12)
Karnataka	2.504 (11)	0.288 (5)	0.484 (4)	0.706 (7)	0.493	0.507 (10)
Kerala	2.823 (14)	0.089 (1)	0.115 (1)	0.784 (9)	0.329	0.671 (15)
M.P.	2.737 (12)	0.458 (13)	0.735 (12)	0.817 (13)	0.670	0.330 (3)
Maharashtra	2.260 (10)	0.282 (3)	0.395 (2)	0.588 (3)	0.422	0.578 (13)
Orissa	1.488 (7)	0.440 (12)	0.624 (1)	0.828 (14)	0.631	0.369 (5)
Punjab	0.516 (1)	0.235 (2)	0.536 (7)	0.277 (1)	0.349	0.651 (14)
Rajasthan	3.076 (15)	0.394 (10)	0.764 (15)	0.785 (10)	0.648	0.352 (4)
Tamil Nadu	2.175 (9)	0.337 (6)	0.401 (3)	0.692 (6)	0.477	0.523 (11)
U.P.	1.186 (3)	0.556 (15)	0.739 (13)	0.803 (11)	0.699	0.301 (1)
W. Bengal	0.947 (2)	0.366 (8)	0.547 (8)	0.677 (4)	0.530	0.470 (8)

Note: Figures within brackets are ranks.

TABLE 3

Levels of Crime Cross-classified According to Levels of Different Types of Deprivation for Indian States, 1995

Level of Deprivation in		*Level of Crime per Thousand of Population*		
		Low	*Medium*	*High*
Life Expectancy:				
	Low	Punjab	Haryana, Maharashtra	Kerala
	Med.	W. Bengal, Bihar	A.P., Tamil Nadu, Karnataka	Gujarat, Rajasthan
	High	U.P.	Assam, Orissa	M.P.
Adult Lit. Level:				
	Low	—	T. Nadu, Maharashtra, Karnataka	Kerala
	Med.	Punjab, W. Bengal	Assam, Haryana, A.P., Orissa	Gujarat
	High	U.P., Bihar	—	M.P., Rajasthan
Real PCI:				
	Low	Punjab, W. Bengal	Haryana, Maharashtra	—
	Med.	U.P.	Tamil Nadu, A.P., Karnataka	Gujarat, Kerala, Rajasthan
	High	Bihar	Assam, Orissa	M.P.
Average:				
	Low	Punjab	Haryana, Maharashtra	Kerala
	Med.	W.Bengal	Assam, A.P., Orissa, T. Nadu, Karnataka	Gujarat
	High	Bihar, U.P.	—	M.P., Rajasthan

Source: Calculated.

the Kerala displays a very high crime rate. The states of Rajasthan and Madhya Pradesh are deprived in terms of health services, education, per capita income and the overall average deprivation. The crime rate per thousand population is also very high in Rajasthan and Madhya Pradesh. But same is not true in the case of the other two states, i.e., Bihar and Uttar Pradesh where average deprivation and deprivation in terms of health, education and per capita income are very high but the crime rate is very low. Thus, crime experience in the Indian states is of two types: First, which is associated with deprivation or poverty and second, which is associated with low deprivation levels. By cross classifying crime with different levels of Human Development Index (Table 4), one finds that both M.P. and Rajasthan have a high crime rate because of low level of human development. On

TABLE 4

Levels of Crime Cross-classified According to Levels of Human Development Index (HDI) for Indian States, 1995

Level of HDI	*Level of Crime per Thousand of Population*		
	Low	*Medium*	*High*
Low	Bihar, U.P.	—	M.P., Rajasthan
Medium	W.Bengal	Assam, A.P., Orissa, T. Nadu, Karnataka	Gujarat
High	Punjab	Haryana, Maharashtra	Kerala

Source: Calculated

the other hand, Punjab has a very low crime rate because of higher level of human development index. But same argument does not hold in the case of Kerala. Kerala has high crime level alongwith higher HDI. Thus, the relation of crime with socio-economic level of development varies significantly both in the temporal and spatial dimensions. This differential behaviour that characterises the Indian states needs a further empirical prognostication to analyse the nature and structure of crime.

In the temporal dimension (Table 5), the crime growth rate is indicative of the fact that for the period 1952 to 1995 the overall growth of crime is 2.31 per cent per annum in India. The decades of sixties and seventies depict a relatively higher crime growth rate. It is of the tune of 4.29 per cent and 3.82 per cent per annum for the sixties and seventies decade, respectively. In the total crime, 'murders and other crimes' category has registered a relatively higher growth rate in comparison with other heads of crime.

TABLE 5

Growth Rate of Crime Under Indian Penal Code by Crime Heads for India

Year	*Murder*	*Dacoity*	*Robbery*	*Burglary*	*Theft*	*Riots*	*Others IPC crime*	*Total*
1952-61	0.88	–5.93	–4.33	–0.87	–0.87	1.88	2.18	–0.16
1961-71	3.76	10.26	11.09	3.06	3.71	8.95	4.45	4.29
1971-81	3.46	2.71	2.25	–0.51	2.33	5.58	6.40	3.82
1981-91	1.84	–3.31	–0.26	–1.98	–2.62	–1.57	2.32	2.14
1952-95	3.04	0.31	2.00	–0.60	0.36	3.39	4.31	2.31
1989-95	2.59	–3.58	–0.74	–1.88	–3.06	–1.29	3.21	1.14

What is the socio-economic or the psychological cause of crime? One fact that needs no further proof is that juvenile delinquency is the nursery of criminals. The nature and cause(s) of crime at juvenile level may give us a clue to society-economy-crime nexus. The figures regarding juvenile delinquency cases (Table 6) show that from among the different heads of crime, the proportion of juveniles who have resorted to theft are the highest and burglars are next to it. But over a time, both of these have shown a declining trend, i.e. 10.23 per cent and 3.08 per cent per annum, respectively. Homicide, kidnapping and abduction, breach of trust and cheating cases have shown the positive growth rate. An overwhelming majority of juveniles, throughout the period, are boys and among them a large proportion belongs to the age group of 12-16 years of age (Table 7). But all the age groups are characterised by a negative growth rate. The most disturbing point, needing the utmost attention, is the increasing proportion of girl juveniles and that too in the age group of 16-18 years of age. It shows a positive growth rate of 12.9 per cent per annum.

To analyse why this tender age group enters the crime, an insight into their educational status, family background and economic status may be useful (Table 8). From among the juveniles, 30 to 43 per cent are found to be illiterate; 36 to 43 per cent have only the primary education and those who are matriculates constitute a very small proportion, i.e., 4 to 7 per cent. It implies that illiteracy is one of the causes of juvenile delinquency. General impression is that most of the juveniles are homeless. It is not so. About 90 per cent of juveniles live with their parents or guardians. About half of the juveniles belong to very low income group (Table 9), i.e., a group with monthly income less than Rs. 500. The next largest proportion belongs to the monthly income group of Rs. 100 to 1000. A negative growth rate of crime is displayed by all income groups and the decline is sharper in the lowermost income group.

To conclude, we can say, that crime in India is not evenly distributed in temporal or spatial dimension. Socio-economic deprivation in terms of education, health and per capita income do lead to crime. Although, so far, juvenile delinquency was dominated by boys but now the involvement of girls of 16-18 years of age groups is growing alarmingly. The root cause of juvenile delinquency is poverty and illiteracy.

TABLE 6

Juvenile Delinquency Cases in India

Year		Murder	Homicide	Rape	Kidnap and Abduct.	Dacoity	Robbery	Burglary	Theft	Riots	Breach of trust	Cheating	Counterfeating	Others	Total
(1)		(2)	(3)	(4)	(5)	(6)	(7)	(8)	(9)	(10)	(11)	(12)	(13)	(14)	(15)
1991	N	348	24	189	141	52	164	1553	4638	1270	21	47	2	4139	12588
	%	2.76	0.19	1.50	1.12	0.41	1.30	12.34	36.84	10.09	0.17	0.37	0.02	32.88	100.00
1992	N	292	19	158	79	51	87	1464	3203	906	21	46	0	4774	11100
	%	2.63	1.17	1.42	0.71	0.46	0.78	13.19	28.86	8.16	0.19	0.41	0.00	43.01	100.00
1993	N	297	15	168	184	51	98	1138	2404	1023	15	63	1	4008	9465
	%	3.14	0.16	1.77	1.94	0.54	1.04	12.02	25.40	10.81	0.16	0.67	0.01	42.35	100.00
1994	N	286	19	176	95	32	49	1294	2346	637	17	24	3	3581	8561
	%	3.36	0.22	2.06	1.11	0.37	0.57	15.12	27.40	7.44	0.20	0.28	0.04	41.83	100.00
1995	N	253	23	174	152	56	76	1285	2835	955	33	54	1	3869	9766
	%	2.59	0.24	1.78	1.56	0.57	0.78	13.16	29.03	9.78	0.34	0.55	0.01	39.62	100.00
1996	N	270	21	157	132	44	87	1315	2356	856	18	60	0	4708	10024
	%	2.69	0.21	1.57	1.32	0.44	0.87	13.12	23.50	8.54	0.18	0.60	0.00	46.97	100.00
G. Rate		–4.82	0.406	–1.68	2.82	–2.87	–11.48	–3.08	–10.23	–6.33	2.05	0.04	NA	–0.28	–4.53

TABLE 7

Juveniles Apprehended Classified by Age Groups and Sex

Year		*7-12 Years*		*12-16 Years*		*16-18 Years*		*All Age Groups*		
		Boys	*Girls*	*Boys*	*Girls*	*Boys*	*Girls*	*Boys*	*Girls*	*Total*
1991	N	5379	458	17822	1065	—	1867	23201	3390	26591
	%	20.23	1.72	67.02	4.01		7.02	87.25	12.75	100.00
1992	N	3282	153	14192	601	—	3130	17474	3884	21358
	%	15.37	0.72	66.45	2.81		14.65	81.81	18.19	100.00
1993	N	3708	221	12683	754	—	2701	16391	3676	20067
	%	18.48	1.10	63.20	3.76		13.46	81.68	18.32	100.00
1994	N	3426	268	10426	627	—	2456	13852	3351	17203
	%	19.92	1.56	60.61	3.64		14.28	80.52	19.48	100.00
1995	N	3147	230	11395	618	—	3405	14542	4251	18793
	%	16.75	1.22	60.63	3.29		18.11	77.38	22.62	100.00
1996	N	3278	193	10790	607	—	4230	14068	5030	19098
	%	17.16	1.01	56.50	3.18	—	22.15	73.66	26.34	100.00
G. Rate		–7.38	–7.97	–9.16	–7.98	NA	12.9	–8.79	6.34	–16.07

TABLE 8

Juveniles Apprehended Classified by Education Groups and Family Background

Year		*By Education*					*Family Background (living with)*			
		Illi-terate	*Prim-ary*	*Below Matric*	*Matric*	*Total*	*Parents*	*Guar-dian*	*Home-less*	*Total*
1991	N	11365	10772	5480	1974	29591	20642	5792	3157	29591
	%	38.41	36.40	18.52	6.67	100.00	69.76	19.57	10.67	100.00
1992	N	7128	9252	4041	937	21358	14945	4056	2357	21358
	%	33.37	43.32	18.92	4.39	100.00	69.97	18.99	11.04	100.00
1993	N	7086	8337	3725	921	20067	12961	3804	3302	20067
	%	35.31	41.55	18.55	4.59	100.00	64.59	18.96	16.45	100.00
1994	N	5141	7493	3613	956	17203	12210	3472	1521	17203
	%	29.88	43.56	21.00	5.56	100.00	70.98	20.18	8.84	100.00
1995	N	6565	7762	3647	819	18793	13247	3968	1578	18793
	%	34.93	41.30	19.41	4.36	100.00	70.49	21.11	8.40	100.00
1996	N	8195	7080	2544	1279	19098	14293	2922	1883	19093
	%	42.91	37.07	13.32	6.70	100.00	74.84	15.30	9.86	100.00
G. Rate		–6.10	–7.51	–11.24	–6.99	–7.50	–6.25	–9.72	–12.22	–7.50

TABLE 9

Juveniles Apprehended Classified by Income Groups

Year		*Monthly Income (Rs.)*					
		<500	*501-1000*	*1001-2000*	*2001-3000*	*>3000*	*Total*
1991	N	17887	6770	2987	1947	0	29591
	%	60.45	22.88	10.09	6.58	0.00	100.00
1992	N	10649	6714	2673	1322	0	21358
	%	49.86	31.44	12.52	6.19	0.00	100.00
1993	N	10433	6391	1887	1356	0	20067
	%	51.99	31.85	9.40	6.76	0.00	100.00
1994	N	9300	4934	1996	973	0	17203
	%	54.06	28.68	11.60	5.66	0.00	100.00
1995	N	9950	5484	2134	1225	458	19251
	%	51.69	28.49	11.09	6.36	2.38	100.00
1996	N	9306	6292	2132	1118	250	19098
	%	48.73	32.95	11.16	5.83	1.31	100.00
G. Rate		–9.74	–3.46	–6.30	–9.09		–7.31

Source: National Crime Records Bureau, Ministry of Home Affairs, *Crime in India.*

REFERENCES

Dennison (1992), *The Source of Economic Growth in the US and Alternatives Before US,* Committee for Economic Development, New York.

Gottfredson, M.R. and Travis, H. (1990), *A General Theory of Crime,* Stanford University Press, Stanford.

Hirschman (1969), *The Strategy of Economic Development,* Yale University Press.

Laufer, W.S. and Fread, A. (1990), *Advances in Criminology Theory,* New Brunswick, N.J., Transactions 1990.

Leontief (1953), "Domestic Production and Foreign, The American Position Re-examined" in *Proceeding of the American Philosophical Society,* Vol. 97, Sept.

Myrdal (1975), *Economic Theory and Underdeveloped Regions,* Vora.

Nurkse (1973), *Problems of Capital Formation in Underdeveloped Countries,* Oxford University Press, Delhi.

Prakash S. (1970), "An Input-Output Model for Educational Planning", *Artha Vijnana,* June, Vol 13, No. 2.

Schultz (1959), "Capital Formation by Education", *Journal of Political Economy,* Vol. 68.

Singh, I. and Singh, R. (1999), "A Modified Measure of Human Development", *Conference Volume,* IEA, Bangalore.

Wilson, J.Q. and Richard, J.H. (1985), *Crime and Human Nature,* Simon & Schuster, New York.

7

Crime and Corruption—Obstacles to Development

Ram Naresh Thakur

I

CRIME IN INDIA

'White collar crimes', 'organised crimes (mafias)', and 'crime syndicates' may be considered as the major obstracles to development. The networks of organised crimes and crime syndicates are widespread and have been functioning for a long period in the economy. These are like parasites which absorb the blood of the economy. The crime syndicates, Mafia and organised criminals have established themselves in the different parts of the country. Those criminal have earned enormous physical and monetary power and have established their liaison with the important government officers, political leaders and others who are economically powerful.

Reported Crimes

The report of the National Crime Records Bureau for 1997, reveals it all. There were 64.11 lakh cognizable offences in the country, of which 17.19 lakh offences were concerned with the Indian Penal Code and the remaining 46.91 lakh were concerned with special and local laws. According to the Report 12 cognizable offences per minute were reported in the stipulated period. The nature of crimes is analysed in this way. Some of the important facts revealed by the report are:

(i) that one out of four crimes were from the North-Eastern states of Nagaland, Manipur, Meghalaya, Tripura, Assam and Bihar;
(ii) that cases of rape and kidnapping were on the rise, though dacoities were on the decrease;
(iii) that there was increase in the cases of loot especially in Nagaland, Karnataka and Tamilnadu;
(iv) that there was increase in dowry-related murders; and
(v) that 31.1 percent cases were reported against scheduled castes and scheduled tribes in which 30.4 percent were in Uttar Pradesh only.

In analysing the data, we find that all kinds of crimes are increasing and thus bring obstacles in the path of development. Some of the factors causing concern are the inadequate police force in some states, longer investigation time and a large number of pending cases before courts.

Population-Police-force ratio:—Among many other causes for increasing crime, one of the important factors is the lack of adequate police force. At the national level, for every one lakh of population, only 134 police personal are available. It is very less in respect of other countries. The police-population ratio differs from state to state. In five states, it is 600 to one lakh people, in 3 states it is 400 to 600, in seven states it is 135 to 200, in six states 200 to 400, in eleven states, it is less than 135 and in Bihar it is only 89.

The load of investigation on the police force is also heavy. At the national level, one investigator investigates 60 cases in a year. This too varies from state to state. In 4 states, it is more than 100, in 2 states, it is 60 to 100, in 7 states, 25 to 60, in 10 states, 10 to 25 and in 9 states, less than 9.

It is evident that due to heavy pressure of investigation of criminal cases, investigation pressure per investigator is intolerable. This will have its impact on the quality of investigation.

Among several reasons of increasing crimes, the important reason is that there is acute shortage of judicial tribunals and courts. A large number of posts of judges remain vacant in different courts. A large number of cases remain pending in the courts. In the district and lower courts of the country, there were more than 2 crore pending cases till December, 1999. There were 20,260 pending cases in the Supreme Court of the country till February, 2000. There were 30 lakh civil and criminal cases pending in the 18 High Courts of the country. There were 136 vacant posts of judges in High Courts till April 2000.

II

A CHALLENGE TO DEVELOPMENT

The increase in crime and corruption has been a major obstacle in the path of development. Industrial investment requires an atmosphere of adequate law and order. The politician-criminal nexus casts doubts in the minds of investors. As a consequence, investment opportunities remain underutilised, production suffers and markets become panicky. This is harmful not only for industrial development, but also for business and agriculture sector. 'Rangdari' taxes are collected, businessmen and industrialists are kidnapped and even big farmers do not escape. They are also kidnapped for *firauti*. By all means, crimes and corruption act as the obstacles in the path of development.

Effect on Foreign Investment

Under climate of widespread crime and corruption, foreign investment also suffers. There is hardly any foreign investment particularly in those states which are lacking law and order. According to a survey of 107 big industrialists conducted by *Business Today* recently, three states were identified as difficult states for investment. These states are Bihar, Uttar Pradesh and Haryana. Foreign direct investment which showed an increase since 1992, still remains very low compared to countries like China. The crime and corruption may be one of the contributing factors.

Investment Preferences in India

The state of south-west states is comparatively far better than that of north-east states in the context of increase of investment, industrialisation and development and decrease of crimes and corruption. The *Business Today* survey of January, 2000 which covered 107 big companies, reported that in the next 5 years most these big companies prefer to make investment only in five states of south-west, i.e. Maharashtra, Andhra Pradesh, Gujarat, Karnataka and Tamil Nadu. Only 10% companies desired to invest in Uttar Pradesh and in Bihar it is only 4 percent. The following Table shows the investment preference.

TABLE 1

Investment Preferences of Big Business Firms

Sl. No.	*State*	*Companies' Preferences for Investment (% age)*	*Sl. No.*	*States*	*Companies' Preferences for Investment (% age)*
1.	Maharashtra	54	11.	Rajasthan	9
2.	Andhra Pradesh	47	12.	Goa	8
3.	Gujarat	44	13.	Orissa	8
4.	Karnataka	36	14.	Punjab	8
5.	Tamil Nadu	32	15.	Pondicherry	8
6.	W. Bengal	15	16.	H.P.	6
7.	M.P.	14	17.	Kerala	6
8.	Delhi	10	18.	Bihar	4
9.	U.P.	10	19.	Arunachal Pradesh	2
10.	Haryana	9	20.	Assam	2

Source: *Business Today*, Jan. 2000.

If we see the graph of total investment in the states of India, it becomes evident that the states situated at the higher points of the crime and corruption graph are on the lower points of investment graph. In 1998-99, more than 50% of the total investment remained concentrated in only five states situated in the south-west. Maharashtra, Gujarat, Andhra Pradesh, Karnatka and Tamil Nadu remained ahead. The position of only one state in the 'Hindi-belt' (or north-east states), Madhya Pradesh, remained better than the southern states. The worst situation is that of seven north-eastern states, whose gross investment remained less than that of even a tiny state like Himachal Pradesh. Bihar too accounts for a very low share of 2.73% of investment.

TABLE 2
State-wise Distribution of Investment, 1998-99

Sl. No.	*States*	*% of Capital Investment*	*Sl. No.*	*States*	*% of Capital Investment*
1.	Maharashtra	16.77	11.	Bihar	2.73
2.	Gujarat	11.15	12.	Himachal Pradesh	2.38
3.	M.P.	9.27	13.	Assam	1.66
4.	Andhra Pradesh	8.37	14.	Punjab	1.59
5.	Karnataka	7.86	15.	Kerala	1.44
6.	Tamil Nadu	7.48	16.	J & K.	1.29
7.	U.P.	6.64	17.	Haryana	1.15
8.	Orissa	4.46	18.	Delhi	1.06
9.	W. Bengal	4.27	19.	Arunachal Pradesh	0.31
10.	Rajasthan	3.18	20.	Mizoram	0.27

Source: Business India, Jan. 2000.

A recent study by NCAER, at the behest of CII, on the situation of the states of India reveals that the conditions in the south-western states are on the upbeat whereas the situation of north-eastern states is worse, comparatively. The economic condition of Maharashtra, Gujarat, Karnataka, Andhra Pradesh and Tamil Nadu is better. The north-eastern states are more backward in several respects. The northern states are in a worse condition. One-third population of whole India resides in this region only. In the gross domestic product (GDP) of India, this region has its share of 27 percent. Due to the grip of crime and corruption, failure of law and order and inefficiency and lack of foresightedness, the condition of this region has become worse. Once Punjab was the fore-runner of green revolution, but it is now in the grip of debts. Hundreds of farmers committed suicides due to the burden of debt. The position of backward condition of U.P. is known. In the 1990s its position had worsened. Until recently only Bihar was considered undeveloped mainly caused by crime and corruption alongwith other factors, and now U.P. seems to be deteriorating into a similar situation.

As a consequence the inequality between the south-western and north-eastern states is increasing. The result of such inequality may be very dangerous. As the foreign capital and consumer culture had divided the nation into two parts, this inequality may divided the nation in the same way.

Although the existence of nexus between criminals and politicians and the representation of Mafias in the different legislative bodies, from 'Gram Panchayats' to the parliament are not unique any one state, there are inter-state difference in the nature of crimes and corruption and the effort towards development. It is this difference that counts in the graph of development, inspite of prevalence of crimes and corruption in all states. It is evident that organised crimes restrict the smooth functioning of the market mechanism in a developing economy. It discourages investment from both internal and external sources. There has been widening differences in the growth and per capita state domestic product, particularly in the 1990s. Punjab and Haryana are on the road of development by virtue of its agriculture. But Uttar Pradesh, Bihar, Madhya Pradesh and Rajasthan (BIMARU states) are falling in the 'development graph' of the country. U.P. and Bihar are agricultural states where there is growing supremacy of land Mafias. There is hardly any improvement in poverty of the villages in the past twenty years. Where villages are poor, the development of state is impossible. In Bihar the land ownership struggles, became severe caste-struggles piloted by the private armies e.g., Bhumi Sena, Ranveer Sena, Bramharshi Sena, M.C.C., Lorik Sena, Kunwar Sena, Kisan Sangh, Sunlight Sena, and Swarn Liberation Army. These rival *Senas* are organised on the caste-basis. And violence is widespread in the country side.

The law and order became totally paralysed in about 18 districts and partially in all over the state. In this situation, state spending could not provide adequate place to rural development. The government officials and bureaucrats themselves act as middlemen in the *'process of development'*. Funds meant for rural development reach the target groups only to the extent of about 10 percent. The rest remains with the bureaucrat-politician nexus. In states like West Bengal due to emergence and implementation of 'Panchayati Raj', there has been development of roads, tanks, canals and resources for agriculture did reach the gross roots. Land reform measures were executed strictly. But this could not happen in U.P. and Bihar were big land Mafias are obstacles in the path of small and marginal farmers' benefits. Still now in West Bengal, Kerala, Tamil Nadu, Gujarat and Andhra Pradesh, Panchayati Raj is very strong. So there the rate of economic development is also fast and effect of crimes, corruption and Mafias is minimised. In U.P. and Bihar there is terror of criminals and Mafias. So no industrialist and businessman wants to set up industries and business in these states due to the criminal system and Mafiaism alongwith corrupt development system. Due to this, a rich state of resources like Bihar has been deteriorating economically. The industrialists observe that in Bihar setting up any industry or business is not possible because of widespread theft of materials. On the contrary, businessmen are compelled to pay continuous and regular extortions in the form of "rangdari tax", "dastoori tax" and "security tax". The businessmen and their sons are kidnapped smoothly for '*firauti*'. Kidnapping and *firauti* have assumed regular business proportions. The efficiency of labour is affected adversely due to chaotic situation, failure of law and order, anarchy and rapidly increasing criminal and corrupt activities. So not more than 5 to 10 percent of the resources meant for development is spent for the purpose.

III

ALTERNATIVE PATH OF DEVELOPMENT

Obstacles by way of the 'vicious circles of the organised crime' to the market mechanism and investment perpetuate the low productivity, low income, low viable employment and ultimately low level of development in spite of a number of economic reform measures. Economic reforms themselves are important, but not capable of delivering goods. This obstacle is not a consequence of poverty. It is imposed by the affluent section of the society influenced from the demonstration effect of the capital surplus developed world. The difference is that large part of the affluence here are more unscrupulous and corrupt. The sufferer is the nation as a whole and the poorer sections, of the society in particular.

It is time to evaluate the political economy of development with more pragmatic considerations to identify the measures to break the "vicious circles of crime and corruption" as a precondition for development. There is a "double vicious circle"—the `vicious circle of poverty' reinforced by the 'vicious circle of crime and corruption'. It is time to create mass consciousness against the `criminalisation of economy'. A crusade for moral regeneration for change must be the need of the hour. People should be awakened and made to campaign against the ethos of crime and corruption".

"Woods are lovely dark and deep
But I have promises to keep
And miles to go before I sleep
And miles to go before I sleep."

REFERENCES

National Council of Applied Economic Research (2000), CII sponsored Investment Survey, *Primary Report.*

Business Today, January 2000.

A.K. Sinha (2000), "Organised Crime and Political Economy of Development—The Indian Panorama, *The Indian Economic Journal,* Jan.-March, 1999-2000, Vol. 47, No. 3

Govt. of India (1995), *Vohra Committee Report,* Ministry of Home Affairs, New Delhi.

Govt. of India (1999), *Crimes in India, 1997,* National Crime Records Bureau, Ministry of Home Affairs, New Delhi.

World Bank (1997), *World Development Report.*

World Bank (1999), *World Development Report.*

U.N.D.P. (1999), *Human Development Report.*

8

The Interface of Corruption and Development in the Third World

S.C. Sharma, Shyam Sunder Singh Chauhan and
Binay Kumar Singh

The present paper takes a generalistic view about corruption and special emphasis has been laid about the magnitude of this very problem in developing countries. The entire discussion rests mainly on secondary data collected from various inter-disciplinary sources as well as personal experience and eternal vigilance.

MEANING OF THE CORRUPTION

Corruption stands for the abandonment of expected standards of behaviour by those in authority for the sake of personal advantage. It is generally acknowledged though grudgingly, that the disjunction between expected behaviour and action generate corruption. Corruption is a relative and relational term and is dependent on the superordination and subordination. *The World Development Report, 1997* opines that the abuse of public power for private gain is corruption. But basically it is a symptom of a more general problem of perverse underlying incentives in public service.[1]

According to N. Vittal, the Chief Vigilance Commissioner, "Corruption is like AIDS, while the disease (AIDS) is caused by uncontrolled sexual behaviour, corruption is caused by uncontrolled financial behaviour[2]." Hence, an individual in power hierarchy, when uses influence at the cost of others and by sideling the institutionalized framework to further one's own financial upliftment, corruption comes to the forefront. Robert Klitgaard is of the view that corruption is a problem of policies and management even more than it is one of the ethics or cultural change.[3] The problem of corruption lies at the intersection of the public and the private sector. It is a two-way process. Private interests, domestic and external, wield their influence through uninstitutionalized means to take advantage of opportunities for corruption and rent seeking, and public institutions succumb to these and other sources of corruption in the absence of credible restrains. Klitgaard has enumerated the phenomenon of corruption in an equation form as follows[4]:

$C = M + D - A$, where

C = Corruption,
M = Monopoly windfalls,
D = Discretion in decision-making, and
A = Accountability.

Corruption has been labelled as not just a political aberration but an economic disaster.[5]

The phenomenon of corruption is a two-way process. Hence it is not the 'bribe-giving' alone which promotes corruption, rather 'bribe-acceptance' with a hidden greed to shoot up in financial-cum-status hierarchy also aggravates the dimensions of corruption. Many politicians and bureaucrats have their close proximity with mafia-dons, underworld chiefs and industrialists. There is enormous evidence to suggest that the shrewd politicians and civil servants by taking resort of legal and constitutional loopholes leave no stone unturned in galvanizing favouritism, nepotism and patronage, in order to make vast fortunes for themselves and the bribe-giver. Hence, bribing is the foundation stone for corruption. Frank Vogl, Vice-Chairman of Transparency International, Berlin, has metamorphically described, "We live in a world of bribe-takers in government and bribe-supplying companies come together with bribe-taking officials in emerging market countries to defraud the people of these countries.[6]

EVOLUTION OF CORRUPTION

The concept of corruption has a historical specific significance. Even though, there have been traces of corruption in ancient days. But the corruption with a rather new paraphernalia has the legacy in imperialism and colonialism. The erstwhile colonial power—the British, labelled themselves as the *messiah* of moral ethic and values in public life and clean government. However, historical contextual specific analyses falsify, their hallow claims. In order to extend their empires, the colonial power used all means akin to corruption. The political ruling elites in U.K., Germany, France, Portugal and others, even did not hesitate to bribe the local/aboriginal rulers. They also used bribe as a prominent and effective weapon to tackle the resistance of local kings, by bribing the opponents. They destabilized the local rulers. The history of many countries of Africa and Latin America which got political independence in the midst of twentieth century is depleted with many evidence that "bribing was used by colonial power underneath the policy of 'divide and rule'. In Indian case, representatives of the East-India Company often received *'dallies'*, in cash or kind, from Indian traders and local zamindars. Even the infamous, the Permanent-Settlement of 1793 in Bengal Presidency functioned as a positive catalyst of bribery—both giving and taking. It is a common belief in India and in other erstwhile colonies of Britain, the English people were faithful to their own country. But in order to strengthen the relationship of superordination and subordination at interpersonal, inter-positional and inter-organisational level, they trained the people of their colonies, in the art of bribery.

Recently, corruption has taken global dimensions in developed and developing countries. In many developed and developing societies corrupt practices, as specified by legal or administrative rules, are customary and widely accepted as normal behaviours. Such behaviours, as in some Third World countries or command economies, are regarded as essential for the achievement of socially necessary outcomes. Nor is corruption confined to less-developed or State-socialist economies, as scandals such as the Watergate Affair or, in the UK, the Poulson Affair, demonstrate.

Multinational companies and other large industrial-trading companies of developed countries, bribe the politicians and bureaucrats of Third World countries for selling their machines, plants, weapons, aeroplanes, warships and also for obtaining contracts for constructing bridges, establishing power plants and getting licences. For industrialized nations, the developing nations are mere dumping grounds and their representatives use bribery as a potent source.

The majority of developing and poor countries of the contemporary world are getting billions of dollars as loans, at concessional rates from the World Bank as well as developed nations like USA, UK, France, Germany, Japan, etc. These loans are meant for the development of basic infrastructure like health, hygiene, primary education, technological upliftment, rural development, poverty alleviation, etc. The entire pattern of loaning address to improvement, transformative prospectives. However, it is a matter of recognition to ascertain whether the assistance are reaching to bottom or to the real beneficiaries down the hierarchy. The developing and the poor nations have been tied in a vicious circle of dependence, in which their economies are conditioned by the deeds of developed countries. Yet, despite enormous efforts of providing loans to poor countries of third world, the process of corruption has not remained aloof.

For over 50 years, the World Bank has ignored corruption in its analysis and prescriptions. Billions of dollars of aid have been hijacked by corrupt rulers. Yet the Bank has ascribed development failures to faulty policies or bad projects rather than plain theft.[7]

During the cold war the USA and its associates gave patronage to many corrupt rulers of Third World in the name of restraining the extension of communism. Not only this they also influenced the World Bank and other doner agencies from going deeper into the political affairs of these countries and keeping their activities confined only to economic affairs.[8] Representatives of these institution working in Third World did not try to investigate the realities of the ultimate use of the money given in the from of loan or assistance.

With the end of Cold War followed by drastic change in World Economy, the economic conditions of Third World have changed in many ways. The whole political and economic system is working with greater openness. The media is more effective and Journalism is equally investigative. Press and Media are bringing the matter of corruption into the lime light. Large scams and scandals in the developed and developing countries have come into the knowledge of general public. Laurence Busse *et. al.* have established an association between financial exposure of corruption and foreign direct-investment. When the current or potential investors take into account country's corrupt practices, as desseminated through the financial media, they react favourably or unfavourably, regarding their expectations about legislative reforms. If the financial media reveals corrupt acts and the government of that country does not seek to readdress or remove them, the capital market reacts unfavourably and it results, ultimately into low level of growth.

Corruption in Third World countries have taken a new shape and dimension under the democratic type of government. Persons elected to the executive, with less or no accountability have themselves become corrupt. In other worlds, State has become a tool and hideout for politicians and bureaucrats. A number of Presidents, Prime Ministers, Ministers, Administrators have been found involved in scandals and scams.

LEVEL OF CORRUPTION

World Bank has surveyed 3600 commercial firms of 69 countries for investigating the real causes responsible for corruption prevalent globalwide. More than 40 per cent firms in this study have accepted that they had paid bribe to get their ends fulfilled. They have also accepted that giving bribe was no guarantee that work will be done. Sometimes these firms greesed the palm of officers of various level to get their file/proposal cleared will in time. If these officers are not bribed they put several unnecessary objections and try to delay the whole process which results in the escalation of project cost. According to this report, the level of corruption is the highest in the Commonwealth of Independent States (USSR) and African countries, while it is the lowest in Europe and in some parts of Asia.

Corruption may however be greatest evil for the community but unfortunately it helps, at least in initial stage of the development developing economies to accelerate their economic growth. As it happened in some East Asian countries where there is a positive correlationship between rapid economic growth and corruption. Many parts of the developing world retain a certain ambivalence towards corruption. A commonly heard view is that corruption merely greases the wheels of commerce and not the growth. Apparent support for this argument comes from the fact that some countries that rank high in surveys of the level of corruption have also excelled the economic growth. The predictability of corruption—both that of the amount one has to pay and that of receiving the outcome one has paid for provides some insights into this apparent paradox. It was found in one of the studies, analysed by World Bank staff, that for a given level of corruption, countries with more predictable corruption have higher investment rates. But even in these countries corruption has an adverse impact on economic performance no matter how high the degree of predictability of corruption in a country, its rate of investment would significantly be higher where there is less corruption.[9] It is true that some highly corrupt countries have achieved high rates of growth (Table 1). But they may find themselves paying a higher price for it in the future, as corruption feeds on itself, creating a widening spiral of illegal payoffs, until development is undermined and years of progress are reversed. And the very growth that permitted corruption in the past produce a shift from productive activities to an unproductive struggle for the spoils.[10]

TABLE 1

Level of Corruption in Selected Countries of Asia (10-highly corrupt, 0-No Corruption)

Country	*Level of Corruption*
Singapore	1.19
Japan	1.97
Hong Kong	2.80
South Korea	4.03
Taiwan	4.22
Malaysia	4.64
Thailand	5.88
Philippines	6.59
India	7.00
Indonesia	7.31
China	7.31

Fortune chart: Political & Economic Risk Consultancy Ltd. Hong Kong in *Times of India*, New Delhi, Sept. 24, 1995.

Hong Kong based firm M/s Political and Economic Risk Consultancy Ltd. through a decadal comparative study of 11 Asian countries has revealed in 1995 that China, Indonesia and India were the most corrupt countries in terms of developmental programmes implementation. Statistics in Table 1 substantiate this view.

Berlin-based anticorruption Watchdog Transparency International, a non-government organisation established by Peeter Eegan, former Director of World Bank, has developed Corruption Perception Index to identify the level of corruption in a country and compare it with other countries. CPI score relates to perceptions of the degree of corruption as seen by business people, risk analysts and the general public and ranges between Ten (highly clean) and Zero (highly corrupt). Standard deviation indicates differences in the values of sources; greater the standard deviation the greater the difference of perceptions of a country among the sources; finding of the surveys and rates of economic growth have been presented in Table 2. The Transparency International has released its fifth annual survey on 26 Oct. 1999, which reveals that Denmark with CPI-10 is the cleanest country of the World while the Cameroon with CPI-1.5 is the most corrupt country among those surveyed. CPI for India is 2.9 and its place is 73rd in order of clean administration. Although the CPI is high in most of the European countries but their annual growth rate is in the range of 0—3.0 per cent, while the growth rate of some of the developing countries like Nigeria, Uganda, Vietnam, India and ASEAN countries is quite high despite high level of corruption. Countries with high level of corruption have shown decreasing trend in growth rate which confirms the hypothesis that the country with high level of corruption may show high growth rate for a limited period but in the long-run corruption will result into a slow growth rate because the creeping accumulation of seemingly minor infractions can slowly erode political legitimacy to the point where even non-corrupt officials and members of the public see little point in playing by the rules.

Economic analysts of South-East and East-Asian countries are of the view that corruption in public life, particularly in corporate sector, does not affect adversally always, sometimes it acts, as an effective tool for development. Western analysts believe that corruption in Third World is a lubricant that makes that system work.[11]

TABLE 2

Level of Corruption and Economic Growth in Selected Countries

Sl. No.	*Country*	*CPI Score (1999)*	*Country Rank (1999)*	*Standard Deviation*	*GNP Annual Growth Rate (0/0)*	
					1975-95	*1990-98*
1.	Denmark	10.0	1	0.8	2.0	2.9
2.	Finland	9.8	2	0.5	2.9	1.6
3.	New Zealand	9.4	3	0.8	0.9	2.2
4.	Sweden	9.4	4	0.6	1.6	2.9
5.	Canada	9.2	5	0.5	2.9	2.0
6.	Singapore	9.1	7	0.9	7.7	8.1
7.	Switzerland	8.9	10	0.6	2.0	0.6
8.	Australia	8.7	12	0.7	2.7	3.9
9.	United Kingdom	8.6	13	0.5	2.3	1.9
10.	Germany	8.0	14	0.5	NA	NA
11.	USA	7.5	18	0.8	2.8	2.8
12.	Israel	6.8	20	1.3	3.8	5.2
13.	France	6.6	22	1.0	2.6	1.7
14.	Japan	6.0	25	1.6	4.2	1.4
15.	Taiwan	5.6	28	0.9	NA	NA
16.	Malaysia	5.1	32	0.5	6.7	6.4
17.	Italy	4.7	38	0.6	2.9	1.2
18.	Poland	4.2	44	0.8	NA	3.9
19.	EI Salvador	3.9	49	1.9	–0.3	5.2
20.	South Korea	3.8	52	0.9	8.4	5.1
21.	Philippines	3.6	54	1.4	3.1	3.3
22.	Turkey	3.6	55	1.0	4.2	4.4
23.	China	3.4	60	0.7	8.4	10.4
24.	Mexico	3.4	63	0.5	3.5	3.0
25.	Thailand	3.2	69	3.2	7.8	4.6
26.	Nicaragua	3.1	70	2.5	–2.5	3.8
27.	Argentina	3.0	71	0.8	–0.1	6.3
28.	India	2.9	73	0.6	4.8	5.6
29.	Vietnam	2.6	79	0.5	NA	8.0
30.	Russia	2.4	83	1.0	NA	–7.1
31.	Pakistan	2.2	88	0.7	6.2	4.3
32.	Uganda	2.2	89	0.7	NA	7.1
33.	Kenya	2.0	90	0.5	4.8	2.4
34.	Tanzania	1.9	93	1.1	NA	3.4
35.	Uzbekistan	1.8	95	0.4	NA	NA
36.	Azerbaijan	1.7	96	0.6	NA	–9.6
37.	Indonesia	1.7	97	0.9	6.7	4.1
38.	Nigeria	1.6	98	0.8	1.5	3.5
39.	Cameroon	1.5	99	0.5	5.4	0.5

Note: CPI - Corruption Perception Index.

Sources: (1) Http/w.w.w. gwd.dein uwvw/1999 Data. htmt.

(2) Human Development Report, 2000, pp. 202-04.

In East-Asian countries, corruption has coexisted with rapid economic growth. It is less debilitating in these countries because:

(a) It is less widespread, being concentrated at the top.
(b) It is more predictable and so reduces risks and delays for investors.
(c) The region has competitive policies.[12]

General public in these countries is of the view that had there been no corruption at the apex level of the State machinery, the level of economic prosperity would have been much higher. Terming corruption as anti-economic and anti-national, N. Vittal has said that if corruption in India was reduced to the level of that of Scandinavian countries the nation's gross domestic product would record a rise of 1.5 per cent without any extra investment.[13]

Most shocking finding, of Transparency International's is that major industrial nations which keep their officials honest at home do not hesitate to indulge in bribery and corruption abroad. Transparency International observed that Singapore, always among the corruption-free countries so far as its officials are concerned, is, nevertheless, one of the major bribe-giving nations abroad to increase exports. CPI for Singapore is 9.1 as corruption at home is concerned. However, when it comes to bribe-giving to boost export, its rank goes down to 5.7. Senior officials were found to be corrupt in two-thirds of the over 99 countries surveyed. Transparency International also developed Bribe-Payers Index (BPI) which has been presented blow in Table 3.

These countries host the companies which are perceived to have engaged in bribery. Interestingly, no country hosting exporters gets 10 in the survey of perceived bribe-givers.

It is worth mentioning here that corruption is rampant in politician-business nexus in Japan, the highly developed nation of the World, that it is institutionalised in countries like the U.S. in the form of paid lobbying, campaign donations and priced dinners.

TABLE 3
Bribe Payers Index for Selected Countries

Country	*Level of Corruption (BPI)*
Sweden	8.3
Australia	8.1
Canada	8.1
Austria	7.8
Switzerland	7.7
The Netherland	7.4
U.K.	7.2
Belgium	6.8
Germany	6.2
U.S.	6.2
Singapore	5.7
Spain	5.3
France	5.2
Japan	5.1
Malaysia	3.9
Italy	3.7
Taiwan	3.5
South Korea	3.4

CAUSES OF CORRUPTION

Electronic analysis of the World Bank survey has concluded that—

(a) High level of distortions in the policies through controls and regulations result in high level of corruption.
(b) Vigilant judiciary minimise corruption.
(c) Better salary and job satisfaction of public servants make them less corrupt.
(d) Appointments on merit leads to lower level of corruption.

Chief Vigilance Commissioner N. Vittal has identified the following three important causes of corruption[15]:

(i) Scarcity of goods and service.
(ii) Red-tape and delay.
(iii) Legal cushions of safety which ensure that a corrupt officer can use to claim that he is innocent until he is proved guilty in a court of law.

It has been observed in many countries that wherever the public servants, ministers and rulers have acquired monopolistic and unlimited powers, corruption gains momentum. Incentives for corrupt behaviour arise whenever public officials have wide discretion and little or no accountability. Public servants tempt to use their position for private gain by accepting bribes in cash or kinds, for their part, private individuals may be willing to make illegal payments to get their work done. Thus, a necessary condition for eruption of corruption is that public servants have rewards and penalties at their disposal.[16]

Under-hand payments received by the government inspectors have increased over the years. This follows their frequent visits to business and industrial outlets purportedly with a view to ensuring implementation of a variety of laws and long drawn procedures[17]. Thus, 'Inspector Raj' is thriving and breeding massive corruption. Sometimes policy distortions also create favourable environment for corruption pay off which are frequent to lower-level officials responsible for assessing and collecting taxes and tariffs, sanctionings subsidies, providing police protection, issuing permits and the like. In case of endemic corruption government officials often create additional red tape and delays to induce even higher illegal payments. Not even this, corruption is more rampant at highest level of government, in the awarding of major contracts, supply order, privatization, the allocation of import quotas, and regulation of natural monopolies. Wider the gap in demand and supply in any of economic goods or services leads to higher level of corruption.

The probability of being caught and punished for a corrupt person affect to a large extent the level of corruption. Corruption is high in those countries where government system does little to deter bribes. Corrupt officials believe that there is a little chance of being caught or if caught, of having to pay the penalty, since they believe that the system of justice itself can be corrupted.

Wages and perks of government officials also play a vital role in corruption. Where wages are very low, officials may try to eke out a middle-class standard of living by supplementing their pay with illegal pay offs. Corruption is often positively associated with the difference between public and private salaries.

MEASURES TO CONTROL CORRUPTION

Corruption in public life leads the country and society towards undulency and sometimes it results into revolt. Many a times, public has revolted against their rulers and compelled them to leave the post. Two former presidents of Republic of Korea have been prosecuted and indicted. One president of Brazil was impeached on charge of corruption. Thousands of people protested the Belgian government's handling of a pedophile ring and alleged corruption in judicial appointments and enforcement. A fierce debate has erupted over the financing of political campaigns and its influence on public policy in the aftermath of the 1996 U.S. Presidential election. At least two former Prime Ministers and several other politicians have been facing legal action in the courts for corrupt practices in Pakistan, former Prime Minister Rajeev Gandhi's name is involved in Bofor's Scam. Another former Prime Minister P.V. Narasimharao has also been accused of bribing members of parliament for saving a no confidence motion against his government. Several ministers and top bureaucrats of India have been found involved in share scam, sugar import scam, urea import scam, telecommunication scam. Former Chief Minister of a State has also been facing court trial in fodder scam case, while another ex-chief minister is involved in T.V. purchase scam and in other cases former President of Philippines—Ferdinend Marcos, and his wife, former ruler of Vietnom—Pol-Pot, former president of Uganda—Idi Amin, Military ruler of Panama—General Noreaga, Ex-president of USA—R. Nixon, former President of Venezuela—Carlos Andress Perraze are some of the other glaring examples of corruption in high echelons of power.

Above examples show that almost each and every country is in the grip of corruption. Although corruption can not be eliminated with a single doze treatment, its level and impact can be minimised by adopting short-run and long-run measures. Prevention of corruption in public life has become so important that without it no further reform in society is possible. There is urgency of raising the moral standard of each individual, so that he/she may fulfil his/her responsibility and duty towards his/her society as well as entire humanity. World Development Report 1997 has suggested the following three important measures.[18]

- Eliminating monopolistic powers by adopting policies encouraging competition;
- Strengthening institutional framework capable to control corruption;
- Democratic decentralization and giving more power to people through strong civil society.

Robert Klitgaard has suggested following measures to check corruption at international level.[19]

- International cooperation can help individual countries develop both the will and the capacity to fight corruption;
- Sponsoring regional diagnostic studies;
- Starting an international 'contest' for the best national strategies to reduce corruption; and
- Regional seminars to be organised. These seminars would broach the idea of a strategy against corruption, with examples, and technical assistance would help countries that wished to enter the contest to design their proposals. The winners (perhaps one or two per continent) would be rewarded with seven years to sustained and additional aid.

Corruption can not be effectively attacked in isolation from other problems as it is a symptom of problems at the intersection of the public and the private sectors and thus needs to be combated through a multipronged strategy based on the following principles:

- Creation of a rule-based bureaucracy with a pay structure that rewards civil servants for honesty;
- A merit-based recruitment and promotion system to shield the civil service from political patronage;
- Credible financial controls to prevent the arbitrary use of public resources;
- Reducing opportunities for officials, to act corruptly, by cutting back on their discretionary authority; and
- Enhancing accountability by strengthening mechanisms of monitoring and punishment.

The above strategy to fight corruption will be effective if following reforms are started with a strong political will.

Administrative Reforms

- Establishing accountability at all levels of administration;
- Adopting 'Hire and fire' policy for the recruitment of public servants, who should be given appointment on contract for a certain period and its terms only be extended with the recommendations of the community and not by the politicians;
- Incentives for honest public servants and disincentives and punishment for corrupt officials; and
- Creation of watchdog organisations who should focus not only on those who receive bribes, but also on those who pay them.

Reforms in Police-Judicial System

- Appointment of judges should be made by an independent commission free from political interference;
- There should be a provision of punishment for judges who deliberately delay the judicial process;
- Accountability should be established for judges; and
- System of judicial predictability should be implemented so as to abolish the endless system of appeals following the 'sunset system' on the line of US administration which automatically makes a legislation or procedure redundant if it does not serve its purpose in the changing socio-economic scenario.

Economic Reforms

- Abolishing regulations;
- Minimising import duties and other trade barriers;
- Price control mechanism should be defunctioned;
- Rampant corruption can be reduced by simplifying procedures relating to income tax, sales tax, excise duty, custom duty and labour laws;
- Monopoly in trade and manufacturing should be abolished;
- Abolishing the system of subsidies;
- More transparency in awarding government contracts;

- Government should not give guarantee of a definite rate of return on any type of investment; and
- Increase competition among traders and manufacturers.

Decentralisation of Power and Public Cooperation

- Decentralisation of power of decision-making;
- Higher cooperation of users;
- Creation of a strong and a vigilant society for her right; and
- Freedom-of-information Act should be enacted in order to make available all the information to the general public. The availability of information helps citizens discipline public officials at the ballot box and through other avenues of protest, such as legal challenges in the form of public interest litigations and direct petitions to decision-makers.

CONCLUSIONS

Hence, foregoing discussion has ranged widely over a number of issues associated with corruption. The central theme of the paper has been that in contemporary geo-politico and geo-economic scenario, corruption is so rampant that there is no sphere of national or trans-national life where it does not exist and people all around the globe have begun to treat it as a normal feature of life.

The exploration of the problems associated with corruption no doubt have proved to be a curse for the developing and poor nations of Third World. Not only the inhabitants of these nations are facing multi-dimensional problems of bewildering varieties, but the very dynamism of the basic infrastructure is bound to be hampered in long-run. The political elite, power elite, bureaucratic elite, intelligentsia etc. will have to make their will stronger enough to tackle the long threatening menaces of corrupt deeds. Globalisation of corruption will stun the development of poor countries and endanger the lives of billions. After independence in India and many other Asian, African and Latin American countries, the prime motto of the ruling and administrative elite has been rapid economic development. The contributions of developed nations, defacto have opened the door of all round development, but only at the cost of deepening corruption. The time is passing out to think in term of "long-sightedness" rather than "short-sightedness". The rational must be strong and courageous enough in policy framing and implementation in which there is competitiveness in economic sphere, democratic decentralisation and maximum public-participation.

NOTES AND REFERENCES

1. World Bank (1997), *World Development Report,* Washington, D.C.
2. Vittal, N. (2000), *The Times of India,* 5 May, Bombay.
3. Klitgaard, Robert (1998), International Cooperation Against Corruption, in *Finance & Development,* March.
4. *Ibid.*
5. World Bank (1997), *op. cit.*
6. Vogal, Frank (1999), Quoted in *The Hindustan Times,* Lucknow, 27 October.
7. Anklesaria Aiyer, Swaminathan S. (1997), The World Bank Discovers Corruption, *The Hindustan Times,* Lucknow, 29 June.
8. Rose-Ackerman, Susan (1978), *Corruption: A Study in Political Economy,* Academic Press, New York, pp. 10-15.
9. World Bank (1997), *op. cit.,* p. 103.
10. *Ibid.*
11. Mohanty, Manoranjan (1995), 'Corruption: Hindu-Chini Bhai-Bhai', *The Sunday Review,* New Delhi, 24 Sept. p. 9.
12. Anklesaria Aiyer, Swaminathan S. (1997), *op. cit.*
13. Vittal, N. (2000), *op. cit.*
14. *The Hindustan Times,* Lucknow, 28 Oct. 1999.
15. Vittal, N. (2000), *op. cit.*
16. Jain, P.C. (2000), 'Inspector Raj Breeding Corruption', *The Times of India,* New Delhi, July 1.
17. *Ibid.*
18. World Bank (1997), *op. cit.*
19. Klitgaard, Robert (1998), *op. cit.*

9

Tax Evasion and Corruption: The Indian Perspective

ANIL KUMAR JAIN

I

INTRODUCTION

The world 'corruption' is a complex phenomenon and has numerous facets. It covers a broad range of human actions and encompasses four distinguishing features: misuse of a position of power; gaining of advantage for those who are, actively or passively, parties to the misuse; undesirable effects on third parties; and secrecy surrounding the transactions. Corruption takes several forms. It is found in politics and the bureaucracy, in police and the judiciary, in the election process and in the private sector. It can be systematic or isolated. Public construction projects have provided the biggest and most dramatic cases of corruption world-wide, although the malady is deeper in developing countries.

At the broadest level, corruption can be said to be the misuse of office for unofficial ends. This may take several forms such as bribery, extortion, influence-peddling, nepotism, fraud, speed money, embezzlement, etc. Robert Klitgaard has rightly observed that corruption follows a formula: C = M + D – A. In other words, corruption equals monopoly *plus* discretion minus accountability. Because corruption is pervasive and it undermines a free and fair system based on trust, it becomes a principal threat to democracy. As corrupt money (which gets transformed into black money) has wings and not wheels, it is often smuggled abroad to safe havens and not ploughed back into the domestic economy. *The South Asian Human Development Report* produced by Mahbu-ul-Haq Centre in Islamabad has rightly observed that high level corruption can be compared to a cancer which, over a period of time, spreads to every organ of the body and finally causes death. If the rules are fine on paper but the officials have a great deal of discretion in their interpretation and implementation, this leads to a higher effective burden and a greater incentive to move to unofficial economy.

The varied and numerous dimensions of corruption are apparent from the fact that today every body in India is talking about *Hawalas*[1], *scams*[2] and corruption. Most of these discussions have been confined to corruption among politicians. But these debates have highlighted the issue of corruption in high places and have opened up avenues for the discussion of different facets of corruption. Although the primary objective of proceeding with the *hawala* diary was political, it has provided an opportunity for the nation towards checking corruption and finding remedies for it. Our object in this paper is to concentrate on economic facets of corruption and suggests measures to check this malady.

II

INTER LINKAGES BETWEEN TAX EVASION AND CORRUPTION

There is a close relationship between tax evasion, black money and corruption and all the three feed on each other. With the passage of time, tax evasion, bribery and corruption have become rampant in India so much so that corruption in India has become cancerous and political corruption has lately come to be virtually legitimized. According to the Transparency International's 1999 rankings, India comes at a pathologically low 72nd position among the 99 countries.

The unsanctioned or black market economy has been created from evasion of both direct and indirect taxes; undervaluation of property, anti-social activities such as smuggling, foreign exchange racketeering, under-invoicing and over-invoicing of foreign trade, remittances from abroad through illegal channels, etc. The prevalence of bribery and corruption has helped in increasing tax evasion which, in turn, has helped in increasing on-payments. Since tax, by definition, is a payment without direct *quid pro quo*, it involves some type of compulsion and, therefore, every person wants to pay the least possible amount of tax. However, the problem is more serious in the case of direct taxes, where the incidence of tax is generally borne by the person on whom it is imposed.

Historical Perspective

Tax evasion and corruption have undergone a significant change in India, both quantitatively and qualitatively, with the passage of time. During the 1930s a large number of wealthy and clever taxpayers started adopting ingenious methods of understating their incomes. The Second World War proved a golden era for tax dodgers and poured fortunes in the laps of skilful tax evaders. Gandhiji wrote in *Harijan* on February 1, 1948 that "the subject of corruption.... is not new. Only it has become much worse than before". The situation did not improve even after Independence; on the contrary, it became worse. To overcome the problem of shortages, different types of controls were imposed but, in practice, such controls generated black markets. The government's licensing policy offered fresh avenues for tax evasion, black market and corruption. Even the integrated system of taxation, introduced on the suggestion of N. Kaldor, did not prove effective. A constant tug of war continued between the tax dodgers and the government in which the former had the upper hand. This was partly due to the fact that until 1973-74, the general trend was to increase tax rates which made gains from evasion very high. A number of complex provisions were added to the tax laws in an attempt to plug the loopholes and curb tax evasion but these changes made the already complex laws more difficult to administer. This encouraged further evasion, generation and accumulation of black income and wealth. Obviously, corruption was further perpetuated. The model of Johnson *et. al.*;[3] on the basis of cross-country data, has found that countries with more regulation tend to have a higher share of the unofficial economy in total GDP, a higher tax burden leads to more unofficial activity and more corruption tends to have a larger unofficial economy.

One can briefly say that with the passage of time, Indian electoral system became more expensive and "we have degenerated from a largely honest society to a dishonest polity".[4] Jawaharlal Nehru and Lal Bahadur Shastri showed serious concern about mounting corruption. Santhanam Committee was set up and code for Central and State Ministers was announced by the Shastri Government in October 1964. Both Indira Gandhi and Rajiv Gandhi started off well, rousing great expectations with their eloquent promises of cleaning up the system. But little was, in fact, done. "Indira Gandhi virtually justified rampant corruption and the failure of her government to combat it on the ground that graft was a 'world phenomenon' and was not peculiar to India".[5] A Survey conducted by MODE for *The Times of India*, in which 1,554 adults were interviewed across six metros, revealed that 92 percent of the respondents opined politicians to be the most corrupt, followed by policemen, government servants and businessmen.[6] They further opined that it had increased since the Rao Government came to power. S. Ambirajan has rightly observed that "It is the result of a cumulative increase in corrupt behaviour on the part of those in government over a long period coupled with a steady increase in the discretionary power vested in the hands of the bureaucracy and politicians to determine the economic fortunes of individual economic agents".[7]

The fact in India today is that tax evasion has developed into a fine art and is accepted as a common feature of life. Today, things have gone to such an extent in India that 'No Harassment Tax' (NHT) must be paid in order to get things done in the right manner, involving no loss to the exchequer.[8] Here, 'No Harassment Tax' refers to the amount of 'on money' or illegal money that the taxpayers generally pay to the tax officials for not being harassed in their tax assessments and getting their assessments completed expeditiously and correctly. The problem is aggravated by the fact that 'black' economy has a close link with 'white' economy and the users of 'black' money can change 'black' money to 'white' money by the sheer force of their genius. Unlike Gresham's law, 'black' money does not drive out the 'white' money; instead it becomes mixed up in the economy in such a way that it becomes difficult to differentiate between the two.[9] Increasing tax evasion, black money and corruption in the Indian economy have had far reaching economic, social and political consequences.[10] There is immediate *quid pro quo* in the case of such money. The vast discretionary powers vested in politicians and bureaucrats, coupled with their low salaries have made them so amenable to bribery that corruption has become order of the day and most people have started accepting small-scale corruption as part of the system or *Suvidha Shulka* and 'grease-the-wheels' strategy is adopted to overcome burdensome regulations and ineffective legal system.

Economic Reforms

The fiscal situation in India, which was under strain throughout the 1980s, reached a critical situation in 1990-91. The macro-imbalance, fuelled by the budget deficit and financed by external borrowings and decumulation of reserves, was accompanied by double-digit inflation. The macro-economic situation, both internal and external, was unsustainable and the economy was left with no soft options and there was immediate need to act. The high point of the 'nineties' has been the clear recognition of the need to press ahead with fiscal reforms as an integral part of the economic reforms programme. Accordingly, comprehensive reform of both direct and indirect taxation was undertaken along the lines recommended by that Tax Reforms Committee (Chelliah Committee). During the nineties, the changes were "geared to move towards a tax structure which is simple, relies on moderate rates with a wider base and better enforcement, serves the objective of equity and provides the incentives and signals consistent with developing an internationally competitive and dynamic economy". In the fields of direct taxes, there has been a gradual increase in the exemption limit, reduction in maximum marginal rate of personal and corporate taxes, widening of tax base through introduction of new taxes and introduction of economic criteria for compulsory filing of tax returns, extension of scheme of tax deduction at source, etc. The aim of indirect tax reforms has been to reduce the level and simplify and rationalise the structure of customs and excise duties. The government hoped that with liberalisation and greater simplification of procedures, tax evasion and corruption would automatically be reduced. While it is true that the total gross tax revenue (centre and states combined) has increased from Rs. 87,564 crores in 1990-91 to Rs. 2,89,238 crores in 1999-2000 (BE) and the share of direct taxes in GDP and in tax revenue has gone up from 2.4 percent and 16.3

percent to 3.6 percent and 24.9 percent respectively, the fact remains that the Tax/GDP ratio has gone down from 15 percent to 14.5 percent during the same period. The experience of the Tax Amnesty Schemes and Summary Assessment Scheme has been far from satisfactory, and many taxpayers have used this confidence as a tool for evading taxes. Further, hardly any serious efforts have been made in recent budgets to improve the administration of direct taxes and several problems such as arrears of assessment and collection, pendency of appeals, delayed disposal of tax refund claims, under-valuation of properties and above all, strained public relations have become more severe with the passage of time. There is a feeling of mutual distrust between tax collectors and taxpayers.

It is a common belief these days that tax evasion, 'black' money and corruption, have increased even after economic reforms. The unearthing of various scams, is a pointer in this direction. "As long as the benefits of tax evasion and corruption far outweigh the risks involved, both maladies are bound to increase. Corruption depends not so much on the extent of controls but more on the ability to influence decisions. A reduction in controls has opened up new potential areas of corruption, and there are still many key areas where discretion is temptingly left with politicians and bureaucrats."[12] Further, as long as social status is determined by such factors as ostentatious expenditure at wedding, there will be pressures to evade taxes and accumulate black money.

III

AN AGENDA FOR ANTI-EVASION AND ANTI-CORRUPTION STRATEGY

To be effective, any anti-evasion and anti-corruption strategy must minimise—if not eliminate—the causes of evasion and corruption. The consequences of tax evasion and corruption can be minimised only if the government has an effective anti-corruption strategy and implements it impartially. So far, corruption has mostly inspired analysis, conferences and writings, rather than a determined and well-thought out action both at the national and international levels. We think that if tax evasion and corruption are to be really fought in India, it is imperative that the risks and costs of being corrupt are sharply increased. "Corruption must generate such a substantial loss of social status that it makes any monetary gain appear as insignificant. Such a loss of social status will only be possible if common people believe that those who break the rules of civil society deserve to be ostracized. This will need a society where most people, if not all, believe that rules that prevail are fair."[13]

To be effective, any anti-evasion and anti-corruption strategy must minimise, if not eliminate, the causes of corruption. It should lay emphasis on four important components; *First,* the government should identify a few major corrupt figures or tax evaders and they should be convicted and punished. Under Indian conditions, we think that there is need for a stricter system of penalties which should be imposed on the basis of gravity of default. In cases of proved tax evasion the tax departments in India should follow a vigorous prosecution policy because imprisonment is a greater deterrent and conviction in a court of law is attended by several legal and social disqualifications. Not only the persons directly involved in tax evasion be prosecuted but those behind such an act should also be prosecuted.[14] *Second,* any such strategy should emphasize greater involvement of people. Citizens are the most fertile source of information about where tax evasion and corruption occurs. People can be consulted through systematic client surveys, hot-lines, educational programmes and so forth. While contacting people, complete anonymity and secrecy be maintained. This would also require that social conscience against tax evasion and corruption be aroused. Towards this end, the veil of secrecy must be removed, all accounts be made public and the names of tax evaders and corrupt officials should be widely publicized. *Third,* experience indicates that efforts at attacking corruption have generated so much red tapism in bureaucracy that costs and losses in efficiency have outweighed the benefits of corruption. What is needed is that frequent workshops be organised to have serious thoughts about different dimensions of the maladies so that a general awareness is created that the government is really serious about tackling evasion and corruption. *Finally,* the government, which is serious about stopping corruption, must provide for a system of disincentives and incentives. There should be stiff penalties for corrupt high officials and such penalties should be simultaneously accompanied by rewards for competent and honest officials. In order to attract honest officials, it is necessary to pay them lucrative salaries and allowances so that he may stand up to 'great men' earning huge sums of money with whom he has to deal. In fact, "when the people pay government functionaries decent salaries, they are buying a layer of insulation against patronage and bribery. And the official gains the security and the self-respect of a civil servant, subverting patrimonialism".[15] Simultaneously, the principle of 'accountability' needs to be introduced.

Nevertheless, the success of any anti-evasion and anti-corruption strategy, which should aim at minimising the causes for the two, is conditioned by two important factors: (1) The adequacy of measures in terms of their comprehensiveness, scope and powers, and (2) the level of commitment of political leaders to the goals of minimising corruption, because ". . . the most elaborate and well-designed anti-corruption measures will be useless unless if they are not enforced by the political leadership."[16]

IV

CONCLUSION

To conclude, we think that lack of consciousness on the part of taxpayers, bureaucrats and political leaders has greatly encouraged evasion of taxes, generation of black money and corruption. People blame the government for difficulties and shortages, but when it comes to the payment of taxes, they feel as if it is their moral duty to evade it. In fact, there is moral crisis in India. These maladies must be fought in the minds and hearts of men. Traditionally, morality is rooted in religion and religious culture. In the name of secularism, we have weakened the moral fabric of our countrymen. It is high time that moral values are rejuvenated in the masses through the education of taxpayers, teaching morality at school level and emphasizing religious values and culture. People should be made to realise their duties towards the State and examples in this direction must be set by the national leaders and top bureaucrats.

NOTES AND REFERENCES

1. Robert Klitgaard, "Combating Corruption", *UN Chronicle,* 1998, Vol. 35, Issue 1, pp. 90-92.
2. Some of the important corruption cases in India include Mundra Scandal (1957), Nagarwala case (1971), Bofors Gum Deal (1987), Airbus Deal (1991), Securities Scam (1992), Sugar Scam (1994), Jain Havala case (1995), Bihar Fodder Scam (1996), JMM Bribery case (1996), Indian Bank Scam (1996), I.T.C. Scam (1996), etc.
3. Johnson, Simon, Kaupmann Daniel and Shleifer, Andrei, "The Unofficial Economy in Transition", *Brookings Papers on Economic Activity,* 1997, pp. 159-239.
4. Inder Jit, "Battling Corruption—Going Beyond Rhetoric and Buzz-words", *The Times of India,* New Delhi, October 1, 1996.
5. *Ibid.*
6. K. Balakrishnan and Gouri Chatterjee, "Corruption All-pervasive: Survey", *The Times of India,* January 14, 1995.
7. S. Ambirajan, "Eradicating Corruption; An Empty Promise", *The Economic Times,* April 30, 1996.
8. Anil Kumar Jain, "Tax Avoidance and Tax Evasion: The Indian case, "*Modern Asian Studies,* Vol. 21, No. 2, 1987.
9. Anil Kumar Jain, "Tax Evasion, Economic Reforms and Corruption in India", *International Tax Review* (INTERTAX), Vol. 25, January, 1997, p. 19.
10. For details, see Anil Kumar Jain, *Taxation of Income in India,* 1975, pp. 202-205.
11. Government of India, *Economic Survey* (1995-96), p. 27.
12. Anil Kumar Jain, INTERTAX, *op. cit,* p. 21.
13. Narendar Pani, "Economic Liberalisation and the Polity", *The Times of India,* 19 March, 1996.
14. Anil Kumar Jain, "Income Tax Penalty and Provisions: A Comparison of the United Kingdom and Indian Experiences", *British Tax Review,* 1987, No. 10, pp. 372-73.
15. Robert S. Leiken, "Controlling the Global Corruption Epidemic", *Foreign Policy,* Winter 1996-97.
16. Jon S.T. Quash, "Bureaucratic Corruption in the Asian Countries: A Comparative Analysis of their Anti-Corruption Strategies", *Journal of Southeast Asian Studies,* Vol. 13, No. 1, 1982, pp. 153-77.

10

Economic Implications of Environmental Crimes

AMITA KUMARI CHOUDHURY AND NIRMAL CHANDRA SAHOO

I

INTRODUCTION

Economic prosperity is the cornerstone of public policy almost everywhere. The unrestrained economic growth based on materialistic individualism undermines socio-cultural, ethical and environmental balance. Individual morality breaks down in an affluent growing economy. Indicators of social disintegration such as divorce, suicide, delinquency and different forms of crime and violence increase with economic growth.[1] Further economic growth and environmental decay are positively correlated. In this context Daly (1973) observed that environmental degradation is an "iatrogenic disease induced by economic physicians who treat the basic malady of unlimited wants by prescribing unlimited economic growth."[2] Growing needs for material aquisition cause environmental pollution, which is nonetheless a crime as it damages human health.

Against this background the paper makes an attempt—(1) to work out the economic dimensions of environmental crimes, (2) to analyse the nature and extent of environmental crimes in Orissa, and (3) to assess the adequacy of policy measures. The paper is divided into six sections. Following the introduction, section two gives a conceptual framework of crime in general and environmental crime in particular. The third section prepares the ground for socio-economic analysis of environmental crimes in Orissa. It has two parts, of which the former provides a brief background of the laws that deal with environment in India and the latter presents the socio-economy and environmental state of Orissa. The fourth section contains an analysis of the environmental crimes in Orissa, which is the core part of the work. The fifth section critically appreciates the strategies that cope with environmental crimes. The paper ends with a summary of the main findings and concluding observations.

II

THE ECONOMIC THEORY OF CRIME AND PUNISHMENT

It is difficult to articulate a correct and precise definition of crime. Glanville Williams (1983) defines crime or offence as a legal wrong that can be followed by criminal proceedings which may result in punishment.[3] Crime refers to any act or omission in respect of which legal punishment may be inflicted on the person who is in default either by acting or omitting to act.[4] The crimes cannot be just felonies—like murder, robbery and assult—which receive so much coverage in the newspapers, but also tax evasion, the so-called white collar crimes and other violations. Another school of thought considers the legal definition to be inadequate and unsuitable for the purposes of criminology. Crime, accordingly is defined as an act which the group (society) regards as sufficient meaning to its fundamental interests, to justify formal reaction to restrain the violations.[5] Raffeale Gorofale, one of the three leading exponents of the Italian School of Criminology, rejected the 'juridical' conception of crime. He stated the natural crime as an act which offends the basic moral sentiments of pity (revulsions against the voluntary infliction of suffering on others) and probity (respect for property right of others).[6] It can be therefore inferred that the definition of crime is one of the thorny intellectual problems of law. But broadly it can be defined as to cover all violations or the written and unwritten rules and regulations of a civil society.

The principle underlying the economic analysis of crimes is based on an idea that those who commit crimes do so because they perceive the benefits of such activity.[7] The crime, when it is committed benefits the criminal, but results in societal costs.[8] Thus, there is a cleavage between individual and public choice.[9] Removal of human organs and exportation of all these 'fictitious commodities' cheaply for transplant operation in developing countries, choosing for abortion of the foetus of a girl, amassing huge profit with prawn culture, the unlawful taking of the last member of species would result in a loss to society equal to the social value of the persistence of species.[10] The social value would be cumulation of economic values such as option, existence and bequest values.[11]

Environmental pollution is a crime against society. Ecological degradation, global warming, biodiversity losses, acid rain, air, water, noise and industrial pollution—all these are environmental crimes, since they impose (health damage cost) societal cost. It is inadequate to address ecological, environmental and social problems by relying entirely on pragmatic utilitarian moral attitude in combination with scientific understanding of natural system. Jenkins (1998) therefore, suggests that some form of 'environmental reverence' is necessary.[12] Cultural heritages may be a starting point for the task of nurturing environmental reverence. Most of the world's main religions have prescription concerning individual and social behaviour towards the social and natural environment.[13] To check environmental crimes, framing of laws and regulations are necessary. But as has been stressed in environmental philosophy, society's behaviour towards the environment and commission of environmental crime depends on the relationship between humanity and nature propounded by its cultural and religious traditions.[14] Further, ethical considerations play a considerable role in shaping the environmental objective, particularly in choosing the economic instruments.[15] From ethical perspectives any polluting activity that endangers the ecosystem is a crime. But under such a perspective, environmental crime is neither quantifiable nor amenable to analysis. So in this paper we take crime in its legal sense, even though it is of limited scope. Under this perspective an environmental crime is one that infringes the environmental statutes of a civil society.

Environmental quality is a typical 'good' for which property rights are not defined and hence no market exists.[16] Environmental pollution is a negative externality, which is typically found in the absence of well defined property rights.[17] Environmental pollution or external effect is that the effect produced is not a deliberate creation but an unintended or incidental by-product of some otherwise legitimate activity.[18] The Coasean solution to check externality may not be fruitful for undepletable externalities due to strategic behaviour and free-riding.[19] Another specific type of technological externality—congestion externality, where each actor is at the same time both supplier and receptor of the effect.[20] It is in this respect Pigou (1920) has suggested for corrective taxation.[21] The Pigouvian insight forms the basis of much further theoretical exploration and the design of environmental policies which attempt to make the polluter pay.[22]

Either through corrective taxation, or penalty or punishment, the polluter must be punished. One goal of punishment is to reimburse the society for the losses it has suffered due to the commission of a crime.[23] Fines provide compensation to victims and optional fines at the margin fully compensate victims. These can restore the *status quo*, so that they are no worse-off than if the offences were not committed.[24]

There may be problems with this approach. It could be argued that fines would be arbitrarily set with no consideration to actual social damage. Another difficulty relating to the fixation of fines is matching with the expected value of the punishment. The last problem concerns the criminal penalty of imprisonment. It has a monetary value, but converting a prison sentence into monetary terms is certainly difficult.[25] Despite all these problems it can be said that the level of fines certainly reflects some manifestation of the marginal damages caused by environmental pollution and degradation.

III

ENVIRONMENTAL STATUTES IN INDIA: A BRIEF REVIEW

In India, the citizens are given the right to clean air, water and environment both at the community level and in the industrial work place. If pollution causes permanent disabilities leading to malfunctioning or non-functioning of vital organs of the body of a person then such disability disallows him to lead a healthy life. Environmental legislation got fresh impetus after the U.N. Conference on Human Environment in 1972.[26] Consequently, a National Committee on environmental planning and coordination (Not Compiled EPC) was established as an apex advisory body on all environmental matters. On recommendation of Tiwari Committee, a separate Department of environment was established at the centre on November 1, 1980. The Water Act, 1974 reflects India's sincerity to deal with the environmental issue effectively. The Forest (Conservation) Act, 1980 was passed to prevent deforestation, which results in ecological imbalance and environmental deterioration. It prohibits forest land to be used for non-forest purposes, except with the prior approval of the central government.[27] The Air Act, 1981, and the Environment Protection Act, 1986, were enacted to implement the decisions reached at the U.N. Conference on Human Environmental degradation coupled with Bhopal gas tragedy forced the central government to enact fresh legislation for adopting stricter environmental policies. These include the 1987 amendments to the Factories Act, 1948 and the rules thereunder, the enactment of a new Environment Act, 1986, and a series of rules thereunder including the manufacture, storage, and import of hazardous chemical rules, 1989, the Public Liability Insurance Act, 1991, the revised Motor Vehicles Act, 1988 and the Central Motor Vehicles Rules, 1989 with latest amendments.[28]

IV

INDUSTRIALISATION AND ENVIRONMENT IN ORISSA

Economy and environment are interwoven. In order to understand and appreciate the state of environment in Orissa a snap and synoptic picture of the economic scene of the state is necessary. It gives a perspective and provides a canvas against which the central theme of the study acquires meaning and significance. The state of Orissa is characterised by poverty and unemployment, low per capita income, low capital formation, inadequate exploitation of natural resources and inadequate development of socio-economic infrastructure.[29]

Comprising 4.74% of India's landmass and with 31.65 million people (1991 census), Orissa accounts for 3.74% of the population of the country. Nearly 87% of its population live in rural areas and depend mostly on agriculture for livelihood. The state has abundant mineral resources. It has also ground water resources of which only 0.5% has been harnessed so far. Planned exploitation and optimum utilisation of rich minerals, land and water and other resources including human resources holds the key to rapid economic development of the state.[30]

The forest area was 58,135 sq. km in 1997-98, which constituted 37.3% of the total geographical area of the state. Due to deforestation the recorded forest cover has come down from 59,963 sq. km in 1981 to 58,135 sq. km in 1997-98.[31]

Orissa, owing to its peculiar geographical location and wide range of physical features, embraces a diversified flora and consequently a vast economic potential. The extensive range of hilly forests, several lofty peaks, long stretch of coastline, excellent river system; brackish water coastal plains altogether have endowed the state with a wide range of ecological habitats for a diverse and broad spectrum of vegetation.[32] The forests of Orissa which have innumerable medicinal and economically important species are dwindling. Since independence till the year 1984-85, the total official deforestation in the state amounted to about 207.4 sq. km. The annually utilisable ground water resource which can be safely utilised for the development of irrigation and other purposes has been estimated at 19,787 lakh hectare meters out of the total potential of 23,279 lakh hectare meters. But so far an irrigation potential of only 275 lakh hectares is created.

In the state, there are three sources of water pollution. These include domestic, non-point and industrial sources of which the last one is relevant here. The waters of Brahmani, Mahanadi, Ib, Rushikulya, Chilkia lagoon, Kolab and Hirakud reservoir system are polluted basically due to industrial effluents and pesticides and agro-chemicals. Most of the major industries of the state discharge their waste waters into the rivers. Rourkela Steel and Fertiliser Plant, Rourkela, Talcher Thermal Power Station, Talcher, Fertiliser Coorporation of India (Talcher), Heavy Water Project, Talcher, National Aluminium Company Smelter and Orissa Synthetic Ltd. (Dhenkanal) are some of the major polluting industrial units. These industries discharge more than 1.2 lakh μ^3 of effluents per day. The untreated effluent are of the Orient

Paper Mill at Brajarajnagar are discharged into the river Ib. The Rushikulya river is indirectly polluted by effluents from the sugar mill and distillery of the Aska. Apart from this the river water is directly polluted by a highly hazardous mercury bearing effluents from the chemical factory at Ganjam. Large quantities of pesticides and agro-chemicals find their way into Chilika through many rivers, rivulets and surface runoff.[33] Throughout the state the major causes of air pollution are the exhausts of industries. The Rourkela Steel Plant contributes criminally to air pollution even to the extent of causing photochemical smog and acid rain. In the Angul-Talcher area there are seven large-scale central and state public sector undertakings: The National Aluminum Company (NALCO), Smelter Plant and Captive Power Plant at Angul, Fertiliser Corporation of India (FCI), National Thermal Power Corporation (NTPC), Talcher Thermal Power Station (TTPS) and Talcher Thermal Power Corporation, TTPC, Talcher Super Thermal Power Plant, Kaniha and The Orissa Chemical Ltd. (ORICHEM). These industries cause severe eco-degradation in the form of forest loss, soil erosion, water and air pollution in the region[34]. These industries emit to the air, sulphurdioxide (SO_2), nitrous oxide (NO), suspended particulate matters (SPRL), carbon monoxide (CO), carbon dioxide (CO_2), fly ash, smoke, fume, dust hydrocarbons and fluoride. All these air pollutants have gradually degraded the biotic and abiotic components of the ecosystem.

In the process of economic development and industrialisation in Orissa, the people in general and entrepreneurs in particular have committed various types of environmental crimes which resulted in severe eco-degradation. In this paper, however, we are concerned with environmental externalities or crimes arising out of the infringement of some of the environmental statutes such as the Air Act, Water Act, and the Forest Act.

V

ENVIRONMENTAL CRIMES

In Orissa, there are 33 industrial units, which come under the 17 categories of highly polluting industries as per the environmental statutes of India. Out of these, 21 units are stated to be complying with the legal conditions. Table 1 shows the

TABLE 1

Status of 17 Categories of Highly Polluting Industries in Orissa, 1996-97

Sl. No.	Name of Industry	Category	Compliance Status Air	Compliance Status Water	Remarks
1.	Talcher Thermal Power Station, Talcher	Thermal Power	Not Compiled	Not Compiled	Two cases have been filed under Water and Air Act on 31-12-91 in the court of SDJM BBSR for non-compliance
2.	Rourkela Steel Plant CPP—I and II, Rourkela	Thermal Power	Not Compiled	Not Compiled	Air Pollution control measures are to be completed by Feb. 98 by the order of the Supreme Court of India
3.	East Coast Fertiliser & Chemicals Ltd. Kalma	Fertiliser	Compiled	Not Compiled	Water Pollution Control measures under upgradation
4.	Rourkela Steel Plant (Fertiliser unit), Rourkela	Fertiliser	Not Compiled	Not Compiled	All pollution control measures are to be completed by Feb. 98 by the order of the Supreme Court of India
5.	Paradeep Phosphates Ltd. Paradeep	Fertiliser	Compiled	Not Compiled	Case has been filed under Water Act for non-adoptation of pollution control measures
6.	Ballarpur Industries Ltd. Choudwar unit, Choudwar	Pulp and paper	Partially compiled	Compiled	No pollution control measures in Rosters (2 nos.) proposed to be replaced by recovery boiler Esp. by Sept. 97
7.	Fertiliser Corporation of India, Talcher	Fertiliser	Complied to some extent	Complied	Compliance is only for the present level of production

(*Contd.*)

TABLE 1 (*Contd.*)

8.	Orient Paper Millls, Brajrajnagar	Pulp and Paper	Complied	Partially complied	Two cases in 1991 and two cases in 1996 have been filed for violation of provisions under Water and Air Act
9.	Dharani Sugar and Chemical Ltd. Nayagarh	Sugar	Complied	Not complied	Asked not to operate without commissioning of full-fledged ETP
10.	Aska Coop. Sugar and Chemicals, Aska	Sugar	Complied	Partially complied	Asked to operate in next crushing season only after commissioning of full-fledged ETP
11.	Umeri Distillery (Pvt.) Ltd. Umeri, Jeypore	Distillery	Complied	Not complied	Industry was closed by the order of the State Pollution Control Board, allowed to operate on trial basis after Pollution Control measures are taken
12.	Rourkela Steel Plant, Rourkela	Integrate	Not complied	Not complied	Air Pollution control measures are completed by Feb. '98 by the order of Supreme Court of India

Source: OSPCB (1996-97).

state of the rest of the 12 industries as against the standards prescribed by Water Act and Air Act. In most of the cases litigation is still pending in the higher courts or the courts have ordered for upgradation of environmental protection measures. As a command and control agency, the Orissa State Pollution Control Board (OSPCB) has ordered some of the units to adopt adequate control measures.

Table 2 shows that up to the 31st March 1997 as many as 101 cases were instituted against the industries. The cases filed were more under the Water Act than the Air Act. So far as decisions of the courts under the Water Act are concerned, seven cases went against the industrial units while in 14 cases the cause of action had ceased, as a result of which the cases were not pursued.

TABLE 2
Pollution Cases in Orissa (1986-87 to 1996-97)

Year	*Water Act*	*Air Act*	*Total*
1986-87	02	Nil	02
1987-88	07	05	12
1988-89	17	10	27
1989-90	05	03	08
1990-91	11	05	16
1991-92	11	02	13
1992-93	01	Nil	01
1993-94	Nil	Nil	Nil
1994-95	04	02	06
1995-96	08	05	13
1996-97	03	Nil	03
Total	69	32	101

Source: OSPCB (1996-97).

There were three convictions leading to imprisonment with fine and four restraint orders. Similarly, under the Air Act, in one case the decision went in favour of the Board which in three cases it went against. Eight cases were not pursued as the causes of action had ceased.[35]

Under the Water Act and Air Act there were 40 and 19 pending cases for hearing in the lower courts. Two cases under the former and one under the latter appealed in High Court. As many as 64 industries including 3 urban local bodies and 9 public sector industries were prosecuted. In Orissa High Court, out of the total of 20 writs filed against the Board, 5 were disposed of in favour of the Board, and 7 were disposed of against the Board. There were 8 pending cases. Out of 39 public interest litigations, 36 cases were filed in the High Court and 3 cases in the Supreme Court. While the High Court disposed off 9 cases in favour of the Board and one case against the Board, the total pending cases in High Court were 20. The Supreme Court disposed only 2 cases in favour of the Board and one case is still pending. Out of the total of nine Consumer Dispute cases 3 were disposed off in favour of the Board and 6 cases are still pending.

During the early 80's number of forest offence cases detected increased from 51 thousand to 57 thousand. But the late 80's witnessed a decline. The total number of cases sent for prosection during 1980-81 to 1989-90 ranged from 16 to 45 hundreds. The total realised compensation and compounding fees was Rs. 2 crore (Table 3).[36] The data analysed here is not up-to-date but still it reflects the environmental crime against infringment of the Forest Act. The total compounding fees realised hardly reflects the social cost.

TABLE 3

Detection and Disposal of Forest Offences in Orissa (1980-81 to 1989-90)

Year	*Total No. of cases detected during the year*	*Total No. of cases sent for prosecution*	*Total No. of cases compounded*	*Compensation and compounding fees realised*
1980-81	51639	3341	35473	Rs. 26,27,308.00
1981-82	62441	2834	45837	Rs. 39,32,264.00
1982-83	64250	4466	48610	Rs. 48,41,171.00
1983-84	57853	4525	35666	Rs. 27,84,558.00
1985-86	31408	2233	15499	Rs. 10,91,497.00
1986-87	29576	1682	15343	Rs. 12,15,622.00
1987-88	29623	2174	16295	Rs. 12,23,836.00
1988-89	33009	2422	18071	Rs. 11,69,000.00
1989-90	12516	2901	18557	Rs. 14,72,000.00
Toal	372315	26578	249343	Rs. 2,03,57,256.00

Source: GOO (1981-90).

The extent of the environmental crimes in Orissa as described above do not indicate the amount of economic cost they impose on society. One can, however, make an informed guess from an illustration of the social cost of industrial pollution generated in the Angul-Talcher area of the state, on which a study has been made.

One comprehensive assessment of environment damage due to industrial pollution has been attempted by Mishra and Sahu (1998) and Mishra (1999) on the Angul-Talcher area of Orissa.[37] The area is one of the 22 pollution hot spots in India because of very high intensity of coal-based pollution of seven large scale public sector undertakings producing thermal power, aluminium, fertiliser and chemcials. The study has considered emissions of all the industries except TSTTP, which had gone into production in 1995 and the HWP, which is a classified industry. All the units come under the 17 categories of highly polluting industries. It is evident from Table 4 that the industries generate about 105 tonnes (t) of SPRL, 114 t of SO_2, 79 t of NO_x, 6205 t of solid waste and 115 thousand cubic metre of waste water everyday. Besides, FCI releases 1.8 t of urea dust and 0.5t of ammonia dust, and the ASP (N) emits 76 kg of fluorides everyday. On the basis of primary and secondary information processed through standard methods (Table 5), the study has estimated five categories of pollution-related damages to human health, cattle health, agricultural crops, forest and biodiversity and drinking water provision. Against average annual value of output of Rs. 11,590 million, the total annual value of damage is Rs. 2170 million. In comparison to the

TABLE 4

Pollution Generated by the Industries in the Angul-Talcher Area of Orissa (per day)

Sl. No.	*Particulars of production and pollution*	*Name of the Industry*						
		TTPS	*FCI*	*ORI CHEM*	*ASP (N)*	*CPP (N)*	*TSTPP*	*Total*
1.	Year of establishment	1967	1980	1983	1986	1986	1995	—
2.	Products	Thermal power	Urea	Chemicals	Aluminium	Thermal power	Thermal power	—
3.	Annual average value of output 1989-95 (Rs. $X10^6$)	932	766	62	7569	2267	—	11596
4.	SPM (Kg)	78863	2592	154	815	9816	13219	105459
5.	SO_2 (Kg)	35256	6864	3	4184	48881	19056	114244
6.	NO_x (Kg)	25512	6336	Nil	—	23414	23640	78902
7.	Solid waste (t)	1836	459	13	18	3879	—	6205
8.	Waste water (m^3)	15076	4757	Nil	12485	71455	11616	115389

Note: TTPS: Talcher Thermal Power Station, FCI: Fertiliser Corporation of India, ORICHEM: Orissa Chemicals, ASP (N): Aluminium Smelter Plant of National Aluminium Company (NALCO), CPP (N): Captive Power Plant of NALCO, TSTPP: Talcher Super Thermal Power Plant.

Source: Mishra and Sahu (1998) and Mishra (1999).

TABLE 5

Environmental Damage due to Industrial Pollution in Angul-Talcher Area of Orissa

Sl. No.	*Damage*	*Method of estimation*	*Total Damage*
1.	Human health	Medicine cost, incidental expenses and earnings lost by indoor and outdoor patients, and value of statistical life (*Shanmugam*, 1997) in death cases under 16 diseases	1775
2.	Cattle health	Treatment cost per cattle under 10 diseases	42
3.	Food crops	Participatory rural appraisal	103
4.	Forest and biodiversity	Annual rental value of forest area lost (*Lal*, 1992)	71
5.	Drinking water	Earnings lost by women in fetching water	179
	Total		2170

Source: Mishra (1999).

social cost of environmental damage, the industries bear annual abatement cost of the tune of Rs. 318 million only. Therefore, for every rupee worth of output of the national industries, the local environmental cost is about 19 paise and abatement cost is only 3 paise. The findings of the study show that with the present low abatement cost, the industries have been able to meet the regulation specified in the statutes of the country. In other words, even after meeting the command-and-control norms, the industries impose heavy damage costs. A generalisation from this case study for all the hot spots, and for all polluting industries implies that environment linked welfare loss is very high in our country, which warrants for careful monitoring of environmental indicators.

Another significant aspect of environmental crime needs further discussion from an ethical angle. The forest is a renewable resource and deforestation for development can be bridged up with keen afforestation programme. Tribals as well as poor people use the forests for their livelihood. The collection of firewood and forest products by tribals enable them to survive. This can be attributed to their utter poverty. And so this should be treated as a subsistence environmental crime. It should not be equated with the high profile and high visibility environmental crimes of industrial entrepreneurs, which may be called 'luxury' environment crimes. The commission of forest crime lies, however, in illegal timber felling by smugglers and contractors in league with corrupt politicians and forest bureaucracy. There is need to consider this on ethical as much as economic cost calculation.

VI

STRATEGIES FOR COPING WITH ENVIRONMENTAL CRIME

So far the basic strategy for dealing with environmental crimes in India and Orissa is of command and control nature. There are statutes and standards which control agencies impose and implement. In cases of infringement, litigations are fought and entrepreneurs are convicted. Such regulatory approaches have some basic loopholes. First, it is a breeding ground of corruption. Second, the administrative cost is very high. Thirdly, for the entrepreneurs environmental statutes are just an addition to the other laws such as Factories Act, Income Tax Act and so on which they have to honour. So for one entrepreneur, a legal cell in the industry is enough to fight the cases in the courts and continue with the polluting activities in the meanwhile. Thus, against the state strategy there is an entrepreneurial strategy which renders environmental crime a pervasive feature of an economy.

The experience shows that command and control measures are not a foolproof strategy to deal with the environmental crimes. Since the crimes have economic benefits for those who commit these economic crimes and thereby imposing heavy cost on the society as a whole, it is necessary to supplement the environmental regulations with economic instruments. Some of the economic instruments which have been argued in environmental economics as sound measures and also have been implemented in some of the countries of the west include emission tax, product charge, input taxes, deposit refund system, and tradeable permits. Though it is true that these measures too would not completely compensate for the environmental damage, their deterrent value may reduce the damage. It is necessary to introduce these measures in Orissa too.

VII

CONCLUSIONS

The main arguments flowing from the paper may be summed as follows:

(i) Crimes are generally defined with a legal perspective, but a legal view is not adequate. Ethical considerations are necessary though not quantifiable.

(ii) Environmental crimes are not just another set of crimes. They have far reaching implications socially, spatially and temporally.

(iii) In economics, the concept and approach to negative externality helps a researcher to make an economic analysis of the environmental crimes such as pollution and ecological degradation. The human health and other damage costs of environmental crimes are much higher than what the courts collect as compensation.

(iv) In a backward state like Orissa, the state of environmental crime is abysmal. The command and control approach alone is not adequate. Economic instruments should be introduced as a part of comprehensive coping strategy and ethical considerations have to be driven home through proper environmental education.

(v) Under an ethical perspective, there is difference between the forest offence cases of a tribal and a contractor or an industrial entrepreneur. The subsistence and 'luxury' environmental crimes call for separate focus and treatment.

NOTES AND REFERENCES

1. Hirsch, F., (1976), *Social Limits to Growth*, Harvard University Press, Massachusetts.
   Mishan, E.J., (1997), *The Economic Growth Debate: An Assessment*, George Allen & Unwin, London.
2. Daly, H.E., (Ed.), (1973), *Towards a Steady-State Economy*, Wlt. Freeman and Company, San Francisco.
3. Glanville, W., (1983), *Text Book of Criminal Law*, Universal Law Publishing Co. Pvt. Ltd., Delhi.

4. Pillai, A.P.S., (1999), *Criminal Law,* N.M. Tripathy Pvt. Ltd., Bomaby.
5. Siddique, A., *Criminology: Problems and Perspectives,* Eastern Book Company, Lucknow.
6. *Ibid.*, p. 4.
7. Becker, G.S., (1968), "Crime and Punishment: An Economic Approach", *Journal of Political Economy,* Vol. 76, pp. 169-217.
8. Posner, R.A., (1986), *Economic Analysis of Law,* Little Brown, Boston.
9. Pigou, A.C., (1920), *Economics of Welfare,* Macmillan, London.
10. Eagel, J.G. and D.R. Betters, (1998), "The endangered species act and economic values: a comparison of fines and contingent valuation studies," *Ecological Economics,* Vol. 26, No. 2, August, pp 165-71.
11. *Ibid.*
12. Jenkins, T.N., (1998), "Economics and the environment: a case of ethical neglect," *Ecological Economics,* Vol. 26, No. 2, August, pp. 161-63.
13. Engel, J.R., Engel, J.G. (Eds.), (1990), *Ethics of Environment and Development,* Arizona up, Tuscon.
    Ching, J., (1994), *Chinese Religions,* Macmillan, London.
14. White, L., (1967), "The Historical Roots of our Ecological Crisis," *Science,* 155, 3767.
15. Tietenberg, T., (1998), "Ethical influences on the evolution of the US tradable permit approach to the air pollution control," *Ecological Economics,* Vol. 24, Nos. 2, 3, February-March, pp. 241-57.
16. Verhoef, T., (1999), "Externalities", in Jeroen, C.J.U. Van den bergh (ed.) *Handbook of Environmental and Resource Economics,* Edward Elgar, Cheltenham, U.K.
17. Baumol, W.J. and W.E. Oates, (1988), *The Theory of Environmental Policy,* Cambridge University Press, U.K.
18. Mishan, E.J., (1971), "The Postwar Literature on externalities: an Interpretative Essay," *Journal of Economic Literature,* 9, 1-28.
    Coase, R.H., (1960), 'The Problem of Social Cost', *Journal of Law and Economics,* 3, October, pp. 1-44.
19. Verhoef, E.T., (1994), "External Effects and Social Costs of a Road Transport", *Transportation Research,* 28A, pp. 273-87.
20. Verhoef, E.T., (1996a), *The Regulation of Road Transport,* Edward Elgar, Cheltenham, U.K.
21. Pigou, A.C. (1920), *Wealth and Welfare,* Macmillan, London.
22. Bohm, P. and E.F. Russel, (1985), "Comparative Analysis of Alternative Policy Instruments", in Allen V. Kneese and James L. Sweeney (Ed.) *Hand Book of Natural Resources and Energy Economics,* North-Holland, pp. 395-460.
    Cropper, M.L. and W.E. Oates, (1992), "Environmental Economics: A Survey", *Journal of Economic Literature,* 30, pp. 675-740.
23. Becker, G.S., (1968), *op. cit.*, pp. 169-217.
24. *Ibid.*
25. *Ibid.*
26. Gupta, S., and M. Gupta, (1997), *Environment, Population and Resources,* Institute for Environmental Development Studies, Lucknow, Anmol Publications Pvt. Ltd., Delhi.

27. Sankar, U., (1998), "Laws and Institutions Relating to Environmental Protection in India", Paper presented at the conference on "The Role of Law and Legal Institutions in Asian Economic Development" held at Erasmus University, Rotterdam, November 1-4.
28. Diwan, P. and P. Diwan, (1998), *Environmental Management Law and Administration; Readings and Cases,* Vanity Books International, New Delhi.
29. Government of Orissa, (1998), *Economic Survey, 1998-99,* Directorate of Economics and Statistics, Bhubaneswar.
30. *Ibid.,* p. 1/1.
31. Council of Professional Social Workers (CPSW), (1994), *State of Orissa's Environment—A Citizen's Report,* Bhubaneswar, CPSW.
32. *Ibid.*
33. *Ibid.,* p. 128.
34. *Ibid.,* pp. 298-309.
35. Orissa State Pollution Control Board (OSPCB), (1997), *Annual Report,* OSPCB, Bhubaneswar.
36. Government of Orissa, (GOO), (1999), *A Decade of Forestry in Orissa, 1981-1990,* Statistical Branch Office of the Principal Chief Conservator of Forests, Orissa, Bhubaneswar.
37. Mishra, M. and N.C. Sahu, (1998), "Environmental Cost of Industrial Agglomerationn in Angul-Talcher area of Orissa, India", paper presented in the Fifth Biennial Conference of the International Society for Ecological Economics on Beyond Growth: Institutions and Policies for Sustainability, Santiago, Chile, 15-19 November.
    Mishra, M., (1999), 'Economics of Industrial Pollution in the Angul-Talcher Industrial Area in Orissa', unpublished Ph.D. Dissertation, Berhampur University, Orissa, India.

11

Economic Analysis of Crime and Punishment

N.B. PRADHAN, B. PATRO AND S.K. PANIGRAHY

I

THEORETICAL FRAMEWORK

Becker (1968) presented an economic approach to crime and punishment analysing economic cost of crime, the determinants of supply of offenses, the economic and social cost of punishment. Becker made an effort to develop a model to combat crime in an optimal fashion by incorporating the behavioural relations between (1) the number of crimes and the cost of offenses; (2) the number of offenses and the punishment meted out; (3) the number of crimes, arrests and convictions and the public expenditure on police and courts; (4) the number of convictions and the costs of punishments; and (5) the number of offenses and the private expenditure on protection and apprehension. The number of offenses by any person depends on the probability of conviction, extent of punishment if convicted and other variable such as income or benefits from offense, willingness to commit a crime. This can be represented as:

$O_j = F(p_j, X_j, Y_j, v_j)$ and

$\partial O_j/\partial p_j < 0$,

$\partial O_j/\partial X_j < 0$,

$\partial O_j/\partial Y_j > 0$

where O_j is the number of offenses a person would commit during a particular period, p_j his probability of conviction per offense, X_j extent of punishment per offense, Y_j gain from offense (monetary plus psychic), v_j is the disturbance term representing all other influences.

According to law only convicted offenders are punished and for conviction sufficient evidence is necessary in the court of justice. Therefore, a person is punished if convicted. This implies that the crime and punishment can be analysed under risk and uncertainty. Generally an increase in either p_j or X_j would reduce the utility expected from an offence or crime and thus tend to reduce the number of crime. On the other hand, increase in Y_j would encourage crime. Thus the net effect depends on interaction of all these legal, economic and socio-psychological variables.

The expected utility $E(U_j)$ from committing a crime is defined as:

$$E(U_j) = p_j U_j(Y_j - X_j) + (1 - p_j)U_j(Y_j)$$

where U_j is N-M (Neumann-Morgenstern) utility function. Both p_j (probability of conviction) and X_j (his punishment) might be considered distributions that depend on efficiency of police and judiciary system.

To achieve the goal of deterrence the probability of conviction, p could be raised close to 1, and punishment, X could be made to exceed gain, Y. Tsebelis (1990a, 1990b) analysed the deterrent effect of punishment using a game theoretic approach. He considered the pay-offs in police-public game, where preferences of police to enforce or not to enforce and preferences of public to commit the crime or not to commit set upon interesting problem. The police-public game has no Nash equilibrium in pure strategy, but the game has a unique Nash equilibrium in mixed strategies. The two-person model of Tsebelis has been criticised on various grounds by Bianco (1990), Ordeshook (1990) and Tullock (1991). Cox (1994) considered n-person model to analyse the deterrent effect of punishment. It is assumed that there are m-different crimes to check with a fixed amount of resources with the police. Thus, to achieve the goal of deterrence of particular crime one has to take into account of the opportunity costs of these resources. In this model the police can raise the probability of catching a speeding motorist only by diverting more resources to this task and thereby lowering the probability of catching a thief or some other types of criminal. Thus, police has to find out optimal use of resources.

Shavell (1987) studied the optimal use of non-monetary sanctions such as imprisonment, the death penalty in a theoretical model of deterrence in which the threat of sanctions may deter persons from committing contemplated crimes. Polinsky and Shavell (1984,1990) have shown that two high value of fine will have no deterrent effect on criminals who cannot pay, rather it will lead criminals to choose imprisonment in lieu of a fine which will increase the cost of maintenance of jail and the judiciary system. Ban-zion, Kawasaki and Spiege (1993) have examined the policy of discrimination in punishment and deterrence effects.

The purpose of the above discussion is not to develop or extend a theoretical frame-work for the analysis of crime in Orissa but to spellout and identify the basic economic factors involved in crime. It is far too difficult to obtain information on gains from crime, more so if they go beyond monetary going to that of psychic. Equally difficult is to calculate the economic loss suffered by a convict. Data to analyse the public-police pay-offs in game theoretic framework are equally difficult to generate. What is attempted in the following section is to examine simple relationships like per capita income and crime rate, police/population and police/crime rate, judicial deterrence, etc.

II

CRIME AND PUNISHMENT IN ORISSA

The present paper is an attempt to analyse the crime and punishment situation in Orissa from the point of view of economics. The theoretical discussion in the preceding paragraphs justifies that even though sociological and political considerations are important to understand criminal behaviour of a human being, the role of economic analysis has gained importance in the recent years due to the twin problems of unemployment and poverty.

The people of Orissa are mostly identified as peace-loving and there is no major conflict in the state since long. Caste-based, class-based and religion-based conflict in the state is practically non-existent barring the current event of Naxalite movement in the South Orissa, a spill-over of the People's War Group movement in Andhra Pradesh. The recent incidents of Hindu-Christian conflict in Keonjhar and Phulbani are more due to economic reasons rather than due to religious considerations. Orissa represents the epitome of poverty in the country and ranks second in the per capita monthly consumption expenditure ladder counted from below. The level of living of the people is quite miserable. The economy is almost fully dependent on agriculture sector due to the absence of an industrial climate. The infrastructure services are very poor. Over-dependence on agriculture manifests significant level of disguised unemployment in the state. The absence of growth in the secondary and tertiary sectors of the economy has caused the problem of educated unemployed a serious one. In the recent years, the Government of Orissa has been compelled even to reduce organised sector employment due to acute financial stringency. Added to all these, is the inefficiency of the successive governments to deliver a system of strong governance. The growing inequality in income and wealth is adding fuel to the fire. It can be safely concluded from all these narrations that the people are to some extent compelled to indulge in criminal activities due to poverty, hunger and starvation.

The purpose of this paper is to identify some economic factors like unemployment, expenditure level on police force, per capita income and examine their relationship with crime and punishment. As discussed earlier, most of the criminal activities have economic roots that may be direct and indirect. The economic analysis can be done from two perspectives. One is the circumstances leading to growth of criminal activities and the other is the steps taken by the Government to control the criminal activities in the state. The theoretical discussion reveals that criminal activities depend on the economic gain and punishment inflicted on the culprit. But due to non-availability of data we confine our discussion to only areas for which data is available.

Using secondary sources of information we have carried out the analysis. The statistical and economic documents of the state reveal the strength of the police force, incidence of different criminal activities, per capita income, educated unemployment, expenditure on police, jails and judiciary, etc.. Quantitative analysis of the situation is carried out to understand the nature of relationship between economic factors and crime in the state.

Crime Promoting Factors

General Crimes

The growth of different types of criminal activities in the state is given below in Table 1. The general criminal activities in the state are classified into nine different categories. These are murder, dacoity, robbery, burglary, theft, rioting, kidnapping, abduction, and misc. Last row of the table indicates the exponential growth rate for each crime. The growth rate of abduction is the highest, i.e. 70.6 percent. Negative growth rate is noticed in case of burglary and theft. For all other crimes there is positive growth rate. The overall growth of general crimes in the State is 7.6 percent. Miscellaneous crimes as such have been of very high

TABLE 1

Incidence of Crime in Orissa: 1983-1996

(in numbers)

Year	*Murder*	*Dacoity*	*Rubbery*	*Burglary*	*Theft*	*Rioting*	*Kidnapping*	*Abduction*	*Misc.*	*Total*
1983	558	361	780	5863	11500	1722	123	3	24077	44987
1984	573	254	766	5358	10374	1913	124	3	23751	43116
1985	571	242	729	4778	9789	1604	516	1	25198	13428
1986	613	267	662	4557	9736	1257	152	1	27195	44410
1987	579	181	575	4110	9307	1040	158	13	26806	42769
1988	577	158	572	4258	9277	1065	232	198	26858	43195
1989	612	198	604	4472	9747	1372	279	207	28733	46224
1990	666	256	666	4876	10731	1532	288	257	30884	50156
1991	712	312	822	4830	10582	1768	287	321	32672	52286
1992	760	335	914	4493	9801	2133	209	349	33991	52985
1993	821	307	957	4315	9626	1653	396	431	35366	53782
1994	813	364	939	4092	8370	1691	384	434	34074	51161
1995	896	264	969	4235	7643	1841	375	590	36771	53614
1996	1019	298	984	4070	7249	1647	408	639	36881	53195
Growth rate	4.5	1.9	3.1	–1.78	–1.99	1.4	7.6	40.6	3.8	7.6

Source: Statistical Outline of Orissa, 1988, 1993, 1997; Directorate of Economics and Statistics, Government of Orissa, Bhubaneswar.

magnitude. The rate of growth of rioting is the lowest (1.4%) among positively growing crimes.

Crime against Women

The crime against women comprises of dowry death, dowry torture and other kinds of torture meted out to women. Table 2 reveals that the growth rate of dowry death due to homicide is the highest, i.e. 40.3 percent followed by dowry torture and non-dowry torture whereas negative growth rate is associated with death due to suicide. It is found that dowry torture was lower than non-dowry torture up to 1990. From 1991, dowry torture exceeded non-dowry torture and dowry death also increased simultaneously.

TABLE 2

Crime against Women in Orissa

Year	*Death due to Homicide*	*Death due to Suicide*	*Dowry Torture*	*Non-dowry Torture*
1987	17	46	62	130
1988	29	47	130	106
1989	46	46	152	177
1990	80	60	175	215
1991	98	71	214	183
1992	155	49	252	168
1993	187	45	341	207
1994	265	43	488	302
1995	314	39	565	377
1996	354	36	710	405
Growth rate (Exponential)	40.3	–3.17	27.6	14.0

Source: *Statistical Outline of Orissa*, 1988, 1993, 1997. Directorate of Economics and Statistics, Government of Orissa, Bhubaneswar.

Crime and Per Capita Income

As per capita income is taken as composite index of economic growth, its relationship with crime can shed light on crime and development. To examine this aspect, regression results are estimated taking particular crime as dependent variable (Y) and state per capita income as independent variable (X). The estimated results are presented in Table 3. Out of the 14 different criminal activities, the per capita income and crime regression relationship gives significant t-values and F-values in case of 11 crimes. The R^2 value is high for 8 crimes. Regression coefficient is positive for all crimes except burglary, theft and suicide. This shows that with economic development criminal activities are also growing.

TABLE 3
Regression Results of Crime and Per Capita Income Relationship

Sl. No.	*Type of Crime*	α	β	*t-test*	*F-test*	R^2
1.	Murder	388.38	0.088	S	S	0.91
2.	Dacoity	210.79	0.018	NS	NS	0.19
3.	Robbery	512.26	0.077	S	S	0.62
4.	Burglary	5308.67	–0.204	S	S	0.38
5.	Theft	11527.26	–0.565	S	S	0.57
6.	Rioting	1327.08	0.075	NS	NS	0.14
7.	Kidnapping	120.42	0.046	S	S	0.34
8.	Abduction	–249.27	0.142	S	S	0.96
9.	Misc.	20038.20	2.914	S	S	0.92
10.	Total	39182.13	2.588	S	S	0.78
11.	Homicide	–202.18	0.086	S	S	0.96
12.	Suicide	61.86	–0.003	NS	NS	0.20
13.	Dowry Death	–299.68	0.147	S	S	0.91
14.	Non-dowry death	47.18	0.066	S	S	0.82

Source: Compiled, S—Significant, NS—Not Significant at 5 percent.

Crime and Unemployment

Absence of gainful employment, both in the public and the private sector is likely to influence the magnitude of criminal activities in the state. This is more so in case of educated unemployed youths because of their dependence on the service sector to a great extent. The regression relationship between crime (Y) and unemployment (X) establishes a positive linkage between the two. The value of R^2 is 0.44 and both t-test and F-test conclude significant regression coefficient for the relationship. This indicates the growth of crime is partially due to increase in unemployment.

Crime Controlling Factors

Maintaining law and order is one of the primary responsibilities of a state government according to the Indian constitution. A conducive work environment is important for the industrialisation of an economy. With the growth of population and the degree of urbanisation, the law and order machinery has to be expanded to cope up with the increasing requirement. In the previous review of literature we have found the number of crimes can be reduced by increasing the probability of conviction and the extent of punishment. For the conviction of a criminal sufficient number of well equipped efficient police force is necessary. Punishment within a scheduled time is very much necessary to decrease the gain from the crime, so that the person can be discouraged to repeat crimes. For this efficient provision of judicial services to dispose growing number of cases of crimes is necessary.

Crime and Police Infrastructure

To evaluate the performance of the Government of Orissa, we are examining the number of institutions and police forces in the state from 1987 to 1995. The expansion in the number of police stations, outposts and beat houses, fire stations, armed police, unarmed police and military police force is given in Table 4 with their growth rates.

TABLE 4
Growth of Police Infrastructure in Orissa

(in numbers)

Year	*Police Stations*	*Outposts & Beat Houses*	*Fire Stations*	*Armed police force*	*Unarmed police force*	*Military Police force*
1987	417	493	89	8924	17453	7052
1988	433	496	90	8306	17474	7052
1989	433	501	93	8903	17679	7188
1990	433	512	93	9003	17853	7189
1991	433	514	93	9013	17838	7189
1992	434	522	96	9013	17884	7484
1993	438	535	98	9230	18036	7579
1994	442	545	98	9300	18096	7560
1995	442	552	98	9294	18011	7615
Growth Rate (Exponential)	0.9	1.6	3.3	0.9	–1.9937	–1.76

Source: Statistical Outline of Orissa, 1988 to 1997.

Table 4 reveals that the police stations and the armed police force have marginally increased by 0.9 per cent during the period 1987 to 1997. Armed police force and military police force have shown negative growth rate.

To adjudge the adequacy of the law and order machinery, there is an attempt to calculate the police/population ratio during period 1987-1995 which is given in Table 5.

TABLE 5

Police/Population and Police/Crime Ratio in Orissa

Year	*Total Police (No.)*	*Population (in lakhs)*	*Police/ Population Ratio*	*Total Crime (No.)*	*Police/ Crime Ratio*
1987	33429	297.32	112	42769	0.782
1988	32832	303.26	103	43195	0.760
1989	33770	309.33	109	46224	0.731
1990	34045	315.52	108	50156	0.679
1991	34040	317.00	107	52286	0.651
1992	34381	322.07	106	52985	0.649
1993	34845	327.23	106	53782	0.648
1994	34958	332.47	105	51161	0.683

Source: Compiled

In 1987, 112 policemen were available per lakh population in Orissa which has declined to 105 policemen in the years 1994. This means the growth of the police force has not commensurate with the growth of population. The linear relationship between crime and policemen available per lakh population gives us a negative value and the fitting is significant at 5% level which shows that crime increases with the declining ratio of police force to check it. This is also supported by the declining police/crime ratio during the period.

Crime and Public Expenditure

Another way of examining the crime control intention (CCI) of the government is to focus on the public spending in the departments associated with the control of crimes. The expenditure on police, jails and judiciary comes under this. The quantum and trend is indicated in Table 6. Table 6 reveals that public expenditure per crime is increasing very fast and within

TABLE 6

Expenditure on Crime-control Activities in Orissa

(Rs. in crores)

Year	*Police*	*Jail*	*Judiciary*	*Total Expenditure*	*Total Crime*	*Expenditure per Crime*
1983	40.87	3.49	5.10	49.46	44987	10995.13
1984	44.81	3.73	5.73	54.27	43116	12586.94
1985	49.66	4.17	6.36	60.19	43428	13859.13
1986	68.74	4.68	8.08	81.50	44410	18351.87
1987	71.97	5.00	9.10	86.07	42769	20123.62
1988	77.94	5.39	9.98	93.31	43195	21601.48
1989	88.27	6.15	11.54	105.96	46224	22922.84
1990	96.53	7.21	12.96	116.71	50156	23269.30
1991	112.13	8.00	14.52	134.66	52286	25753.65
1992	129.20	9.01	17.24	155.45	52985	29338.30
1993	135.40	10.07	18.26	163.72	53782	30441.94
1994	151.97	12.53	22.51	187.01	51161	36553.34
1995	177.36	13.53	24.68	215.56	53614	40206.84
1996	211.58	14.36	28.54	254.48	53195	47838.28

Source: Finances Accounts, Govt. of Orissa from 1983 to 1996.

13 years it has gone up by more than four times. It has gone up from Rs. 10995 per crime in 1983 to Rs. 47838 per crime in 1996. The crime-expenditure regression line exhibits a significant positive relationship over time. This means in spite of increased expenditure on the law and order machinery, there is no reduction in the crime rate in the state.

Crime and Punishment

The role of judiciary is very important to introduce a sense of fear to conduct a crime. The quantum of criminal cases pending in the judicial system is presented in column 2 of Table 7. There is consistent rise in the number of cases pending and it has doubled within a period of twelve years. The number of cases for which trial is over and punishment inflicted, however, is more or less stagnant. It is around one lakh with slight variation in the aforesaid period. The disposal ratio has fallen continuously from 53% in 1983 to 31% in 1994. The linear regression between crime and disposal ratio gives a negative regression coefficient indicating rise in crime due to reduction in the disposal ratio. The shows an inadequate judicial deterrence in Orissa.

TABLE 7
Judicial Deterrence to Crime in Orissa

Year	*Total for Disposal during the year*	*Disposed off during the year*	*Disposal Ratio*	*Total Crime*
1983	154147	82190	0.533192	44987
1984	164977	82731	0.501470	43116
1985	167062	76616	0.458602	43428
1986	169301	77112	0.455473	44410
1987	175522	82342	0.469126	42769
1988	212135	99393	0.468537	43195
1989	235175	107548	0.457311	46224
1990	254567	101735	0.399639	50156
1991	261835	99975	0.381824	52286
1992	276303	115188	0.416890	52985
1993	280420	100507	0.358416	53782
1994	307384	94306	0.306792	51161

Source: Statistical Outline of Orissa, 1988, 1993 and 1997.

Findings

The main finding of the study are:

(i) The crime rate has increased invariably over the years. The growth rate of general total crimes is around 8%. Crime against women is much higher than the general crime in the state. Growing cases of dowry death and dowry torture indicate the plight of women in the state.

(ii) The relationship of crime with income and unemployment is found to be positive.

(iii) The provision of police infrastructure is completely inadequate as is evident from the comparative growth rate of crime and police forces.

(iv) Public expenditure per crime has increased over the years without decreasing the quantum of crime.

(v) The disposal of criminal cases by the judicial system results into very much delayed punishment.

III

CONCLUSIONS

Even though the crime rate in Orissa appears to be high, any final conclusion on this matter requires inter-state comparison of various crimes in India. The increasing rate of crime against women appears to be an economic as well as a sociological problem. In most of the cases, this is due to incomplete information and absence of clear-cut negotiation on the quantum of dowry before marriage. In spite of Anti-dowry Act prevalent in India dowry is given under compulsion. In the marriage market, bride's parents are in disadvantageous position mainly because of patriarchal system of family and lower status of women in terms of education and power. The prevailing caste system limiting the marriage market reduces it to a oligopolistic situation. In general, many criminal cases remain uncontrolled because of economic and political pressure imposed on the police and the judiciary. In the present fiscal scenario of the state, it is not desirable to allocate more resources to the police department by reducing other developmental expenditure. What is required now is to reallocate the given resources to modernise the police force and enhance their capabilities.

REFERENCES

Becker, Gary S. (1968), "Crime and Punishment: An Economic Approach," *Journal of Political Economy*, Vol. 76, No. 2; pp. 169-217.

Ben-Zion, U. Kawasaki, S. and Spiegel, U., (1993), "Discrimination in Punishment and Deterrence Effects," *Public Finance/Finance Publiques*, Vol. 48, No. 1, pp. 10-18.

Bianco, W.T. (1990), "Crime and Punishment", *American Political Science Review*, Vol. 84, pp. 569-73.

Cox, G.W. (1994), "A Note on Crime and Punishment", *Public Choice*, January, 1994, Vol. 78(1), pp. 115-24.

Government of Orissa, *Finance Accounts*, 1983-84 to 1996-97.

Government of Orissa, *Economic Survey*, (1998-99), Directorate of Economics and Statistics.

Government of Orissa; Directorate of Economics and Statistics, *Statistical Outline of Orissa*, (1988, 1993, 1997).

Ordeshook, P.C. (1990), "Crime and Punishment", *American Poltical Science Review,* Vol. 84, pp. 573-75.

Polinsky, M.A. and Shavell, S. (1984), "The Optimal Use of Fines and Imprisonment," *Journal of Public Economics,* Vol. 24, pp. 89-99.

Polinsky, M.A. and Shavell, S. (1990), 'A Note on Optimal Fines when Wealth Varies Among Individuals', NBER Working Paper Series, No. 3232.

Shavell, S. (1987), "The Optimal use of Non-monetary Sanctions as a Deterrent," *American Economic Review,* September, pp. 584-90.

Tsebelis, B. (1990a), "Crime and Punishment," *American Political Science Review,* Vol. 84, pp. 576-86.

Tsebelis, B. (1990b), "Are Sanctions Effective? A Game Theoretic Analysis," *Journal of Conflict Resolution,* Vol. 34, pp. 3-28.

Tullock, G. (1991), "The Effect of Fines on Regulated Industries: Game Theory Vs. Decision Theory," *Journal of Theoretical Political Economics,* Vol. 3, pp. 81-101.

12

Economic Crimes: Key Issues

SATYA PAL SINGH

I

INTRODUCTION

"Arthasya Purusho Daaso"—man is subservient to money and means—thus sadly echoed Bhism in Mahabharata.[1] As Jean Girandoux has remarked, to have money is to be virtuous, honest, beautiful and witty. And to be without is to be ugly and boring and stupid and useless.[2] The current dominant economic trends of liberalisation and globalisation sweeping the world have brought in their fold an emergence of new forms of economic crimes, more sophisticated and more damaging to the democratic and economic development of a nation. Reforms not only open the barriers to business, they also create a thousand areas where economic crimes can proliferate.

Economic crimes, once popularly known as 'white-collar crimes', are committed by persons of relatively high social or economic status in connection with their regular occupations. Those forms of crimes in general were known to cover embezzlement, misappropriation of funds, criminal breach of trust, securities theft, bribery and kickbacks, cheating, fraud, forgery and counterfeiting. In a shrinking borderless world coupled with fast changing economic and trade policies, these forms of crimes have taken an ominous hydra-headed transformation as 'Economic Crimes' encompassing many more new generation crimes from misappropriation to money-laundering, from simple frauds to floating fictitious firms, from breach of trust to bank manipulations, from smuggling to narco-terrorism, from selling secrets to subverting systems, to quote a few illustratively.[3]

Feature of Economic Crimes

These crimes are committed often by non-violent means and deceit for pecuniary gain. These crimes constitute a separate class by virtue of the scale and dimension, *modus operandi,* and in making individuals, society and State as collective victims of financial loss. These crimes are sophisticated and complicated. These are of high gains and low risk. Not even 25% of the cases are reported. Of this 70% are detected, investigated and sent to the courts. But the conviction rate is abysmally low as compared to traditional crimes. Therefore, economic criminals are rarely afraid of enforcement agencies. Their criminality is generally persistent. A large proportion of the offenders is recidivists. Many types of violations of law are industry-specific, in the sense that practically all companies or persons in particular industries violate the same law, more or less following the same *modus-operandi*.

Other important characteristic of economic criminal is that he does not generally lose his status among associates. The general principle in this regard is that a violation of the legal code is not necessarily a violation of the business code or even the moral code, as determined by the class to which the economic offender belongs. It has a queer democratic dimension too. Unlike other crimes, it can be committed by a bank clerk or the chairman of the bank. The offender can be a lower division clerk or a Secretary to the Government of India. This crime thus transcends the barriers of sex, status and nationality. Filthy lucre is what all economic criminals wish to amass.

Unfortunately, in our country we have differential implementation of laws with regard to economic crimes. An economic criminal despite the fact that he can be most devastating to a society or a nation, more often than not carries an air of respectability with him and accordingly the attitude of law enforcement agencies also is less rigorous towards him. People in general have diffused resentment against economic criminals as no particular person suffers much at any particular time. Media also, exceptions apart, appears to avoid coverage of economic crime because of class similarities between an economic criminal and magnates controlling the media. The sardonic criticism of C.S. Lewis, a criminologist and his telling indictment of an economic criminal is, "The greatest evil is not now done in those sordid dens of crime that Dickens loves to point out, not even in the concentration camps; but it is conceived, ordered, moved, carried and minuted in clean, carpeted, warmed and well-lighted offices by quiet men in white collars and cut fingernails and smooth-shaven cheeks, who do not need to raise their voices".

Economic crimes generally concern money and matters of finance. White-collar crimes, commercial and financial frauds are the species of the same family. Economic crimes encompass a wide range of activities which include banking, commerce, chit fund and insurance frauds; tax and duty evasion and smuggling; import-export and foreign exchange violations (*hawala*); violation of industrial, labour and environmental regulations; hoarding and black-marketing; adulteration of food and drugs; drug trafficking; money laundering; bribery and other corrupt practices; violation of intellectual property rights; counterfeiting of currency, stamps, bonds and shares; racketeering in passports and illegal migration; trade in human organs; smuggling of cultural and antique objects; and computer-related crimes. The list grows as the economies grow to diversify.

II

IMPACT ON NATIONAL ECONOMY

The Magnitude

The economic crimes cause considerable damage to the general economy of the country, adversely affecting the growth and development of the nation. They rob the masses of the assurances of the State. Internationally, it erodes the confidence reposed in the financial credibility and financial stability of the nation, thus weakening its global competitiveness and further becoming unattractive to investments from within as well as outside. Where there is high incidence level of economic crime, the government and bureaucracy are also viewed as being corrupt and weak. Rider states that "once organised criminal cells are established in a country, particularly a developing one, there is strong incentive for them to seek to infiltrate the political structure indeed, in the long to survive and prosper, it must do so.[4]

The National Institute of Finance and Public Policy, New Delhi had estimated in 1996-97 that total amount of undisclosed income in the country was Rs. 500,000 crore. In 1996, the Central Board of Direct Taxes reported that total number of people who ought to have paid income tax was around 30 million while their number rose only to around 12 million in 1996 from around 8 million in 1992.[5] Directorate of Enforcement guess that every day hawala transaction in India is to the tune of Rs. 100 crore. Enforcement agencies similarly believe that there is huge tax evasion worth about Rs. 100 crore every day at Mumbai port alone. At the time of serious crunch of foreign exchange payment in 1991-92 in the country, the World Bank officials had estimated that about US $ 250 billion are slashed in foreign banks by Indian corporate predators, criminals and politicians. However, RBI estimates it approximately US $ 180 billion.[6] Corrupt money has wings, not wheels. Also, Gresham's law of bad money driving away good money was allowed to become a norm.

Enforcement Agencies in India

Besides Police, the Central Bureau of Investigation, the Government of India has set up a number of investigations and enforcement agencies, which function under the Department of Revenue in Union Ministry of Finance. The enforcement work done by these agencies during 1994-98 is given in Annexure I.[7]

III

CURRENT TRENDS IN ECONOMIC CRIMES

Loopholes in Economic Policies

Most of the current economic crimes are committed by taking advantage of certain loopholes in the law or by evading law. A few exemplary instances could be mentioned here. In the Voluntary Disclosure of Income Scheme (VDIS) implemented during 1996-97, Rs. 31,000 crore of black money was disclosed and regularised by the government thereby foregoing nearly Rs. 10,000 crore.[8] The persons who disclosed were taxed at the rate of 30 percent only though the honest tax payers had to 34-40% tax on their income. Over the years tax evasion has become the national sport of India. Chapter III of the Banking Manual provides for secrecy about the bank defaulters, thus giving respectability to criminals. Similar is the case in industry. In our country, industry gets sick but not an industrialist. The role of Sick Industrial Company Act (SICA) and Bureau of Industrial Finance and Reconstruction (BIFR) indirectly favour and encourage economic players to enjoy at the expense of State and honest taxpayers. The loopholes in regulation relating to drugs is another instance. We know that opium is the raw material for hard drugs like heroin. The government's compulsory procurement price for raw opium, purchased from authorised poppy cultivators in UP, MP and Rajasthan is about Rs. 650 per kilogram.[9] But the illicit price in the nearby markets in these States varies between Rs. 5,000—10,000 per kg. This impractical approach of government prompts local cultivators to conceal the opium production from the government and sell it in the illicit markets where it gets diverted into the manufacturing of hard narcotic drugs.

Liberalization seems to have added much limbo to economic crimes. The liberalisation process in the country has repealed the Import-Export Act, 1947 and in its place the Foreign Trade (Development and Regulation) Act, 1992 has dispensed with the prosecution and imprisonment of offenders engaged in export-import business. The violations of licence conditions now attract only the adjudication and a dilatory appellate process where not even 10% economic offenders get punished. We have no law to fix the price of a commodity. There is no authority for valuation of goods. Therefore, the misuse of exports incentive schemes like DEEC and Duty Drawbacks has defrauded the country. In the name of promoting exports, the mandatory provisions of realising export proceeds in foreign exchange has been liberalised for the exporters dealing in gems, diamonds and jewellery. Similarly, our Restricted and OGL lists for import items have not been made crystal clear for example pamphret fish has been put in OGL while hilsa in restricted list. Similarly, the ginger and roasted breads have been put in different lists. Who will examine and exactly find out which fish or bread is being imported.

For the last few years, the circulation of fake currency in the country has created upheavals. Large amount of counterfeit currency has the potential of damaging the national economy. Neither our agencies have kept a record of persons importing photocopying/printing machinery nor we felt the need to ban the import of fake currency into the country until 1998. We all know our snail paced judicial system. It would be appropriate to quote the President of India while speaking at the golden jubilee celebrations of the Supreme Court, where he referred to an old saying "Law is not a cathedral but a casino where so much depends on the throw of the dice". He said mysterious are the ways of justice. Judges are not here to do justice but to decide cases according to the evidence on record.[10] Our system convicts about 6% accused, it bothers more about the human rights of accused but appears neutral to the victims.

The former American President Franklin Roosevelt had observed much before computers came of age, "A man who has never gone to school may steal from freight car, but if he has a university education he may steal the whole rail road". Elaborating it a little further we may say that if he happens to be a cyber-savvy, he might even steal the whole world". Looking into the experiences of intelligence and enforcement agencies in India, we may safely state that this country has become poorer not because of large population (as some economists claim) but because of almost unfettered loot by rich and educated. Our economic and trade policies are influenced during their formulation stage by the pressure groups of business community. Most corporate criminologists agree that corporate and economic crime inflict far more damage on society than all street crimes combined.[11]

Corporate Crimes

Economic offences are of much larger magnitude compared to traditional poverty offences. Table 1 shows the Mumbai experience.

TABLE 1

Economic and Traditional Offences in Mumbai

Year	*Economic Offences*			*Traditional Property Offences*		
	No. of Cases	*Property involved (Rs. Crore)*	*Average per case (Rs. Crore)*	*No. of cases*	*Property involved (Rs. Crore)*	*Average per case (Rs. Crore)*
1997	75	180	2.4	18389	324	0.02
1998	61	67	1.1	17483	235	0.01
1999	142	343	2.4	15091	101	0.01

Source: Crime Branch, Mumbai Police.

Industrial, banking, finance company and other violations are the major sources of economic fraud. In a survey of 800 largest companies in India conducted by KPMG about 200 companies responded.[12] Loss was reported to be a Rs. 2,307 million. Main areas of fraud included expense accounts, false invoices, and secret commissions/kickbacks. Typical fraudster was male (93%) and just 7% female. Age of fraudster was 26-40 years, (68%) and (22%) between 45-55 years. The income level was found to be Rs. 1-2.5. lakh per month of (38%) fraudsters and above 2.5 lakh in 26% cases. Surprisingly only 37% cases were reported to police. Similarly, in one of the most substantial surveys of fraud in U.K in recent years, published in '*Security Gazette*' revealed that more than two-thirds of the British companies admitted that they had suffered from fraud, most of it perpetrated by the management.[13]

It is common knowledge that frauds in banks are on the rise and every year it is about to the tune of Rs. 800 crore. The common fraud prone areas are: deposit accounts, issue of DDs and other transfer accounts, discounting of bills, letter of credit/guarantee and co-acceptance, investments, credits, cash and where accounts are not immediately reconciled. Also NOSTRO & VOSTRO accounts and inter-bank call money markets are susceptible to frauds. It is to be noted that non-performing assets in scheduled banks are over Rs. 58,000 crore. Out of it, Rs. 11,000 crore are due to the wilful default of 200 big companies and large industrial houses including Dalmia, Khetan, Irani, Ram, Shah, Modi, Goenka, Duggal, Singhania and Bansal.[14] More than half of the non-performing assets is due to the other businessmen. The Default, Recovery Tribunal Act, 1993 has failed to make any dent for recovering the huge amounts, though RBI has come out with detailed guidelines to monitor and control the delinquent banks. The banks, almost every one, have invented a novel way of setting up its own subsidiaries as Non-Banking Financial Companies (NBFCs) where RBI circulars are not applicable.

Then we have chit funds, non-banking financial companies, plantation companies and capital market frauds. We will perhaps all agree that such firms and companies are the handiworks of educated and well-of people. The Securities and Exchange Board of India (SEBI) came out in its 1998 report that 80 companies vanished after collecting Rs. 360 crore through issue of public shares. In Nov. 1999, SEBI acting on a High Court order gave an option to plantation companies to either register themselves with the board or to wind up their business. Out of 700 companies, 690 preferred to close shop. And by doing this, they locked in almost Rs. 2,600 crore put in by the investors. The remaining 10 companies, in which Rs. 265 crore had been invested agreed to follow the rules.[15] Recently, Department of Company Affairs, Govt. of India had collected the information that 142 companies have disappeared with Rs. 668.61 crore of investment. In Mumbai alone, it is estimated that non-banking financial companies have cheated 30,40,000 small investors. We all know what happened in banks and securities scams worth Rs. 5000 crore in late 1980s and early 1990s involving Harshad Mehta, Dalal and others and financial institutions.

In its latest report,[16] the Comptroller and Auditor General (CAG) has pointed out that big exporters corner bulk of the advance licences issued by the Directorate General of Foreign Trade (DGFT). TISCO was issued value-based advance licences (Vabal) worth Rs. 797 crore during the year ending March 31, 1998. Other companies were Ganapathy Export, Ispat Alloys, RSI, Tosh Picture Tubes, Raymond, Dunlop, HLL, Allanasons, Reliance, Balmer Lawrie, Tata Exports, ITC, Luxor, and Satnam Overseas. These companies were issued licences totaling an import value of Rs. 2,068 crore. CAG found irregularities in 23 percent of the licences examined, involving a revenue effect of Rs. 3,532 crore. Among the major violations, by the above firms, were found mis-declaration of export/import value and non-fulfilment of export obligations. M/s Shalini Exports Pvt. Ltd., Mumbai, one of the Mittal Group of Companies, which was incorporated in the year 1991 had no activity till the year 1998. The said dormant company suddenly became active and projected itself as a software developing and export company. This firm in connivance with one Sanjay Patel, an Indian born U.S. citizen at California, obtained two 64 kbps International Private Leased Connections (IPLC) from VSNL for Digital Data Transmission from Mumbai to US. Simultaneously, M/s Shalini Ltd. obtained 40 new MTNL telephone lines, which were connected to the IPLC line for receiving telephone calls from USA to Mumbai subscribers. Similar arrangements were also made at California. These lines were offered to prospective customers who wanted to contact Mumbai over phone, on concessional rate by bypassing VSNL route. Within a period of about 1 year, more than 20 lakh telephone calls were received from USA and the revenue loss to VSNL came out to more than Rs. 15 crore. While firm paid only Rs. 15 lakh to VSNL.[17]

Enforcement Directorate is investigating the over invoicing and foreign exchange frauds by ITC which set up a number of fraud companies abroad with the help of NRIs and duped the country with hundreds of crore. Similarly, Shaw Wallace has committed an inter-corporate frauds worth Rs. 420 crore through a host of paper companies.[18] In one of the biggest trade scandals in recent years, known as Switch Trade Scandal, inside experts believe that this country was defrauded to the tune of about Rs. 15,000 crore. India was having Rupee Trade Agreement with Russia and other East Eurpoean countries. Exporters' ships, instead of going to Russian and East European ports, were being diverted to hard-currency areas of the world. In one of the enquiries, where I was associated in the beginning, the CBI got the documents establishing that out of 92 ships originally booked for Russian ports only 4 reached there. All others were diverted to Europe and American ports. Vostro accounts (held in India by Russia) were grossly misused.

Emerging Trends

Today, thanks to computer and communications technologies which enhance the capacity of criminals and corporate predators to perpetrate serious offences with a greatly diminished task of apprehension. Dimensions of economic data are becoming transnational. Every day about US $ 3 trillion are being transacted at the speed of light. With the emergence of a new world of e-commerce, traditional paper-based procedures are fast getting replaced by new mechanism, such as Electronic Data Interchange (EDI), Electronic Funds Transfer (EFT), etc. With information technology where the legal business will get multifold, the economic offenders will be using it in a borderless world where tracking and prosecution will be quite difficult. The complex financial transaction, in the course of an economic crime, that may have taken one hour to complete now might take law enforcers in the most advanced countries at least one year to trace. U.S. Justice Department officials estimate that sophisticated computer techniques permit thieves to steal US $ 10 billion annually from American financial institutions. Millions lost their savings in the MMM pyramid scheme in 1990s in Russia, at least two millions lost their savings in Romania and Albania was totally destablished by a pyramid scheme that went sour.[19] As Jack Blum has noted, "International financial fraud, commercial fraud, money laundering and tax evasion will be the most important enterprise crimes of the future."[20] With new technologies, the inherent weakness of established systems are getting exposed for example, the credit card frauds are mounting. Magnetic strip is easily reproduced. VISA and Master card companies are losing about US $ 5 billion annually for their old technology.

Drug trafficking coupled with narco-terrorism is emerging quite fast and will be a challenge for law enforcement agencies. India is considered to be one of the leading staging posts of the international narcotics network. In the world economy, the largest illegitimate trade is attributable to narcotic drugs, where annual turnover is estimated at US $ 500 billion by the United Nations Drugs Control Programme (UNDCP).[21] Illicit trafficking in arms, people and endangered species has also reached high levels. For example, the International Organisation of Migration estimates that 'people smuggling' is now a US $ 5 to 7 billion business. Each of these areas of illicit commerce represents a multibillion-dollar business annually.[22] Recently, one surprising incident took place on internet. When the Mumbai producer of film *'Dil Se'* was trying to know about RDX explosive on internet, one person from somewhere asked him that supply of RDX can be arranged if he was interested. It signals serious portents for the world community at large.

For economic criminals, the illegally gained money must be introduced into a nation's legitimate financial system and hence *money laundering* has become an integral part of present day crime. The UNDCP estimates that US $ 1 billion of illicit capital moves through the world's financial system on a daily basis.[23] The problem of illicit capital movements is compounded by the fact that technology permits the rapid transfer of funds to new financial centres where controls are purposefully limited and the possibility of effective enforcement is insignificant. In offshore banking centres, the absence of regulation is attractive to the money launderer because he is provided with secrecy, a tax haven and the ability to move capital with ease. The IMF has identified over a dozen major offshore centres, many of them in the Caribbean, South East Asia and Europe. For example, in the Cayman Islands, which has total population of 30,000, there are 550 banks only 17 of which maintain a physical presence. The rest conduct business primarily through high technology. The UNDCP estimates that "more than half of the world's stock of money transits through offshore centres", and about US $ 2 trillion of private wealth—20 percent of the world total invested there.[24]

Of late, the violation of Intellectual Property Rigths is becoming a major issue. These rights mainly concern to Copyright, Patents and Trademarks. Copyright given by the law to creators of literary, dramatic, musical and artistic works and producers of cinemagraph films and sound recordings. Piracy of films, music and computer softwares has assumed serious dimensions. Similarly, the trade marks violation of mass-consumer items like Scotch Whisky has become quite serious as well as risky. In one of the studies conducted by United Breweries it was found that 95% Scotch Whisky available in India is spurious.

IV

THE COUNTER MEASURES

Law enforcement is becoming complicated when on one hand crimes are getting increasingly sophisticated and on the other individual rights recognition is growing in stringency. The growing complexity and diversity of economic operations and the global concern for circulation of dirty money, flight of national capital, money laundering and growing trends in terrorist activities have attracted the attention of United Nations and other world bodies. The G-7 Economic Summit in 1989 constituted the Financial Action Task Force (FATF) that addresses the global problem of money-laundering. The FATF is comprised of 22 countries, the European Commission and Gulf Cooperation Council.[25]

Similarly, the UN Declaration on Organised Transnational Crime (Warsaw-1998) asked member countries to consider largely legal reforms involving measures to amend and upgrade existing laws and introduce special laws to deal with emerging forms of sophisticated crimes. The Financial Action Task Force at its meeting in July, 1999 in Tokyo has further expanded its work and membership. Its efforts have resulted in the establishment of Financial Intelligence Units (FIUs) in various countries around the world to protect the banking community, to detect criminal abuse of its financial system and to ensure adherence to its laws against financial crime. Such units exist in UK, France, Belgium, Netherlands, Argentina, Australia and US.[26] In India, a number of Special Laws have been enacted to deal with various forms of economic crime. The enactment of FEMA, 1999, the Information Technology Act, 2000 and passing of Ant-money laundering bill, 2000 by Lok Sabha are the serious efforts of the government to streamline Indian trade and to put a dent on economic crime. However, the pressure groups of vested interests are able to exert sufficient pressure on law-makers to dilute the provisions of new efforts. Under FEMA, which has come in place of FERA, 1973, the prosecution and imprisonment of offenders have been taken out and now only penalties can be imposed through the adjudication process. It means law has become weak instead.

Expensive to investigate and highly elusive, these economic crimes are potentially much more dangerous than individual acts of violence. If the society or nation is to avoid the high costs of economic crime affecting the national economy, sovereignty and stability, critical planning and analysis must be addressed immediately.

NOTES AND REFERENCES

1. Vedvyas, *Mahabharata*, Bhandarkar Research Institute, Pune.
2. Girandoux, Jean (2000), 'Thought for Today', *The Times of India*, August 7, Mumbai.
3. Amarnathan, L.C. (2000), Economic Crimes in India and Effective Countermeasures, *CBI Bulletin*, Vol. VIII, No. 4, April, New Delhi.
4. *Commonwealth: Secretariat* (1980): *Law Ministers' Conference*, London, (Rider, Barry AK—Economic crimes).
5. Parthasarathi, Ashok (2000), Illusion of Growth, *The Times of India*, August 2, Mumbai.
6. Kapoor, Sanjay (2000), Politics of Hawala, *One India One People*, Feb., Mumbai.
7. Crime in India (1998), *National Crime Records Bureau*, MHA, New Delhi.
8. Parthasarthi, *ibid*.
9. Office of the Narcotic Commissioner of India (2000), Gwaliar, M.P.
10. *The Times of India*, New Delhi, Jan., 28, 2000, New Delhi.
11. Mokhiber, Russell & Weissman, Robert (1999), *Corporate Predators: The Hunt for Mega-profits and the Attack on Democracy*, Common Courage, Washington, D.C.
12. *India Fraud Survey Report*, (1998), KPMG.
13. *The Times*, June, 1995, London.
14. *Nav Bharat*, Jan., 12, 2000, Mumbai.
15. *The Times of India*, Feb., 2000, New Delhi.
16. *The Economic Times*, Feb., 2000, New Delhi.
17. Jain, M. (2000), Money Laundering: The Challenge of New Century *CBI Bulletin*, Vol. VIII, No. 4, April, New Delhi.
18. Press Relase (1999), *CBI*, New Delhi.
19. Shelley, Louise (1998), Crimes and Corruption in the Digital Age, *Journal of International Affairs*, March.
20. *Ibid*.
21. *United Nations International Drug Control Programme*, (1996), Drugs and Development.
22. Shelley, Louse, *ibid*.
23. *Ibid*.
24. United Nations International Drug Control Programme (1997), *World Drug Report*, Oxford University Press, Oxford.
25. FinCen Report (1999), *The Global Fight Against Money Laundering*, U.S.
26. *Ibid*.

ANNEXURE I

The Investigating Agencies under the Department of Revenue, Union Ministry of Finance

- The Central Economic Intelligence Bureau (Apex body).
- Directorate General of Revenue Intelligence (for customs-related offences).
- Directorate of Enforcement (for Foreign Exchange-related offences).
- Directorate General of Anti-Evasion (for Central Excise-related offences).
- Directorate General of Income Tax (for Income Tax-related offences)
- Narcotics Control Bureau (for Drugs-related offences).

(1) Smuggling
Seizure made by Customs under Customs Act (1994-1998)

Sl. No.	*Year*	*Total No. of seizures*	*Value of seizures (Rs. in crores)*
1	1994	49997	535.2
2.	1995	55947	1062.0
3.	1996	49580	553.4
4.	1997	48993	983.9
5.	1998	39906	1274.4

Source: GOI, Directorate of Revenue Intelligence, New Delhi.

Nature and Value of Commodities Seized by the Customs (1994-98)

Sl. No.	*Commodities*	*1994*	*1995*	*1996*	*1997*	*1998*
1.	Gold (Qty. in Kgs.)	1147	1169	1100	1325	552
	(Value in Rs. crores)	(53.4)	(58.3)	(65.7)	(61.9)	(23.2)
2.	Silver (Qty. in Kgs.)	6404	678	3700	—	—
	(Value in Rs. crores)	(4.5)	(0.5)	(3.0)	—	—
3.	Diamonds					
	(Value Rs. in crores)	2.9	NA	NA	—	—
4.	Synthetic fibres	7.2	NA	NA	33.2	55.7
	(Value Rs. in crores)					
5.	Electronic goods	37.2	63.3	38.8	33.1	39.0
	(Value Rs. in crores)					
6.	Drugs/Narcotics	54.3	85.7	44.9	70.1	63.7
	(Value Rs. in crores)					
7.	Others					
	(Value in Rs. crores)	347.7	854.2	410.0	532.0	549.1
	Total (Value Rs. in crores)	535.2	1062.0	562.4	730.3	730.7

NA—Data not available.

Source: GOI, Directorate of Revenue Intelligence, New Delhi.

(2) Money Laundering
Money Laundering: 1994-98 (Cases under FERA)

Sl. No.	Year	No. of		Currency Seized (in Indian Rs. in crores)		Currency confiscated (in Indian Rs. crores)		Fines (in Indian Rs. in crores)	
		Searches Raids	Seizures recovery	Indian	Foreign	Indian	Foreign	Impo-sed	Reali-zed
1.	1994	1540	1046	9.8	8.1	1.8	2.2	24.8	3.4
2.	1995	1175	832	10.2	6.5	1.2	2.3	10.6	2.2
3.	1996	1164	868	12.4	7.8	4.0	2.2	78.0	1.6
4.	1997	1238	946	11.6	5.1	3.4	2.3	86.8	1.9
5.	1998	544	361	5.7	1.4	4.6	1.8	—	1.8

Source: GOI, Enforcement Directorate, New Delhi.

(3) Tax Evasion—Income Tax
Seizures by Income Tax Department (1994-98)

Sl. No.	Year	No. of searches conducted	Assets seized in (Rs. crores)
1.	1994-95	4830	381.41
2.	1995-96	4612	458.14
3.	1996-97	4299	405.63
4.	1997-98	3653	306.85
5.	1998-99	5746	300.54

Source: GOI, Central Board of Direct Taxes, New Delhi.

(4) Offences under Export and Import Act (1992-196)

Sl. No.	Year	Inspections Condu-cted	Cases Regist-ered	Cases Adjudicated Imposing penalty	Fine in crore of Rs.	
					Imposed	Realised
1.	1992	344	600	546	34.2	35.7
2.	1993	334	983	268	34.5	28.3
3.	1994	545	1106	140	83.7	28.4
4.	1995	255	1020	129	54.0	44.3
5.	1996	557	1468	186	40.9	24.4

Source: GOI, Director General of Foreign Trade, New Delhi.

(5) Drug Trafficking

Seizures of Narcotics and Drugs (No. of Cases) during 1994-98

Sl. No.	*Drugs*	*1994*	*1995*	*1996*	*1997*	*1998*
1.	Opium	1171	871	977	1333	868
2.	Morphine	145	35	37	75	45
3.	Heroin	3331	3236	3043	2990	2713
4.	Ganja	6827	5737	5833	7062	5809
5.	Hashish	2672	2691	2593	2233	1771
6.	Cocaine	6	6	8	6	4
7.	Methaqualone	457	196	405	207	112
8.	Phenobarbital	—	—	—	—	—
9.	L.S.D.	—	1	7	—	1
10.	Acetic anhydride	40	26	14	12	7

Source: Narcotics Control Bureau, New Delhi.

Quantity of Drugs Seized in Kg. (1994-98)

Sl. No.	*Drugs*	*1994*	*1995*	*1996*	*1997*	*1998*
1.	Opium	2256	1339	2875	3221	1834
2.	Morphine	51	4	4	76	14
3.	Heroin	1011	1678	1257	1332	597
4.	Ganja	187896	121873	62992	808666	62591
5.	Hashish	6992	3629	6520	3285	8478
6.	Methaqualone	45319	20485	2212	1740	2087
7.	Cocaine	1.6	40	3	24	1

Source: Narcotics Control Bureau, New Delhi.

Value of Property Forfeited and Frozen of Drug Traffickers (1994-98) (Amount in Lakhs)

Sl. No.	*Value of property*	*1994*	*1995*	*1996*	*1997*	*1998*
1.	Forfeited	10.2	3.0	13.7	10.6	238.5
2.	Frozen	851	2104.2	16.6	154.8	306.4

Source: Narcotics Control Bureau, New Delhi.

(6) Trafficking in Cultural Property
Cultural Porperty Stolen, Recovered (1994-98)

Sl. No.	*Year*	*No. of cases in which Property was*		*Value of property (Rs. in lakhs)*	
		Stolen	*Recovered*	*Stolen*	*Recoverd*
1.	1994	1484	513	239.7	124.6
2.	1995	3759	1226	253.5	98.5
3.	1996	2870	856	648.8	133.4
4.	1997	1677	485	400.8	168.5
5.	1998	2600	796	877.7	464.8

Source: National Crime Records Bureau, New Delhi.

(7) Bribery and Corruption
Details of Cases Registerd and Persons Arrested under Prevention of Corruption Act (1994-98)

Sl. No.	*Years*	*No. of Vigilance cases registered by*		*Persons Arrested*	
		CBI	*States/UTs*	*CBI*	*States/UTs*
1.	1994	1106	2104	463	2296
2.	1995	825	2064	297	2604
3.	1996	845	2361	304	2922
4.	1997	746	2788	239	3603
5.	1998	884	2817	163	2504

Source: Naional Crime Records Bureau, New Delhi.

Details of Public Servants Involved in Corruption Cases (Investigated by the CBI) and the Punishment Awarded (1994-98)

Sl. No.	*Year*	*Persons reported for regular Dept. action*	*Persons reported for suitable action by Dept.*	*Departmental punishment*				*Categories of public servants involved in regular Dept. Action*		
				Dis-missal	*Remo-val*	*Major*	*Minor*	*Gaze-tted offi-cers*	*NGO's*	*Pvt.*
1.	1994	1922	149	23	22	137	256	249	187	1
2.	1995	735	44	27	11	133	194	392	322	21
3.	1996	544	72	42	20	148	228	250	280	14
4.	1997	428	64	28	7	122	384	209	192	27
5.	1998	700	128	32	16	132	274	297	374	27

Source: NCRB, New Delhi, Crime in India, 1998.

Details of Public Servants Involved in Corruption Cases in the States/UTs Investigated by States/UT Vigilance Bureau (1994-98)

Sl. No.	*Year*	*Persons reported for regular Dept. action*	*Persons reported for suitable action by Dept.*	*Departmental punishment*				*Categories of public servants involved in regular Dept. Action*		
				Dis-missal	*Remo-val*	*Major*	*Minor*	*Gaze-tted offi-cers*	*NGO's*	*Pvt.*
1.	1994	318	103	7	3	27	115	464	1176	229
2.	1995	295	87	27	14	33	76	1114	1278	499
3.	1996	168	144	9	2	27	97	612	1634	462
4.	1997	212	163	9	3	53	64	451	2568	493
5.	1998	133	42	2	2	46	59	930	2775	541

Source: NCRB, New Delhi, Crime in India, 1998.

13

Socio-Economic Aspects of Organised Crime: A Case Study of Illegal Coal Mining

DIPANKAR SEN AND SANDIP MITRA

The thrust of the paper is to analyse the process of operation of the criminal gangs, mafia, in the coal belt and the resulting social and economic welfare implications, with the help of a case study. The paper is divided into five brief sections. The second section provides a brief historical background of the study area. The third section describes the methodological approach. The fourth section sets out the analysis of the mafia activities. And the fifth is concluding observations.

I

INTRODUCTION

Study on organised crime is a very sensitive area of research with vast theoretical literature. The studies by Sociologists, Economists, and Historians with different objectives in mind have attempted to analyse the phenomenon of crime. Reference may be made of Fiorentine (1995). There had been references of crime and corruption in Kautilya's *Arthasastra* too.

This study is an attempt to get a snapshot view of an organised crime (carried on by coal mafias) in an underdeveloped region. These mafias have been carrying on their activities quite smoothly for a long time. The State power even could not confront their operation. The mafias have nearly established their legitimate claims on abandoned coal mines and have emerged with an alternative industry. They have engaged displaced agricultural labourers or displaced mine workers to meet their goal of collection and distribution of coal by perpetuating a system of competition among labourers for greater share of profit and thereby transferring the risk factor to the heads of labourers. The labourers who are vulnerable to more risk gets greater share of profit. The labourers who are vulnerable to more risks gets greater share of profit. This trade off between risk and profit in this system and the nature of society backed by illegal trade is an interesting area of research. Moreover, the labour market here is unorganised and in the absence of any scope of employment larger and larger number of labourers flock together to make the system sustainable. Questions normally arise if this system uplifts the economic condition of these labourers and thereby brings a social upliftment. This is the point from which the relation between crime and social change via social stratification is derived. In this study a general improvement of the life style of the participating workers was observed. Before dealing with the exact mechanism of control and the incidence of crime, it should be stated that these mafias have historically developed taking advantage of the weakness of the governance or through the inspiration of local landlords and industrialists or often as a remnant of excess bureaucratic control of power. Schelling (1971), Catanzaro (1992), Chubb (1989), have discussed this quite elaborately. One should argue that private control of state resources, illegal distribution and depriving the state of fiscal contribution incurs a huge loss to the economy in terms of its revenue and generates an inefficient economy with misallocation, maldistribution and instability. However, modern state often can not take care of the exploding population and guarantee welfare. Here is a risk that the state confronts in a system (though inefficient) that promotes upliftment through illegal market organisation. Some economists like Lane (1985), Findlay (1980), Gambatta (1988), have tried to model the economic effects of criminal organisations who provide alternative public services. In that sense the State faces a competition from the mafias. This highlights the positive role of the mafias. Inspite of penalty and premium being highly correlated in these illegal markets, the workers and the entrepreneurs planned their activities based on their individual perceptions of risk and reward and their motivation to reach at a threshold level of earnings. An indepth study based on Case History Approach can lead to interesting findings about the activities of mafias and the proliferation of illegal markets. The region selected in our study is located in the Giridih district which is a plateau with labour surplus economy and a backward region with least infra-structural facilities. A short account of the history of the region might reveal how the growth of mafias have taken place in the region.

II

BRIEF HISTORICAL NOTE

Since the study deals with organised crime, the historical linkage must be stated to explain the current state of activities. The Cicilian or Italian mafias which are active in both urban and rural societies, have emanated from families which grown powerful historically through developing their networks. However, the mafias in our study does not represent the ramification of a family but have grown because of the adverse socio-economic condition originating from power transfer by the British and the low productivity resulting from unemployment. The district in our study (Giridih) had been one of the heartlands of Chootanagpur plateau. It had immense stock of mines and wide coverage of forests. Right from the colonial rule down the history this area had been an area of focal interest to the traders. Naturally, it had been a breeding ground of struggles and conflicts for supremacy over the resources of the region. The landed class in order to build greater marketable surplus increased exploitation on labouring class. Being a region of low fertility, surplus could not be generated without these means (e.g., lowering wage, increasing working hours, etc.). On the contrary, the agricultural labourers for the sake of subsistence ventured out for alternative employment. These labourers comprised the displaced labouring class later. On the other hand, the miners started using the mines extravagantly without considering the consequences. Their aim was to establish monopoly control companies like the Equitable Coal Company and to establish their sway in and around Giridih.

Bengal Coal Company was a later addition to this race. East Indian Railways appeared to be the sole authority of the region.

After independence, National Coal Development Corporation (later renamed as Coal Authority of India) with its three wings, Eastern Coal Fields Ltd., Bharat Coking Coal Ltd., and Central Coal Ltd. came into existence. However, nationalisation of coal mines after independence could not achieve its goal. One by one, mines were declared abandoned because of huge losses. The possible causes, as stated in various reports, were the lack of appropriate low cost technology, mismanagement and corruption. These phenomena gave birth to a huge army of unemployed labourers. With sickness and closures, the mines in Giridih triggered-off a social unrest. The miners, in order to control their resources and to protect their interest, tried to build a private force. However, due to the growing loss the miner started winding-up. The private army which the private miner maintained earlier now arose as a separate controlling force (who reappeared as mafias). Our study deals with the activity of this newborn center of power. They have been active since 1960s in all the abandoned mines (e.g., Upper Khandia, Dhobidih, Khandia Saktight). They started with the new gesture of raising coal (often under dangerous circumstances) by making use of the displaced unemployed labourers and tactically maintaining connection with the landlords and administrator.

III

METHODOLOGY

Very few studies have deal with a methodology of analysing organised crime. It is really difficult to impose any standard methodology to study this objective. Broadly, indirect method of inquiry with open ended questionnaires has been followed. Case study approach has been undertaken to get an overview of the system. It is true that the questionnaire could not be tested with the mafias or the carriers, because there is a threat. On the other hand, the small traders and people in different public places have been interviewed and the information has been analysed to get an overall picture. In this way, indirect survey method can serve as important instrument to study a sensitive area like crime and corruption. Fifteen people in the mining vicinity, two traders and three administrators were interviewed.

It was rather a difficult exercise to compare and contrast the level of living with the earlier positions of the persons involved. Our objective was to capture the extent of social change (including change in role and status) if any. On a revisit after an interval of three years, it was observed that significant changes have occurred in their socio-economic activities.

In this way often resurvey methods helped a large extent to unfold changes in several dimensions of socio-economic parameters. Rigorous survey methods using sample procedure could not be done in our study because of the complexity of the content. Nevertheless Sociologists-Anthropologists have agreed in principle to adopt such methods to attain their goals.

IV

BRIEF ACTIVITIES

The activities of the mafias in the coal belts differ partially with the other Indian, Sicilian or American mafias in the sense that these groups are never family groups. Many of mafia groups are first generation mafias. They monitor sequential chain-wise operation and accumulate profits through making suitable contracts. This might be treated on par with that Transaction Cost Analysis in Economics (*Oliver Williamson*, 1985). People in this set up strive to fulfil their desires by taking advantage of the opportunities available and their contracts never cover all aspects because of the existence of uncertainty. The individuals in this system are highly vulnerable to risk. More an individual is close to a mafia more is his threat. On the other hand, remuneration increases with greater risk. Risk is from threats of mafia, police etc. On this basis, a utility function of an individual labourer can be derived:

$u = u\,(w, p)$ $\quad w$ = wage or reward

$\quad p$ = punishment or threat

$$du = u_w dw + u_p dp$$

$$U_w > 0,\ U_p < 0,\ \frac{du}{dw} = u_w,\ \frac{du}{dp} = u_p,\ \frac{d^2u}{dw^2} \geq 0,\ \frac{d^2u}{dp^2} \geq 0$$

The signs of the second order conditions depend on individual attitude. On the same indifference curve.

$$du = 0$$

or,
$$\frac{dp}{dw} = \frac{u_w}{u_p} < 0$$

$$\frac{d^2p}{dw^2} = -\frac{1}{u_{p^3}}(u_{ww}u_p^2 - 2u_{wp}u_p + u_{pp}u_w^2)$$

$$\frac{d^2p}{dw^2} \leq 0$$

depending on the type of indifference curve. Otherwise speaking, individual's attitude to risk determines the sign of $\frac{d^2p}{dw^2}$. If an individual is a risk lover he gets less wage with more rise, (when the indifference curve is strictly quasi-concave) $\frac{d^2p}{dw^2} > 0$. If he is a risk averter (that is he wants more wage with less risk), the indifference curve is got to be strictly quasi-convex. The $\frac{d^2p}{dw^2} < 0$ following the same logic $\frac{d^2p}{dw^2} = 0$ for risk neutral persons. The existence of all these types of persons were found in the chain; every individual tries to find out optimal w^* and p^* to maximise his utility, we avoid rigorous modeling for optimal solution here. One may look into Polo (1995) where such problems has been taken care of in Principal Agent framework. Coming directly to the coal mafia activity one can find that mafias operate at two terminal stages directly (see Diagram 1). In one end there is the mine where coal is collected from the holo-cast mines and in the other end where the coal is distributed by the depo-holders (authorised dealer of coal). They allow the "malkatris" (the lifters of coal) to raise to coal and transfer the same to the carriers (who may be innumerable in number). The carriers by relay system reach the depo-holders and work on commission basis.

DIAGRAM 1

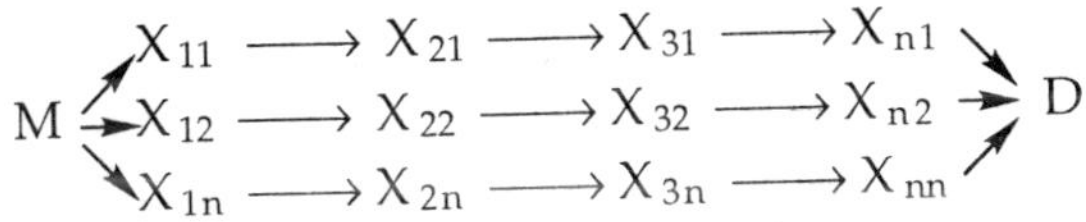

"M" denotes site of mining, "D" denotes the site of distribution, Xij denotes ith stage and jth batch. The innumerable ramification of the chains is indicated by dotted lines. X_{ij} ......X_{nn} denotes the carriers of different stages and batches. X_{11}, X_{12}......X_{1n} belongs to 1st stage who receives the coal from the malkatris. As we move to second or third stage the carriers move away from the mafias. The risk or threat from mafias also decreases with distance. However, there is distance d where from the risk increases as one approaches closer to D. d may be anywhere between M and D. It depends on the power of the mafia. If mafias in m (Mm) is more powerful than mafias at D(Dd) then d will lie close to Mm. If mafias in m (Mm) is more powerful than mafias at D (Dd) then d will lie close to Mm. If *vice versa* d will lie close to Dd. If they are similar, d is expected to lie at mean distance from Mm and Dd. The relations between distance and risk (or threat) can be explained from following Diagram 2.

DIAGRAM 2

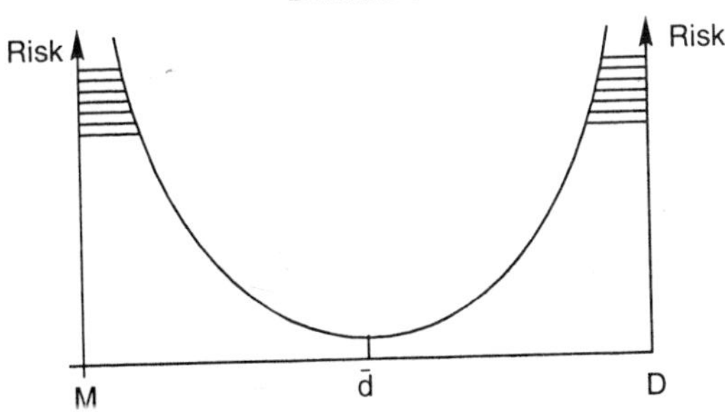

Distance from M & D is shown in X-axis and risk in Y-axis. At d risk is minimum. In the study it was observed that risk lovers operate in the shaded portion while risk neutrals and risk averters operate in the neighbourhood of d. It is true that all the chains are often not complete and equally spaced. However to get an essence of the whole idea Diagram 2 has been shown. If the population distribution is shown it can be found that more people are clubbed in the neighbourhood of d.

However, after the resurvey, it was observed that there has been a tendency of the individual carriers to be more closer to M and D. This might be because of the expected higher remuneration and the gaining of their skills in the trade. By assimilation and acculturation in their society they adopt such ways and means that they often change their roles and status to move to their new positions. Social change in the long run comes from this tendency of movement upwards. However, such changes are never the obvious consequence of every individual. This point becomes more clear when the remuneration frame is discussed.

It has been increasingly observed that reward and penalty are highly correlated in this set up. If an individual is closer to a mafia he gets not only higher remuneration but is also exposed to greater threat (from mafia or state). The most intimate to the mafias, the malkatris and the first batch of carriers (X_{11}, X_{12}, X_{1n}) or last batch of deliverers (X_{n1}, X_{n2}, X_{nn}) have almost identified themselves as primary relations of the mafia families. They have 'face to face relationship' following C.H. Cooley. As one move away from mafia, wage starts decreasing (details explained in Diagram 2). It was found that carriers who were in the neighbourhood of d often did not know the mafia. The study showed how average reward per individual is changed with distance (which is ranked in absence of data on absolute distance, details in Table 1).

TABLE 1

Distance (from Mines/Depo)	Wage/Reward	Approximate persons engaged
(1)	(2)	(3)
1	100	5
2	70	27
3	65	30
4	60	40
5	50	42
6	40	60
d		.... d
7	30	100
8	40	90
9	70	30
10	100	4

Some distinct characteristics for different stages of carriers has been observed: (i) Carriers in stages 1 to 3 and 9 to 10 are the richest. They have better dwelling and clothing. They are generally tribals and scheduled castes. Alcoholism is most among them. They have left their caste occupation and represent comparatively modern society with different amenities. (ii) The carriers of stages 4, 5, 6, 7, and 8 have lower level of earning. They often comprise of the migrants or currently displaced labourers. They have comparatively traditional societies with caste stratification. Their values differ largely from the types stated in (i). The mafia is a demi God to the group stated in (i) while a demon to the group stated in (ii). Given proper scope these people are ready to leave these jobs. Their behaviour is deviant while the group behaviour of (i) is ethnocentric. These persons are mostly displaced agricultural labourers.

The statement of activities becomes incomplete if we do not focus on the real intention of the mafias in operation. The mafias (M and D) try to shift the burden of risk in illegal trade to the agents by carefully designing their sequence and operation. The agents (carriers and malkatris) can never form cartels, because of the existence of competition among them. Thus, the system of contract has nullified the possibilities of organised move of the labouring class. Had the mafia been acting as employers, the picture would have been quite different. The mafias thus extort super-normal profits by maintaining monopoly cartel among themselves and perpetuating a system of contract.

The possible role of the state is worth mentioning here. In the mining operation the state has earlier failed. Some kind of privatisation in the score of mining can accrue some revenue. However, the carriers can not be taxed because they have marginal profit. They need to be supported by state with amenitities so that more efficient transportation is possible. On the other hand, state can charge higher taxes from depots without directly taxing the carriers. The operation at the terminal ends perhaps might be beneficial to mop up resources and provide efficient allocation. Nevertheless it might not be so simple an operation. Giving a free hand to the illegal traders would lead to detrimental social and economic consequences.

V

CONCLUSION

Understanding the proliferation of organised crime and the communities involved is essential for analysing social transformation. It is of course premature to comment anything in totality about social change brought about in this process. However, distinct changes in role, status, value systems have been found. Society built on illegal trade is qualitatively different from traditional societies. Strict compare and contrast exercises have not been undertaken here in this study. In these new type of societies individual's role, status in the family and outside, need a careful examination. Social tension which might erupt in the absence of these types of trade is expected to be too heavy for a nation state to manage. If the system is to sustain, the state might loose a sizeable portion of revenue. However, the state might operate somewhere and somehow in order to minimise its losses. This aspect can also be an interesting area for a social researcher. Our study has only taken care of the characterisation of the illegal activities and their significance in the society. Last, but not the least, this study has highlighted that illegal trade under increasing monopolisation has led to exploitation with optimal contract. The aspect of social welfare in totality has not been taken care of due to paucity of data.

REFERENCES

Catanzaro, R., 1992, *Mean of Respect: A Social History of the Sicilian Mafia,* New York: The Free Press.

Chubb, J., 1989, *The Mafia and Politics: The Italian State Siage,* Western Societies Program Occasional Paper, I thau, N.Y., Cornell Centre for International Studies.

Findlay, R., 1990, "The New Political Economy: Its Explanatory Power for LDC's Economics and Politics," 2, pp. 193-221.

Fiorentine, G. and Sam Pelzman, 1995, *The Economics of Organised Crime,* Cambridge University Press.

Gambatta, D., 1988, "Fragments of an Economic Theory of the Mafia", *Archives Europeannes de Sociologies,* 29, pp. 127-45.

Kautilya, 1991, *Arthasastra,* Penguin Books, New Delhi.

Polo Michele, 1995, "Internal Cohesion and Competition among Criminal Organisations" in Fiorentine *et. al.* (eds.) *The Economics of Organised Crime,* Cambridge University Press.

Schelling, T.C., 1971, "What is the Business of Organised Crime?" *Journal of Public Law,* 20, pp. 71-84.

Williamson, O.E., 1989, "Transaction Cost Economics" in R. Schmalansee and R.D. Willing (eds.), Handbook of Industrial Organisation, Amsterdam and N.Y., Elsevier Science Publishers, Vol. 1, Ch. 3, pp. 135-82.

Lane, F., 1958, "Economic Consequences of Organised Violance", *Journal of Economic History,* 18, pp. 401-17.

14

Micro Theoretic Issues in Generation of Crime, with Reference to Mafia as an Oligopolistic Firm

Santanu Ghosh

I

With the growth of civilisation of human society, the world has experienced a rather rapidly rising crime graph. It is, indeed, an irony as well as a paradox that while civilisation, especially science and technology, has been scaling new heights, on one hand, the society, on the other hand, is being increasingly plagued by different kinds of offences and crimes. The nature and extent of crimes do obviously differ across societies, countries and regions and also, possibly, vary over time. In recent years, the developing countries in particular and the globe in general have been badly hit by a spurt of crimes. This phenomenon is not only a hurdle before social development, but also is posing a major obstacle in the way of smooth, speedy economic development.

In this paper, we are, however, trying to focus on a large proportion of criminal activities that are basically motivated by "economic rationality". Economic rationality is one of the vital driving forces in the progress of human society. While, through social, political and religious reforms it is a bit easier to tackle a large number of crimes, economic rationality and instinct—to be more precise, self-interest—are difficult to control and supress.

In today's world, it is possible to visualise crime as a product—a product which is produced and consumed and also can be exported and imported. Part of the crime production is for self consumption, while part of the crime production is for the market. Social crimes are basically for self-consumption. For instance, atrocities on women and weaker sections are basically non-marketable output, though sometimes we find situations where criminal acts are performed by hired persons on behalf of others. On the other hand, production or manufacturing of unlicensed guns, bombs, hand grenades, etc. are basically meant for sale to the prospective, select group of customers. Production of crime may be supply determined or demand determined. The former is basically produced for self-consumption, while the latter is meant for the market. For example, when a person or a gang is engaged in extortion of money or bank robbery or kidnapping for reasons, then that act should basically be treated as supply side phenomenon. On the other hand, manufacturing of illegal arms, smuggling of drugs and contraband goods, contract killings, etc. are actually demand determined phenomena. A person or a group does these activities on behalf of others and in exchange of cash. However, these are often situations where production structure of crime becomes vertically integrated. A criminal gang may be conceived as a firm. This firm, say, is engaged in a variety of activities. It may be engaged in extortion of money from rich firms and families, kidnapping, bank looting, currency faking, anti-state terrorist activities and so on. This firm can be classified as a multi-product firm. The chances of vertical integration of this firm are much higher.

II

Let us now consider some microeconomic aspects of crime. The basic approach/assumption, in the following discussion, is that crime and corruption are products. Before proceeding further we seek to distinguish between crime and corruption. While commitment of corruption and crime both inflict a loss on society, the former does not usually lead to loss of human lives and/or property—it does not usually pose a threat in terms of death and injury. Crime, on the other hand, happens to be more serious and is, often, violent in nature. It poses a potential threat to human lives and property. We can illustrate this distinction with a few examples: tax erosion, foreign exchange violation, taking bribe and the like are basically corrupt practices. Looting a bank, kidnapping someone and demanding ransom, drug trafficking, manufacture of and trade in illegal arms, etc. should, on the other hand, appropriately be treated as crime. Corruption and crime both cause damages to society; but the former is performed in rather subtle and covert forms, devoid of any element of violence, while the adverse effects of the latter are generally evident, clearly realised and it frequently contains some violence. Another point can also be raised here; corruption is basically related to economic aspects (e.g. tax evasion, bribe, smuggling); but crime can be linked to economic as well as social, political and other factors. Profit and utility motives dominate in corruption. For instance, when someone is engaged in smuggling of contraband goods, (s)he is primarily guided by profit/utility considerations. On the other hand, when someone or some group resorts to subversive, antinational activities or resorts to, say, electoral malpractices then that may be linked to achieving certain political goals. Again, manufacturing of illegal aims, food adulteration etc. are undertaken with a view to earn extra and fast profits. So, we may say, that corruption is basically a subject of crime: all corruptions are crimes, but all crimes are not corruptions. This sort of distinction has indeed, policy implication—different approaches need to be taken so as to control or wipe out each form.

On the basis of the foregoing discussion, we may now move over to some micro-theoretic aspects of crime and corruption, with special reference to the formers, i.e. the broader set.

We recall that the crux of the present paper is to emphasise that crime is a commodity—it is produced by an individual or a group of individuals so as to reap some benefit: profit and/or utility. By concentrating on this angle, we are, accordingly, leaving out from our domain of discussion other sorts of crime—e.g. electoral malpractices, murdering for personal revenge and so on. Our focus is on those activities which have "direct" connection with economic gain (or loss).

III

There is a considerable body of literature on labour contract in traditional text book firms, i.e., firms in overground world. It will be interesting to explore the implications of alternative wage contracts in case of an underworld firm. Unlike overground business, underground business runs on oral contracts and mutual trusts. Since the business is illegal in nature, and, therefore, risky, written contracts, are not feasible. Any breach of trust by any person is, again, hazardous on his/her part. Even if the contracts are oral in nature, that would not necessarily have any adverse effect on resource allocation process. Rather, because of the oral nature of the contracts, the underworld firms are able to save a lot of transaction costs, which often become quite high in today's corporate world.

A worker working under a mafia leader has to bear a lot of risks and occupational hazards, along with the employer. In modern industrial structures, it is the entrepreneur who bears the risk, and not the workers. The workers are basically paid staff, having fixed salary and/or productivity linked income. A labourer in a mafia firm, on the contrary, usually works on commission basis; the success in a particular operation and the resulting return from this operation determine the compensation package. The income is also erratic and not necessarily a steady one. If the worker is caught at the time of operation or at any other stage, then target remains unfulfilled. Naturally, the employer also looses. Under such circumstances we may conceive of a set of alternative scenarios. The worker has to face penalty and/or has to go to prison. This will entail a cost of legal battle, which often become prohibitively high; the employer may also land in legal trouble; further there will be some time cost—opportunity cost of serving prison term. The employer, under such circumstances, may have to share a maintenance cost of the employee's family; (s)he may offer compensatory employment to some family member. Another probable situation is that the worker will be paid higher reward, while (s)he is required to bear all the costs in case of arrest. We can examine the implications of these different wage contracts with respect to the size and nature of criminal activity and, thereby, resort to micro-economic modelling exercises for production of crime.

Such modelling exercises should incorporate game theoretic and bargaining solutions, aspects of resource allocation (including labour time) under asymmetric information and contingent markets and probabilistic solutions. These are, indeed, some of the vistas along which further research in economics of crime and oligopolistic mafia can be done.

III A

Let us now revert to analysis of production of crime. Since, as already hinted, criminal activities can take various forms and are guided by different motives (e.g. social, political, economic, etc.) we shall concentrate here only on economic crime; to be more specific, we focus mainly on mafia as an oligopolistic firm. The mafia under consideration may have specialised in kidnapping businessmen or illegal arms dealing or smuggling or any such activity.

Consider first the organisational, locational and other aspects of mafia firm. A mafia or a criminal firm, unlike the traditional firm of micro theory, may take longer period to come to limelight. We often find that initially an individual or a small group of individuals starts resorting to some petty and sporadic crimes—snatching, wagon breaking—on small scale. This individual or group, indeed, might have been forced into these activities as a result of unemployment and frustration, social and political environment. But, gradually, lured by making fast buck and because of the prospects of reaping large profits, the person or the group beings to expand the horizon of operation. In the process, a crime syndicate or a firm engaged in crime production (here production for self/internal consumption, unlike the case of, say, manufacture of illegal arms or drug trafficking which is marketed to prospective clients) comes into its nascent stage which ultimately begins to assume a concrete and well organised shape. We can cite many instances of today's dreaded underworld dons who made a humble beginning in their criminal careers and have steadily built up large empires. Though initially frustration and social environment play a crucial role in the emergence of criminals, at the end, economic rationality assumes greater weightage.

While social and political environment may explain the rise of many criminals and crime syndicates, economic rationality can, perhaps, account for their sustenance. As long as economic rationality survives, mere social and political reforms will not be able to stem the growth of crime world. As a result, crime is ultimately adapted as an alluring profession by these persons. Even if these individuals are in a position to obtain loans, start other forms of business or take up alternative occupations they would still not abandon their criminal careers. The simple reason is that in case of a traditional micro firm, raw material or intermediate costs usually account for substantial part of total cost; profits and value added, accordingly, are relatively small. But for a criminal firm, raw material costs are usually low. On the other hand, because of the risky nature of business the prospective returns are quite high. The net income, i.e., profit margin, is also, therefore, quite attractive. There is always the scope of substantial premium income.

While production of crime involves a lot of risks, it also involves a lot of information—to be more precise acquiring as much information as possible as well as optimal use of available information. The cost of information in various criminal activities is quite high. The more costly is it to gather information, the more profitable may be the business; also the very act of collecting, i.e., buying information is itself a risky venture. Information cost may take a wide variety of forms. For example, a crime syndicate planning a bank robbery needs to know the arrival and departure timings of its target clients, whether the security staff would be present or not at a particular time and so on; someone or some group carrying out cross-border smuggling or engaged in drug trafficking needs to know as much information as possible regarding patrol duty, patrol staff roster, etc. While some of the information can be obtained through proper planning and deployment of manpower—which, again, involves risk factors—some of the crucial/vital information may be directly purchased by bribing contact person(s) of the relevant agency. We may assert, then, that while some of the informational inputs are produced by the firm, the rest may have to be purchased through underhand dealings. It is, in this context, we may raise another aspect of crime, viz. corruption in public organisations. In India, we normally find government purchases and stock disposals are not very much transparent. Moreover, the right to information is still absent. Hence, there is substantial degree of asymmetric information. The public authority and its staff possess more information than others (common people). There is always, therefore, monetary temptation among some unscruplous staff to leak some secret documents and policies and in exchange, earn some money illegally. Firm—both criminal and traditional/non-criminal—find it worthwhile to spend money in bribing some staff, and, thereby, enjoy economically advantageous position *vis-a-vis* rival firms or reap sheer benefits. We often find that firms are directly bribing higher authority or decision-makers in order to restrain them form taking certain decision (e.g., stalling replacement/transfer of, say, a police officer who is friendly with the criminals). The highly controversial Bofors deal fracas could, possibly, not have reached its crescendo had there been greater transparency in government's functioning system. The lack of transparency gives rise to the germs of asymmetric information, which in turn facilitate crime and corruption.

III B

Let us now consider some aspects of production technology of crime. Criminal output may be labour-intensive as well as capital-intensive. On the whole, however, crime is basically a labour-intensive product. The sheer spurt of crimes and the present magnitude of employment in crime world in India and elsewhere basically highlight this. Petty crimes are actually labour-intensive products, though persons, while committing such offences, often require to carry some simple, crude capital instruments—e.g., razor, pistol, etc. Firms and syndicates specialised in production of serious, and hence highly profitable crimes, on the other hand, may need to deploy capital-intensive techniques. For example, execution of some crimes needs sophisticated electronic devices (remote), highly costly equipments (AK-47), materials (RDX) and so on. A small group of persons can cause a serious impact on society or can reap large monetary dividends by successfully engineering it (the enemy nation may offer a lucrative sum for executing it). An important aspect of crime production is that in many cases we have to distinguish between notional use and effective use of capital as a factor of production. The traditional theory of production function shows that actual output level of firm depends, among others, on the actual employment of labour and capital. Mere addition to or possession of capital stock does not mean enhanced output unless and until this capital is actually deployed. Idle capital, in fact, results in wastages and a fall in profit margin. The case of criminal firms, in this respect, is, however quite different. For such a firm, capital—i.e., weapons, ammunition, etc., has a dual role to play; it can be used to attain the desired target (firing or throwing bombs at the time of looting a bank) or used to demonstrate simply for intimidation purposes, and thus, realise the actual objective. In some cases, in fact, dummy capital instruments even do the trick—a toy pistol, e.g., may be intelligently used to snatch a gold chain.

Of late, society has been experiencing another sort of crime, thanks to revolution in information technology, viz., cyber crime. It is a crime which does not necessarily need ownership of sophisticated equipments as such; rather it can be performed only by a highly skilled person, who prefers to direct his/her time and energy into something which may have a telling effect on business, commerce and normal lives, without inflicting any loss of lives. The computer hackers are now a cause of worry in every nation. Very recently, the U.S. government has even been forced to come with attractive pay offers to these hackers, i.e. the government is trying to hire hackers so as to prevent itself from being hacked. As science and technology, especially information technology, scale increasingly new heights, organisation of cyber crime syndicates is likely to receive a fillip. The development of e-commerce in the "true" sense—which entails transactions purely through credit cards—will not be possible unless and until adequate means of protection against hacking and cyber crime are available.

III C

In the traditional theory of firm, there is a considerable body of literature on splits, take overs, mergers and ancillary issues, as well as on issues like limit pricing, entry barriers, etc. When one attempts to explore the behaviour of mafias as oligopolistic firms, then one finds dearth of adequate research; consequently there is a lot of scope of exploration of new avenues along these lines.

Since crime syndicates and mafias have been dominating in many pockets of industrial society, it is important to gauge the economic effects of the activities of the underground world. This is more so because of the organised nature of crimes and, often existence of covert collusion among the mafia gangs, which even spreads across national boundaries. It has already been hinted that a mafia gang does not spring up over night or in a short span of time. It evolves at the initial stage, gradually and stealthily. In its nascent phase a person or a core group usually forms the nucleus of the gang. The "learning by doing" aspect is extremely important for the survival and growth of mafia firm. Successful operation of a big mafia firm entails a meticulous planning of various aspects and a detailed division of labour. For instance, in case of drug trafficking, a chain of human beings may be needed to transport drugs across places. In many cases, the "workers" or the carriers may not be aware about who is the ultimate boss—which is in sharp contrast to modern firm. In modern industrial world, recruitment and placement of labour is independent of regional bias; a firm recruits best or most suitable candidates and places them in those plant locations where their services are required. In other words, in a truly industrial society, labour has the mobility across regions, if not across sectors (because specificity of skill). In contrast, a mafia firm operates basically on the basis of service of local people. This is mainly because local persons—i.e., where the mafia concentrates its operation—will be much more aware of the local environment, locational hazards of their works and, accordingly, possess more information than rank outsiders. Moreover, outside residents or unknown faces may create suspicion. This is not to say that workers associated with criminal firms are not mobile across spaces. In the long-run, "criminal workers" may and do switch over from one activity or region to another.

III D

At this juncture, some locational aspects of mafia firms can also be emphasised. We find mafias are often working/ concentrating in one region. If mafia firms are producing different products—e.g. one specialised in fraud, robbery, one in kidnapping, one in drug peddling and so on—then chances of conflict between the firms are relatively low. The firms are not competing with each other. The concentration of a variety of mafia firms can be due to a series of factors—lopsided development that creates a sharp wedge between 'haves' and 'have not', poor law and order machinery, unemployment and so on. But the real problem crops up when the firms are engaged in producing the same/similar products, i.e., in similar activity. This leads to intense inter-firm rivalry, or the so-called "gang war", each firm wants to expand its market share by eliminating or cornering its rivals. Modern firms basically produce for market—there is a large number of consumers of each product. In order to wean away customers from rivals' fold into its fold, a firm has to resort to various marketing strategies, offer incentives to prospective customers and other measures. Naturally, advertising forms an important pillar of business decisions. Mafia firms, in contrast, can not go for advertising and marketing decisions since it is producing for self-consumption and not for the market (we are leaving out the case of firms producing illegal weapons for sale to under world, mercenary firms—specialised in contract killing and firms of such nature). A mafia organisation would like to operate within its domain of control as in that case its effectiveness in intimidating people and extorting money is quite high; it would prefer to shun away, other things remaining same, from venturing into 'foreign' territory—territory not under its effective control and territory where it is yet to make a dent through recruitment of contact persons. Naturally, within a geographic zone mafias of same class often get entangled in fierce internecine war. This phenomenon may sought to be captured in terms of a spatial duopoly model, a la Hotelling. Consider the following illustration:

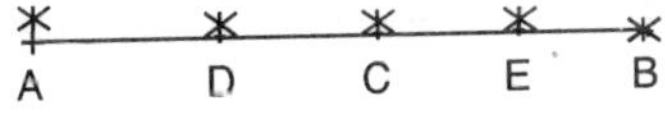

The length of the line, AB, indicates the given market size and it is assumed that each dot on the line represents one consumer only. In terms of our framework, a consumer means a prospective client or a target person whom a mafia group can fleece for monetary benefits. Unlike standard micro theory, a criminal product is usually not voluntarily demanded or purchased (sometimes, though entrepreneurs are forced to come into some monetary understanding so as to ward-off threats from other gangs and smoothly run their operations). A gang would find it risky and costly to do business in those areas where it is not on an advantageous footing. The further is the prospective client from its main centre of decision-making, the more risky and costly will be its business operation. In other words, we may conceive of cost of transporting crime, a cost which is reflected in risk factors. Suppose, initially mafia firm was located at point A and firm II at point B. If firm I shifts its location to D, then all clients (target persons) lying to the left of the point D, will become firm I's captive market. It will be more costly, e.g., for firm II to target someone (say for extortion) who is located to the left of point D as firm II will have to overlap into rival's territory and thus incur higher transport cost (may be in terms of asymmetric information, risk, etc.) than firm I. Similarly, firm II will also find it judicious to shift its location from point B to a point like E. In its case, all clients lying to the right of E will become its captive consumers. The logical corollary of this type of behaviour is that each mafia—in its attempt to enlarge its size of captive market—will tend to locate to the central point, which is C. As a result, the two mafia firms tend to localise their presence at or around C. After reaching point C, firm I will not find it worthwhile to move further to right of C, firm II, similarly, will not also attempt to move further to the left of C. Some sort of *status quo* is likely to emerge at C. With this kind of exercise—which is an application of Hotelling's duopoly model—one may try to rationalise the locational concentration of criminal activities. However, rather than sharing a market or booty, an oligopolistic criminal firm will always find it attractive to eliminate its rivals so that it can reign unchallenged. This attitude, which is quite strong among mafia gangs, is bound to give rise to better and bloody underworld struggle—struggle for the market.

This battle over market control creates an entry deterrence too. Oligopolistic mafias will always attempt as rational economic agents and like traditional text-book firms, to stall entry of a new mafia in their zone of operation. Whenever another mafia group attempts to enter the market, the existing ones fiercely resist the entry; in the process, again, gang wars are likely to erupt. Though entry of a new firm becomes difficult, often, however, new mafia groups come into existence through splits in existing ones. In fact, underworld firms multiply through the processes of splitting and regrouping. A person initially engaged in petty crimes under the umbrella of a big don, may ultimately be found to build empire of his/her own. The mentor is often betrayed and the "learning by doing" phenomenon is quite strong among the criminals.

An important aspect of market of crime production is that not only there is entry barrier, but also there is exit barrier, which is virtually absent in overground markets. The logic of entry barrier is quite obvious—profit seeking firms would not like presence of rivals and/or increase in the member of competitors. The exit barrier operates because of the factors emanating from high risk and asymmetric information associated with underworld activities. Success and profitability in crime business are very much linked to secrecy of information. If a firm or a gang contemplates to close down its operations voluntarily, existing rivals fear leakage of vital information by this party to the law enforcing agency. The same point applies to an individual also. A worker associated with crime production and working under a particular don will find it risky to quit the work and lead a normal life. The market of crime production is like a blind or dark alley: once you are in or manage to be there, quitting will become a highly hazardous proposition. Even, switching loyalty—i.e., shifting from one employer to another—is very risky. The survival of a criminal firm is very much dependent, among others, on the exclusive possession of some vital information; these informations, and not the raw materials as such, form useful factors of production, which are often firm specific in nature. So when a labourer slips out and seeks engagement with another enterprise, that means the original firm may have to share some vital information with another one as the worker is likely to divulge some secret information to his/her new boss. So, even exit of a worker is not at all an easy affair—exist form one firm as well as total exist form the underground market. In other words, there is not enough scope of (occupational) mobility of labour in the market dominated by crime syndicates.

IV

Let us now persent a fairly simple mathematical exercise to obtain some insights into the behaviour pattern of crime world.

The Model

Consider an economy where people have two options: to work in legal or overground sector or to get associated with underground world. The wage rate in overground activity is lower than that prevailing in the crime world. But, working in the underworld is itself risky. While there is the incentive of earning fabulous sum of money, there is also the chance of being caught and arrested. Once a fellow is caught or detected, the authorities will impose fine or penalty, which might be quite substantial. The imposition of fine signifies a loss element. Apart from fine, the individual may have to spend money towards lawyer's fees, bail bond and so on. The chance of being detected or caught during the act of committing crime is higher, the higher is the involvement—measured in terms of labour hours—in the crime world. Consequently, if there is no labour allocation in crime world, the chance of being caught is naught.

In the following analysis we assume, for simplicity, the case of a labour surplus economy—i.e., an economy where labour supply does not pose a constraint on the decision-making and working of overground as well as of underground sectors.

Let us now define the following notations:

- W_1: Wage rate in the underground market (i.e., in crime world);
- W_2: Wage rate in the overground market;
- L_1: Volume of labour service (say, in hours) rendered to the illegal sector;
- L_2: Volume of labour service rendered to the overground activities;
- P: Probability of being caught/detected (in case of labour);
- q: Probability of escape or not being caught/detected; and
- f: fine incurred by the labourer in case of detection.

We may treat 'P' and 'q' as probability of failure and probability of success, respectively too. We measure p and q in the following fashion:

$$p = \frac{L_1}{1 + L_1} = \frac{1}{1 + \left(\frac{1}{L_1}\right)} \quad \text{and} \quad q = \frac{1}{L_1 + 1}; p + q = 1$$

It can be verified that if $L_1 = 0$, $p = 0$ and $q = 1$; i.e. if no labour is allocated to underworld activity, probability of being caught is zero or there is 100% chance of not being caught. The way the two probabilities have been defined further shows that as L_1 increases, the chances of being detected rise or the chances of slipping out fall. In other words, as L_1 rises p rises and q falls. Hence, unlike many analysis, probability values have been taken as variables—the values varying with the magnitude of illegal activities.

In order to determine how much labour is allocated to crime world or to determine the size of employment in crime world, we resort to expected income hypothesis. Labour will move from overground to underground activities as long as expected wage income from illegal activities exceeds actual income from overground sector. So, labour movement will come to an equilibrium state when the following condition holds:

$$W_1\left[\frac{L_1}{(1+L_1)}\right]-f\left[\frac{L_1}{(1+L_1)}\right]=W_2L_2 \qquad \ldots (1)$$

We are, therefore, using the assumption that the labour allocation decision is motivated by expected income from crime world (which often turns out to be quite attractive) and actual income from legalised sector (which may not be high in a labour surplus economy). While calculating expected wage rate, we have to consider the penalty (fine) factor also. When a labourer is caught and fined, that entails a loss of income. The amount of penalty is assumed to be lump-sum in nature. The moment someone is caught, a fine is charged, without considering the length of the service in the underworld—i.e., for how long (s)he has been carrying on this illegal operation. Alternatively, we may assume that the person calculates the volume of fine taking into account direct cost, litigation cost and all other costs (indirect cost). Depending on the nature of the activity, the value of 'f' is likely to vary. For simplicity we have refrained ourselves from these intricacies. It is reasonable to assume that $W_1 > f > W_2 > 0$. Equation (1) can be rewritten in the following manner:

$$W_1 L_1 - f L_1 = W_2 L_2 (L_1 + 1) \qquad \ldots (2)$$

or, $$(W_1 - f) L_1 = W_2 L_2 L_1 + W_2 L_2$$

or, $$(W_1 - f) L_1 - W_2 L_2 L_1 = W_2 L_2$$

or, $[(W_1 - f) - W_2 L_2] L_1 = W_2 L_2$

or, $$L_1 = \frac{W_2 L_2}{[(W_1 - f) - W_2 L_2]}$$

or, $$L_1 = \frac{W_2 L_2}{[W_1 - (f + W_2 L_2)]} \quad \ldots (3)$$

From equation (3) we observe that for meaningful solution of L_1 (i.e., $L_1 > 0$) the condition $[(W_1 - f) - W_2 L_2] > 0$ must hold.

In other words, as long as "net" (the nomenclature "net" should be interpreted in a rather careful manner since the fine/penalty element has been assumed to be lump-sum in nature) wage rate from underground activity exceeds actual income from overground activity, there will be some labour allocation in crime world. Moreover, as $(W_1 - f) \rightarrow W_2 L_2$ or *vice versa*, the size of labour employment tends to become infinitely large.

We can now also easily verify a couple of comparative static results derivable from this simple framework. From equation (2) one can easily check that:

$$\text{(a) } \frac{\delta L_1}{\delta L_2} > 0, \text{ (b) } \frac{\delta L_1}{\delta W_1} < 0, \text{ (c) } \frac{\delta L_1}{\delta W_2} > 0 \text{ and (d) } \frac{\delta L_1}{\delta f} > 0$$

Result (a) indicates that, in terms of our model, there is a positive correlation between employment in overground and underground activities: with the growth of overground economy or legalised sector (in terms of employment level), labour absorption in criminal sector rises. The other three results are quite interesting too. Result (b) indicates that with a rise in wage rate in the illegal activity, labour employment/allocation in such activity declines (i.e., a possibility of backward- binding or, rather forward falling, labour supply curve looms large), while with a rise in wage rate in the legalised sector, labour allocation in the illegal occupation rises. These results, indeed, are contrary to normal expectations. The fourth result also seems quite paradoxical. Usual belief is that a higher monetary penalty or fine acts as a deterrent before criminal or illegal activity. However, our analysis indicates that, *ceteris paribus*, a rise in amount of penalty/fine will induce greater labour allocation in illegal activities. This means a policy of imposing stronger penalty in arresting crime is counter productive. These results, indeed, require further investigation.

Let us now relax the hypothesis that labour allocation decision is governed by the comparison between expected income from illegal occupation *vis-a-vis* actual income from legal sector; instead, we now use the assumption that migration or labour allocation decision is dependent on the expected wage rate in illegal sector and actual wage rate in the legal sector. In that case, the labour-flow equilibrium condition will be:

$$W_1\left[\frac{1}{(1+L_1)}\right]-f\left[\frac{L_1}{1+L_1}\right]=W_2 \qquad \ldots (3)$$

This equation can be rewritten in the following fashion too:

$$W_1 - f\,L_1 = W_2\,(1 + L_1)$$

Or,

$$L_1 = \frac{(W_1 - W_2)}{(W_2 + f)} > 0 \qquad \because \quad W_1 > W_2 \qquad \ldots (4)$$

This time, however, it can easily be verified that

$$\frac{\delta L_1}{\delta W_1} > 0, \frac{\delta L_1}{\delta W_2} < 0 \quad \text{and} \quad \frac{\delta L_1}{\delta f} < 0$$

where all the signs are intuitively simple. A major reason for arriving at sharply opposite conclusions is that in the previous case we compared income levels between overground and underground sectors, while fine element was considered fixed irrespective of the magnitude of labour involvement in criminal activities. In the second case we considered, on the other hand, wage rates—and not income levels—even though the penalty aspect was treated in the identical fashion. This is a bit rigid assumption since it implies that when someone is caught, (s)he is charged with a penalty, no investigation is pursued regarding the past activities of the labourer. If this is not so, then magnitude of penalty or cost of detection (from the criminals' point-of-view) should positively depend on the size of L_1 or the duration of involvement in crime world. It will, indeed, be an interesting exercise to introduce greater realism into the story and explore the qualitative and/or quantitative changes in our results. But since we strongly believe that labour allocation decision (between legal and illegal activities) is primarily influenced by total earnings, and not so much by wage rates, we would like to put greater weightage on the paradoxical findings rather than on standard ones. Moreover, these paradoxical findings should incite greater interest as far as policy implications are concerned.

So far we have concentrated on the supply aspect—labour allocation decision from the view point of the prospective criminals and/or households. Let us now briefly turn our attention to the probable behaviour patterns of a firm engaged in production of crime.

We have already said that production of crime may take tangible (arms, bombs, etc.) as well as intangible (robbery) forms; it may be produced for the market (i.e., for sale) or for self-consumption. Here we confine ourselves, for simplicity, with the case of a criminal firm which is producing intangible good and the output is being used for self-consumption. Let us conceive a situation where the output of the firm is represented in terms of money; this may be the case where, say, the firm is specialised or doing 'business' in extortion of money or bank robbery/fraud or collection of ransom money through kidnapping. The output of the firm has no market price as such (unlike in the case of manufacture of illegal weapons or banned drugs); the revenue of the firm is the total money collected through its operations.

Under the above circumstances, the revenue and production functions become identical. The revenue/production function can take various forms, depending on the nature of the technology. Under the assumption of constant returns to scale (CRS) we can postulate, at least, following two functions:

1. $Q = a\sqrt{L_1 K} = Q\,(L_1, K) = M, a > 0$ and

2. $Q = a(\sqrt{L_1 K} + L_1) = Q\,(L_1, K) = M, a > 0$

where 'M' stands for money (i.e., monetary output), 'a' is a constant and L_1 and K stand for employment of labour and capital (equipments, weapons, etc.), respectively.

While the first form of the production function is quite familiar and, hence, does not need any clarification, a few words can be spared for the second function. Our presumption is that income from criminal activity can't be earned without any labour involvement, though without capital it can be earned. This means labour is a necessary input, which should be quite obvious. A firm or a gang can earn money simply by its muscle power and threats/intimidation tactics, and without even resorting to the use of pistols, knifes, etc. So, when $L_1 = 0$, $Q = M = 0$, i.e. no income is earned. But $K = 0$ does not mean $Q = M = 0$ (i.e., $Q = M > 0$ even when $K = 0$).

When we consider the issue from the view point of the firm, then probability of detection (of criminal activity) or being caught is measured in a slightly different way (though the previous formula type is retained). We write or define:

$$p^* = \frac{M}{M+1} = \frac{Q}{Q+1} \quad \text{and} \quad q^* = \frac{1}{M+1} = \frac{1}{Q+1}$$

where p^* is the probability of detection and q^* is the probability of escape. ($p^* + q^* = 1$). The hypothesis is that the larger is the output or income of the firm, the higher is the chance of detection; i.e., as the firm expands its racket (by employing more labour or capital or both). It faces greater risk of being caught. When, $Q = M = 0$, $p^* = 0$, too: the question of detection simply does not arise. As Q or M increases, p^* tends to unity (i.e., q^* tends to zero). If the criminal firm is caught, a fine/penalty is slapped on it, the magnitude of the cost (to be incurred by the firm) being F (> 0). Let W_1 and r stand for wage rate and rental, respectively. Given this scenario, the oligopolistic firm may pursue a number of alternative strategies or goals. Suppose, the firm seeks to maximize its profits (π)—to be precise enough, expected profits, denoted as $E(\pi) = \pi^*$. We write done the expected profit function:

$$E(\pi) = \pi^* = \frac{1}{Q+1}[Q - W_1L_1 - rK] - \frac{Q}{Q+1} \cdot F \quad \ldots (5)$$

or

$$\pi^* = \frac{1}{M+1}[M - W_1L_1 - rK] - \frac{M}{M+1} \cdot F$$

Putting the value of Q or M from the production function, we get:

$$\pi^* = \frac{1}{[Q(L_1, K)+1}[Q(L_1, K) - W_1L_1 - rK] - \frac{Q(L_1, K)}{[Q(L_1, K)+1]} \cdot F \quad \ldots (6)$$

In short run, if $K = \overline{K}$, then the choice before the firm is to choose the value of L_1 in such a fashion that $E(\pi) = \pi^*$ is maximum. In long run, the firm has to choose both L_1 and K such that profits are maximised.

Let us consider, for simplicity, short run situation (note that firms in fact, operate in the short run, but plan in the long run and also recall that long run is basically a relative concept) so that $K = \overline{K}$. Then we can write:

$$\pi^* = \frac{1}{[Q(L_1, \overline{K}) + 1]}[Q(L_1, \overline{K}) - W_1 L_1 - \overline{C}] - \frac{Q(L_1, \overline{K})}{[Q(L_1, K) + 1]} \cdot F \tag{7}$$

where $r\overline{K} = \overline{\varepsilon}$ = a constant (the fixed cost).

Putting $\dfrac{d\pi^*}{dL_1} = 0$ (the first order condition for maximum profit),

we get:

$$(1 - F)\, Q_L - (Q + 1)\, W_1 + W_1\, Q_L\, L_1 + \overline{C} Q_L = 0 \quad \ldots (8)$$

or

$$Q_L = \frac{(Q+1)\, W_1}{[(1-F) + (\overline{C} + W_1 L_1)]} \quad \ldots (9)$$

where $\quad Q_L = \delta Q / \delta L_1 > 0$

Equation (9) can be rewritten in the following form too:

$$W_1 = \frac{Q_L\, [(1-F) + \overline{C}]}{[(Q+1) - L_1 Q_L]} = \frac{Q_L\, [(1-F) + \overline{C}]}{L_1\left[\left(\dfrac{Q}{L_1} - Q_L\right) + \dfrac{1}{L_1}\right]}$$

$$= \frac{Q_L\, [(1-F) + \overline{C}]}{L_1\left[(AP_L - MP_L) + \dfrac{1}{L_1}\right]} \quad \ldots (10)$$

Since $Q_{LL} < 0$, i.e. marginal product of labour is diminishing (which can easily be verified from the production/revenue functions), the second order condition, presumably holds. (AP_L and MP_L denote average and marginal products of labour, respectively).

From any of the above relations we may investigate the nature of relation between W_1 and L_1—i.e., between the wage rate in the illegal sector and labour demand emanating from that sector.

Suppose, starting from an initial equilibrium position, L_1 rises. Now, in terms of signs or symbols we can assert that $O_L \downarrow$ ($\because Q_{LL} < 0$), $1/L_1 \downarrow$ and $(AP_L - MP_L) \downarrow$ ($\because$ with fall in both AP_L and MP_L, consequent upon an increase in labour employment, the difference between average and marginal products declines). So, while the numerator falls as L_1 increases, the effect on denominator is apparently ambiguous. The net result is W_1 may fall or rise or remain same. However, we can try to derive the exact nature of the relation using simple mathematics.

Consider equation (10), again, where

$$W_1 = \frac{[(1-F)+\overline{C}]}{[(Q+1)-L_1 Q_L]}$$

$$\therefore \qquad dW_1 = [(1-F)+\overline{C}]\, d\left[\frac{Q_L}{(Q+1)-L_1 Q_L}\right] \qquad \ldots (11)$$

A little bit of calculation and manipulation yields the following:

$$dW_1 = (1-F+\overline{C})\left[\frac{\{(Q+1)-L_1 Q_L\} Q_{LL}\, dL_1 + Q_L\ (L_1\ Q_{LL}\, dL_1)}{\{(Q+1)-L_1 Q_L\}^2}\right]$$

$$\text{or} \qquad dW_1 = (1-F+\overline{C})\left[\frac{(Q+1)\, Q_{LL}}{\{(Q+1)-L_1 Q_L\}^2}\right] dL_1 \qquad \ldots (12)$$

(note $dQ = Q_L\, dL_1$)

Since $Q_{LL} < 0$, so

$$\frac{dL_1}{dW_1} < 0 \text{ \{assuming } (1 - F + \overline{C}) > 0\}$$

Thus we can now unequivocally state that the labour demand schedule for illegal activities will be negatively sloped. We are now reasonably equiped to determine the equilibrium level of criminal activity and also carry out some simple comparative static exercises. We consider negatively sloped demand curve for labour as well as negatively sloped labour supply curve, the possibility of which has already been established. We concentrate on forward falling labour supply curve since this case is deemed to be more interesting than the traditional type.

In Fig. 1 we have represented an equilibrium configuration by the point *E*. In this figure D_C^L and S_C^L indicate demand for and

FIG. 1

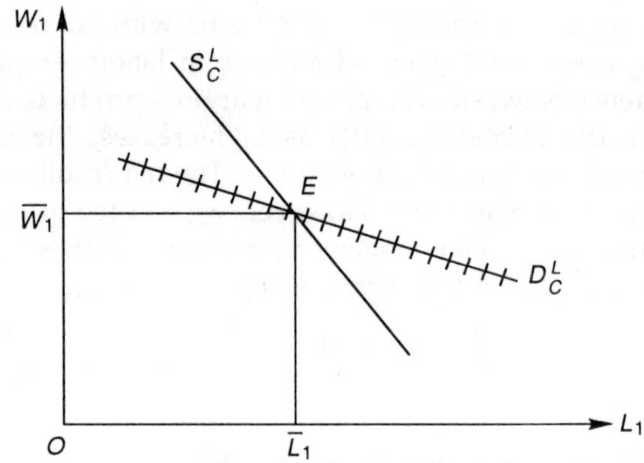

supply of labour in criminal activities. Walrasian stability requires that demand curve be flatter than the supply curve. At any wage rate below W_1, for instances, there is an excess demand for criminals and, accordingly, wage rate of criminals rises. (Interestingly, explosion of criminal activities in many societies can, perhaps, sought to be explained in terms of an unstable model, where the supply curve is flatter than the demand curve.).

FIG. 2(a)

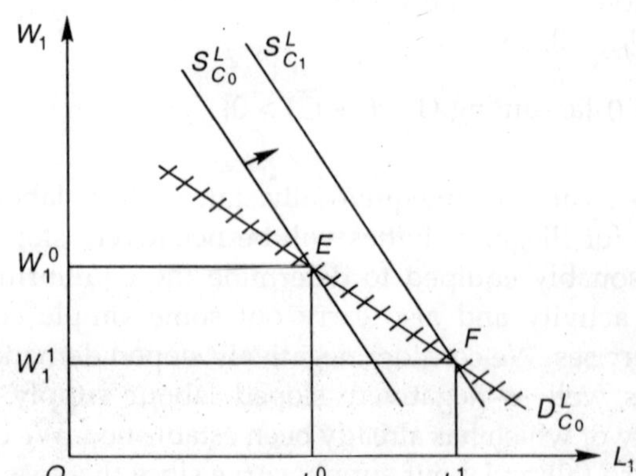

FIG. 2(b)

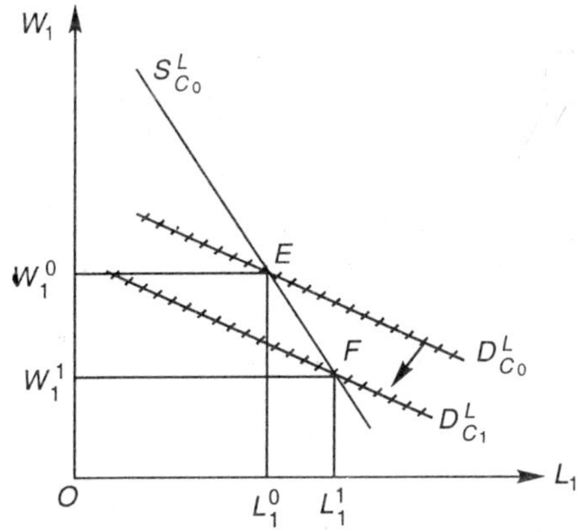

In Figure 2, we have analysed a couple of comparative static exercises. In both Fig. 2(a) and Fig. 2(b), point E denotes initial equilibrium, where $D^L_{C_0}$ and $S^L_{C_0}$ denote initial demand and supply curves respectively. Now, consider a situation of sterner government policy with respect to the criminals (as suppliers of labour) so that the magnitude of fine or penalty is now higher than before. This means, as per our previous findings, a rightward shift of the supply curve. Consequently, labour involvement or labour allocation in criminal activities rises, even though the equilibrium wage rate declines. Also, given the condition $\dot{Q}_L > 0$, higher volume of labour allocation means enhanced income generation from mafia activities. In Fig. 2(b), we have examined, on the other hand, a parametric shift in the demand side—e.g., imposition of a higher penalty/fine on the criminal firm. We observe from equation (10) that as F rises, at any given L (and, hence, given Q_L. and Q) W_1 falls. This means labour demand schedule of the mafia firm shifts to the left. Once again, we find larger labour involvement in illegal production. In other words, a policy of imposing stricter penalty either on the mafia firm or on the individuals supplying labour towards underworld activities or on both is found to be counter productive as it ultimately leads to greater criminalisation of the society.

Before winding up our discussion, we should keep in mind that we have only tried to present a fairly simple demonstration of economic rationality inherent in criminals' world. Our analysis needs further elaboration in different directions and, especially, it would be fruitful to modify some of the assumptions of our model. For instance, we have assumed that while mafia firm seeks to maximize its expected profits, household and individuals, offering labour for illegal activities, are guided by expected income consideration; i.e., in case of the latter, we have abstained from any explicit optimising behaviour. It is quite possible that households as suppliers of labour are motivated by utility maximising calculus. The firm, again, may attempt to follow the goal of attaining or retaining a certain market share or of erecting entry barrier to prospective rivals and so on. Clearly, we can conceive various scenarios under different permutations and combinations. Given the paucity of existing research, it will, indeed, be rewarding to carry on further investigations along these lines. With the use of this type of models, as well as of dynamics, it might be easier to explain growing criminalisation of society in terms of economic rationality.

REFERENCES

Anderson, A., "Organised Crime, Mafia and Governments" in *Economics for Organised Crime,* ed. Fiorentini, G. and Peltzman, S.

Andreano, R. and Sigfried, J., *The Economics of Crime*.

Becker, G.S., "Irrational Behaviour and Economic Theory", *Journal of Political Economy* (JPE), Vol. 70, Feb. 1962.

Becker, G.S., "Crime and Punishment: An Economic Approach", *JPE*, Vol. 78, Mar./April 1968.

Becker, G.S. and Landes, W.M. (ed.), *Essays in the Economics of Crime and Punishment*.

Bhagwati, J.N., "Fiscal Policies, the Faking of Foreign Trade Declarations and the Balance of Payments", *Bulletin of the Oxford University Institute of Statistics*, Feb. 1967.

Bhagwati, J.N., *Illegal Transactions in International Trade*.

Bhagwati., J.N. and Hansen, B., "A Theoretical Analysis of Smuggling", *Quarterly Journal of Economics*, May 1973.

Bhagwati, J.N. and Srinivasan, T.N., "Smuggling and Trade Policy", *Journal of Public Economics*, 1973.

Buchanan, J.M., "A Defense of Organised Crime" in *The Economics of Crime and Punishment* ed. S. Rottemberg.

Cowell, F.A. and Gordon, J.P.E., 'Auditing with "Ghosts" ' in *Economics for Organised Crime* ed. G. Fiorentini and S. Peltzman.

Ehrlich, I., "Participation in Illegitimate Activities: An Economic Analysis" in *Essays in Crime and Punishment*, ed. G. S. Becker and Peltzman.

Fiorentini, G., "Oligopolistic Competition in Illegal Marekts" in G. Fiorentini and S. Peltzman (ed.), *op. cit.*

Fiorentini, G. and Peltzman, S. (ed.), *The Economics for Organised Crime.*

Grossman, H.L., "The Mafia versus the State" in G. Fiorentini and S. Peltzman (ed.), *op. cit.*

Polinsky, A.M. and Shavell, S., "The Economic Theory of Public Enforcement of Law", *Journal of Economic Literature,* Vol. XXXVIII, No. 1, March 2000.

Rottemberg, S., *The Economics of Crime and Punishment.*

Schelling, T.C. (ed.), *Choice and Consequences.*

Schelling, T.C., "What is the Business of Organised Crime?", *Journal of Public Law,* Vol. 20, 1971.

Skaperdas, S. and Syropoulos, C., *Gangs As Primitive States.*

Stigler, G.J., "The Optimum Enforcement of Laws", *JPE,* Vol. 78, May/June 1970.

15

Corruption and Development: Bangladesh Perspective

M. ZAINUL ABEDIN

1. INTRODUCTION

Criminology may be defined as "a body of scientific knowledge about crime, including its causes and prevention, the handling of offenders, and the pursuit of such knowledge regardless of where it stems from." It may also be defined as a didactic discipline that assembles, analyses and integrates the observations and findings of criminological research for suggesting the best measures with a view to solve the crime-related problems and to secure socially desirable ends.[1] In order to include white-collar violations within criminology, it is necessary to define crime in such a broad sense that any corrupt behaviour of any person should be punishable regardless of the offenders' social status.[2] When crime is considered from a development point of view, the white-collar crimes and organised crimes emerge as the main limiting factor of development.[3] Corruption is an act of turning from right to wrong. It is the perversion of a person's integrity in the performance of his official duty or works. Corruption includes a departure from purity, moral deterioration, depravity, manifestation, etc. Corruptionist is a person who supports or practices corruption.[4] The respondents of a baseline survey (of 2500 households) conducted by Transparency International—Bangladesh Chapter viewed corruption as misuse of position and power (76%), negligence of duty (75.7%), taking bribe for personal gain (57.8%), misuse of funds (50.6%), etc. However, the said organization in its another document attempts to define corrupt activities as that include corruption, misuse of public resources, and misuse of public offices. Crime causation theory explains the statistical distribution of criminal behaviour in time and space which can be used to derive predictive statements about unknown statistical distributions.[5] This also helps to undertake corrective measures. Crimes are broadly classified as : (1) Homicide including murder and manslaughter; (2) offenses against person including sex offenses and violence; (3) offenses against property including burglary, robbery, etc. and (4) social disorganization including drunkness, disorderly conduct, petty larency, etc.[6]

Development means the attaining of reasonably high rates of growth of real GDP for a longer period and changing the structure of the economy from the backward one to modern and progressive one. Higgins observes, "Fundamentally, growth consists of rising national and per capita real income; development entails a good deal more—structural change, technological advance, resource discovery, and closing sectoral and regional gaps."[7] With this, reasonable progress in social sector, practice of democracy and good governance are added characteristics to the term development. Development is not only an economic and administrative exercise but also "a bold and massive movement emanating from and depending on the immense potential of the human spirit."[8]

This article attempts to analyse the recent dimensions of corruption in Bangladesh and their relations with the development potentials. In this regard Wahid observes, "Instead of democracy, it is corruption that has been institutionalised in the last 29 years with the covert support of some unscrupulous people belonging to politics and bureaucracy. Corruption could find a solid berth because of total lack of accountability and transparency in the country, from the lowest to the highest strata of administration. The failure of the two respective governments (during 1990s) in containing this menace from percolating down to all the vital sectors like education, health care and law enforcement is too glaring to be overlooked".[9]

This article is mainly based on secondary and some primary sources of data which are available in different research studies, periodicals and newspapers. The main findings of a report of Transparency International—Bangladesh Chapter have been very briefly stated here in precise form as an illustration of the levels of corruption in Bangladesh.

2. NATURE AND INTENSITY OF CORRUPTION

Recently a baseline survey was conducted by the above organization among 2500 households for collecting information on corruption occurring in different sectors of the economy. These include police, judiciary, education, municipal services, trade licenses, system loss in electric and water bills and the new media.

2.1. Police

While mentioning about corruption in police department, nearly 71 percent of the respondents reported that police deliberately delayed sending the cases to the court. Over 49 percent of the plaintiffs made prior arrangements with the police for disposal of their cases, 55 percent made the same for not sending the disputes to the court and 38 percent did the same for sending the complains to the court for disposal. Over 68 percent complainants made payments to the police for filing complains as First Information Report (FIR). Payments were made to the police by 40 percent plaintiffs directly, 34 percent through office employee, and 26 percent through local dalals.

2.2. Judiciary

Over 88 percent of the households said that it was almost impossible to get quick and fair judgement from the court without money or influence. In total, 63 percent of the households involved in court cases paid bribe to court officials. These figures for rural and urban areas are 64 percent and 51 percent respectively. Among them 53.3 percent paid bribe directly while 28.1 percent through the lawyers and the rests through other mediums.

2.3. Social Sector

About 74 percent of the households used extra regular methods for admission of their children into schools. Among those 41 percent mentioned about payment of donations, 28 percent used their political influences, 10 percent engaged school teachers as private tutors and the rest used other methods.

About 70 percent households reported that there existed unethical practices in the procedures for admission into the hospitals, in the supply of medicines and providing with treatments in the hospitals. About the use of extra regular methods for admissions into the hospitals, 20 percent reported that they had consultations with the doctors at their private chambers, 18 percent paid extra money to the hospital staff, 9 percent used influential persons, another 9 percent took the help of hospital staff, and the rest used other methods.

2.4. Municipal Services

The survey revealed that only 44 percent of urban dwellers had municipal water supply facilities. Among them 23 percent households reported about the difficulties in getting water connections. Of them 17 percent paid extra money, 16 percent made repeated visits, 12 percent reported long wait and red tape while the rests used other methods.

About 80 percent of the urban households reported that they had electric connections. Over 70 percent of them faced difficulties in getting connections. About 33 percent of them paid extra money to the officials for getting electric connections, 21 percent made frequent visits to the offices, 12 percent reported undue delays and the rests reported about other unstated difficulties.

Around 56 percent of urban households considered the assessment of municipal holding tax on houses and property was acceptable while 44 percent found that unacceptable. The excessive assessment was reduced by 53 percent of those through the Review Board while the rest 47 percent of those made arrangements with municipal staff on payment of extra money for reduction of holding tax.

2.5. System Loss

System loss (Theft or breach of trust) was reported by 32 percent of urban households. Over 30 percent of urban households possessing electric connections reduced their electricity bills while 32 percent of the same who had water connections reduced water bills by extra arrangements with meter readers.

2.6. Trade Licence

The survey revealed that 35 percent of urban households were involved in some business or trade and 56 percent of them had trade licenses. About 65 percent of them said that getting trade licenses without extra money or influence was impossible. The survey shows that among the trade licence holders, 49 percent paid extra money, 40 percent made repeated visits to municipal offices and the rest faced other difficulties in getting those.

2.7. News Media

Over 83 percent of the households expressed the views that the newspapers were professionally unethical and partisan. They opined that the newspapers should be factual and impartial in furnishing the news.

The report finally remarked that the two important elements of a civilized society, i.e. protection of life and property, and dispensation of justice in Bangladesh were partially absent. This is a devastating comment on the state of affairs. Unfortunately, the conditions are recently deteriorating instead of improving.

2.8. Some Other Reports on Corruption

A recent World Bank report mentioned about widespread practices of corruption in Bangladesh. It says that many utility services are delivered poorly and corruptly, while many officials of regulatory bodies are involved in various types of malpractices. It opines "in a situation where corruption flourishes and also where political, social, legal and economic systems that constitute the pillars of integrity for any society, lose their strength as supports for rule of law, governance will hardly have any relevance to the conditions of life and living for the people at large".[10]

US State Department's recent report on Bangladesh observes that the judiciary is subject to executive influence and suffers from corruption. It states that civilian authority's control over the police is weak and there are widespread corruption and indiscipline in the police administration. The report also narrates that police committed a number of extra-judicial killings and some persons died in police custody; while they routinely use torture, beatings, and other forms of abuses when interrogating the suspects. The police frequently beat the demonstrators of opposition parties and even the members of the parliament are not safe from their beating while they are on the streets in processions. Citing the government's records, the report claims that 101 persons died in prisons and police custody during the first nine months of 1999. During the same period 1320 persons were detained under Section 54 and 739 persons were arrested under Special Powers Act in the capital city alone. A two judge High Court panel in a recent ruling criticised the police force for rampant use of detention laws and powers.[11]

A recent report of Dhaka Chamber of Commerce and Industries (DCCI) states that at present the business community and the industrialists have become the main targets of the rent seekers. Inability to meet their demands for money may risk the lives of the businessmen and the industrialists. In a statement the members of DCCI demanded the safety of their lives and properties.[12] Manik Manir reported in the *Daily Inqilab* that 19 persons were murdered in the capital city[13] alone in the month of May, 1999. In an illustrated article Mansoor Mamoon reported that violent crimes against women registered an alarming upward swing by about 20 percent in 1998 compared to 1997. He also stated that in the month of October, 1998 alone there were 166 incidents of rape, 11 incidents of dowry murder and 24 incidents of acid throwing. It was also shameful that about 200 female students of a public university were raped at gun point and sexually abused by their powerful male counterparts (who were mainly student leaders of the student wing of a political party) and on protest of that happenings the girl students had to go on strike and other movements. But the results were not very encouraging.[14] However, they could at least organize themselves against such violence. Faruq Choudhury states in another article that "corruption and the lack of performance by the education sector in Bangladesh is doing irreparable damage—a damage that will take decades and generations to make up, even if corrective measures were to be undertaken now."[15]

Menon states in a recent article that a nexus of the musclemen and gangsters with local police and political leadership has developed in recent periods. Police use them for different purposes, sometimes as sources of black money while political leaders patronige and induct them in their own parties for using them in election vote-cutting. The criminals are now not only the master of the situation, but they are now up in the ladder of political leadership. He opines ". . . this criminalization process goes on while the political leadership is keeping their eyes shut, because they need them to bolster their own political prospects."[16]

Farooque in an article observes that, if politics is accepted as a business, it establishes high corruption as an accepted behavioural norm. The two major political parties open the doors for those who did everything in their lives except politics. As a result, dedicated party workers are left far behind. So, in a high stake political game, the persons who are able to raise money for the party and capable to manage musclemen, terrorists and extortionists to work for the gains of the party, become in the frontline; and are usually getting nominations for fighting in the parliamentary elections. Honesty, quality and dedications sometimes become meaningless under such circumstances. As a result, some god-fathers of underworld crime syndicates can easily become members of the parliaments.[17]

3. IMPACT ON DEVELOPMENT

To what extent corruption damages the national income of Bangladesh can easily be understood from a recent World Bank's report. It states that a reasonable elimination of corruption in Bangladesh, can easily add about 3 percent to its Gross Domestic Product (GDP). It adds, "per capita income in corruption-free Bangladesh could have nearly doubled to US $700 instead of US $350". All these reflect the harmful impact of corruptions including "bribery, kickbacks and similar under-the-table payments in investment levels and misallocated resources."[18]

A recent publication of Asian Development Bank (ADB) titled: *Asian Development Outlook 2000* states on the growth prospects of Bangladesh that the country's annual growth target of 7 percent envisaged in the Fifth Five Year Plan remains unattainable, not because the country lacks economic potential, but because the country have been seriously clouded by political conflicts, strikes, endemic corruptions and lack of good governance.[19]

All these hamper the climate of investment and the inflow of foreign direct investment (FDI). Sinha[20] argues that "obstacle by the vicious circles of organised crimes to the market mechanism and investment, perpetuate the low productivity, low income, low viable employment and ultimately low level of development". So, corruption does innumerable harms to our society and nation.

4. WHAT CAN BE DONE IN NEAR FUTURE?

Poverty, illiteracy, over population, backward technology, low levels of savings and investments, etc. are usually identified as the main causes of corruption. But, if we study the recent cases of corruption, new causes are added to old ones. At present, most of the leaders of crime syndicates come from affluent society. They are educated and wealthy persons. So, there is something wrong with our education. We do not provide our young generation with proper education. Hence, before eradicating poverty, we must eradicate the devils from the education sector. A total reform of the education sector is urgently needed. This reform, must equip our young generation with modern scientific knowledge as well as with our religious and cultural values. But, side by side, we must eradicate poverty, illiteracy and take care of development issues.

For improving the overall socio-economic conditions of Bangladesh, the World Bank offered some valuable suggestions which I want to mention here. These are : (1) placing the highest emphasis on human development; (2) improving governance and building strong institutions; (3) enhancing the competitiveness of the private sector; (4) managing and attracting foreign direct investment; (5) establishing the soundness of the financial system; and (6) maintaining a stable macro-economic environment.[21] Political commitment is a must for implementing these and other suggestions.

5. CONCLUSIONS

A more neglected area is the poor level of social capital which includes also social institutions within which individuals work and operate. These protect individual, civil and political liberties and freedom. A strong civil society needs the existence of diversified and active social organizations and the operation of a free media. Our conscious citizens must organize themselves for improving and developing our social capital.

In this country good governance remains a far cry for long. Poor governance is the existing real phenomenon. It includes lack of accountability for the actions of a government, lack of voices for the governed, existence of ineffective and partisan executives, political instability and violence, the absence of rule of law and, the prevalence of corruption. Our civil society and the political parties must come forward to improve the governance for leading towards good governance. The sooner our leaders understand it, the better for the nation as a whole.

NOTES AND REFERENCES

1. Sellin, Thorsten, (1968), "Criminology" in David L. Sills (ed.), *International Encyclopedia of the Social Sciences*, Vol. 3, The Macmillan Company & The Free Press, USA, p. 505.
2. Clinard, Marshall B., (1968), "White-Collar Crime" in *Ibid*., p. 483.
3. Sinha, Ajit Kumar, (2000), "Organised Crime and Political Economy of Development: The Indian Panorama". *The Indian Economic Journal*, Vol. 7, No. 3, January-March, p. 1.
4. Brown, Lesley (ed.), (1993), *The New Shorter Oxford English Dictionary*, Vol. 1, Clarendon Press, Oxford, p. 518.
5. Cressey, Dunald R., (1968), "Causes of Crime" in *International Encyclopedia of Social Sciences*, Vol. 3, p. 472.
6. Wilkins, Lesile T., (1968),"Offense Patterns" in *ibid*., p. 482.
7. Higgins, Benjamin, (1968), *Economic Development: Problems, Principles and Policies*, W.W. Norton & Company Inc., New York, p. 106.
8. Shelley, Mizanur Rahman, (1999), "28 Years of Bangladesh". *The National Weekly Holiday*, 15 October, p. 24.
9. Wahid, Shahnoor, (2000), "Democracy in Distress". *The Daily Independent*, 30 April, p. 28.
10. Hossain, Moazzem, (2000), "Fighting Corruption a Tall Order for the Government". *The Financial Express*, 12 April, Dhaka, p. 12.
11. Ahmed, Reazuddin (ed.), (2000), "US Report". *The Financial Express*, 27 February, p. 1.

12. Alam, Akhtarul (ed.), (2000), "Evaluation of the Latest Economic Situation of the Country by DCCI" (Bengali). *The Daily Dinkal,* 16 July, p. 8.
13. Manir, Manik, (2000), "Dhaka Megacity is the Heaven of Corruptionists". *The Daily Inqilab,* 13 June, p. 9.
14. Mamoon, Mansoor, (1999), "Violence Against Women". *The National Weekly Holiday,* 15 October, p. 34.
15. Choudhury, Faruq, (2000), "Corruption: Bangladesh's Major Challenge". *The Independent,* 30 April, p. 5.
16. Menon, Rashed Khan, (1997), "Criminalization of Politics". *The National Weekly Holiday,* 5 September, p. 9.
17. Farooque, Mahmud, (2000), "Money, Muscle and the Electroal Process". *The Daily Star,* 15 July, p. 4.
18. Hossain, *loc. cit.*
19. ADB (2000), *Asian Development Outlook 2000,* p. 126.
20. Sinha, *op. cit.* p. 10.
21. World Bank (1999), *Bangladesh: Key Challenges for the Next Millennium.*

16

Globalisation of Economy and Conflicts in South Asia

PRAMOD KUMAR

Conflicts are inevitable in the process of development. The conditions which generate conflict derive their life force from the interface of economic development, social structures and politics. These conflicts manifest into denial of, and restricted access to resources, which in other words, perpetuate conditions of deprivations and discriminations. For instance, corruption diverts resources meant for life enhancing facilities resulting into multiplication of conditions of structural violence. The life threatening deprivations directly leads to death and starvation.

The conflicts arising out of deprivations remain in the realm of invisibility and hence the relationship between the factors causing these remain obscure. In most of the exploitative situations, people fail to perceive that their interests are being harmed or they are being injured (physically or psychologically) because of the actions of others or because of the nature of exploitative social structures.[1] In fact, most of the conflicts that occur in societies remain latent. It is possible that the non-observance of conflicts give rise to the belief that there is a genuine consensus about the prevailing location of values. To draw such a conclusion is to rule out the possibility of false or manipulated consensus.

The institutionalisation of conflict involves just a kind of unspoken adoption of key assumptions behind which there is a pragmatically dictated agreement but not legitimisation of positive consensus. What actually happens in this case is that the structure remains in the forefront and the subject whose interest these structures serve is pushed into the background. Therefore, the conflicts emanating from such a processes do not find easy resolution. In contrast to this, the conflicts which arise between parties, involved in pursuance of incompatible objectives, are empirical, observable and a conscious act.

Any attempt to understand these two forms of conflicts, it is necessary to place them in the context of specificities of historical experiences and the nature of socio-economic, political, cultural and religious formations. In other words,the interactions of the state with the path of development and consequential denial of legitimate claims produce conditions of structural disequilibrium.

The process of integrating countries into the global market has accentuated conflict. The developing countries have become more vulnerable to these dangerous trends.[2] 'Countries in transition from planned to market economies and from communist rule to parliamentary democracies are particularly hard hit by both corruption and the rising opportunities for "Frontier capitalism" and organised crime (*Shelly*, 1994; *White*, 1996).'[3]

The globalisation syndrome represents a kind of dualism. On the one hand, there is globalisation of capital and, on the other, there is localisation of human capital (labour), their aspirations, culture, history, language, etc. This phenomenon has provided impetus to the "sons of the soil" movements throughout the world and has led to the explosion of ethnic identities. 'The worldwide magnitude of ethnic rebellion, for example, increased nearly fourfold between the period 1950-55 and the years 1985-89".[4]

The emerging phenomena of localisation of conflicts can further be captured from the data, which show that most of the conflicts that erupted in the world were intra-state in the decade of 1990s.

TABLE 1
Interstate and Intrastate Armed Conflict, 1988-89

Type of conflicts	*1989*	*1990*	*1991*	*1992*	*1993*	*1994*	*1995*	*1996*	*1997*	*1998*	*All years*
Intrastate	43	44	49	52	42	42	34	33	30	32	92
Intrastate with foreign intervention	1	2	1	2	4	0	0	1	3	2	9
Interstate	3	3	1	1	0	0	1	2	1	2	7
All armed conflicts	47	49	51	55	46	42	35	36	34	36	108

Source: Peter Wallensteen and Margreta Sollenberg (1998), *States in Armed Conflicts, 1998*, Report No. 54, Deptt. of Peace and Conflict Research.

The situation has nurtured those factors which made both latent (life reducing mechanisms like corruption etc.) and manifest (ethnic, gender atrocities) violence more pervasive.

Most of these conlicts erupted in Asia and Africa. Out of the total 36-armed conflicts in the year 1998, the Asia (15) and Africa (14) experienced 29 conflicts.[5]

TABLE 2

Number of Armed Conflicts by Region, 1989-98

	Europe	*Middle East*	*Asia*	*Africa*	*Americas*
1989	2	4	19	14	8
1990	3	6	18	17	5
1991	6	7	16	17	5
1992	9	7	20	15	4
1993	10	7	15	11	3
1994	5	5	15	13	4
1995	5	4	13	9	4
1996	1	5	14	14	2
1997	0	3	15	14	2
1998	2	3	15	14	2

Source: Peter Wallensteen and Margreta Sollenberg (1998), *States in Armed Conflict, 1998,* Report No. 54, Deptt. of Peace and Conflict Research.

The phenomena of explosion of identities has become more visible in the post-colonial South Asian countries. The assertion of these identities transcend territorial boundaries. For instance, the assertions of *Panjabi identity* transcend the territorial boundaries of India and Pakistan, *the Tamil identity*–India and Sri Lanka, *Bengali identity*–India and Bangladesh, *Gorkha identity*–India and Nepal, *Sindhi identity*–India and Pakistan. The explosion of these identities has the potential to disintegrate the whole of South-Asian region. The assertion of these identities questions religion as well as communal-based identities. Therefore, the expedient politics order to weaken the process of identity formation excessively relies on communal and religious mobilisation. This explosion of identities in fact is a negation of the ideological basis on which the nation-building project has been conceived–a case in point is the partition of India on the basis of religion and the formation of Pakistan.

To illustrate, the post-colonial state responds to the autonomy assertions within the same framework. For instance, the Liberation of Tamil Tigers Eelem's (LTTE) armed resurgence could not get the support of the Indian establishment inspite of the pressure put by the Tamil alliance partners in the central government. The arguments reported in the media were that such a support would result in a movement for a separate Tamil state in the region. Similarly, in Kashmir, both the Indian and the Pakistani establishments present it as an Islamic *Jehad* rather than a movement for the preservation of the ethno-cultural identity of Kashmir. The fear is that this would in turn result in restructuring the territorial boundaries of the two countries.

The manner in which these countries have pursued the project of nation building and coupled with the adverse realities of the market has accentuated the crisis.

The quest of the post-colonial states for emerging as a nation by melting diverse interests into a monolith entity has led to the subversion of the rights of cultural and linguistic identities. The process of homogenisation by undermining multi-cultural realities and disparate aspirations and identities has led to the negation of the rights of the collectivities. These collectivities started redefining their boundaries by reinforcing the 'traditional purity of culture.'[6] They felt threatened by a superimposed dominant culture. In a multi-cultural society extremism survives and even thrives on the state of mind of a group arising out of a feeling that a threat, real or imaginary, exists to their faith which should be combated by collective action.

This was mainly the result of the institutionalisation of the western notion of inalienable rights of the individual, whereas the politics and social discourse relied on ascriptive categories for the mobilisation and maintenance of their support base. The western notion of inalienable rights was antithetical to the interests of the colonial powers which, therefore, were slow to promote the notion among the colonialised.[7] On the contrary, the focus of British colonialism was to sharpen the distinctions by institutionalising practices on the basis of group identities. There was a conscious policy of misappropriating perceived notions about the ethnic superiority and inferiority of the groups and providing accesses to economic and political or social opportunities on the basis of these notions. The policy of group distribution of colonial opportunities was set in motion. The underlying assumption of these policies was the incompatibility of economic and political interests of the groups and, therefore, need for separate politics. This kind of political activity emphasised the particularistic aspects of social existence. It is this specific nature of socio-cultural or economic and political development in the presence of traditional structures and organisations that acquires retrogressive assertions. The interaction of these deformed group identities with modern institutions have reaffirmed and consolidated the already existing reservoir of mistrust and suspicion among the various castes, regions and religious groups.

The project of nation building took the initiatives away from the community to the sub-system, from the sub-system to the state and ultimately to the dominant powers in the global system. This was justified on the basis of common good and majority rule being the divine goals pursued by the state. Therefore, participation of the people became symbolic and their role in conflict identification and resolution was marginalised. Each hierarchical layer abdicated its responsibilities to the higher layer. For instance, community systems abdicated their responsibility to the sub-system and sub-system to the state and state to the dominant power in the global system. "What was not brought to the surface was that this philosophy was a power philosophy, the common good turned out to be both at domestic and international level, the common good as interpreted by the powerful".[8]

In this scheme superior position and knowledge to resolve conflict has been attributed to the external "interventionist". This system has failed to resolve conflict. On the contrary, it has reinforced the existing conflicts and nurtured the conditions for their growth. In response to the ineffectiveness of the existing interventionist mechanisms, the states and within the states sub-systems have started abdicating their responsibilities regarding resolution of conflicts to and in favour of the community at the grassroot level. In fact, catch phrases such as power back to the people are being bandied about, to cover their inability to perform the necessary functions for the resolution of conflicts. In nutshell, these countries lack resources to respond to the welfare and security needs of a large number of their population.

Therefore, it is not surprising to find that most of the violent conflicts are erupting in countries without resources. Data show that of more than 150 major violent conflicts have erupted, since the Second World War, 130 have been fought in the developing world in general and the South Asian countries in particular. These countries have suffered a major set back because of the recurrent armed conflicts. The escalation of these conflicts has led to the multiplication of military spending, a diversion of funds from life supporting systems.

Developing countries devote on average only 13 per cent of their national budgets ($57 billion a year) to basic human development concerns. They have considerable scope for changing their budget priorities, by reducing their military spending around $125 billion a year.[9]

The report further exemplifies the human development cost of arms import in certain countries. For instance,

India–ordered 20 MiG-29 fighter aircraft from Russia at a cost that could have provided basic education to all the 15 million girls out of schools.

Pakistan–ordered 40 Mirage 2000E fighters and three Tripartite aircraft from France at a cost that could have provided safe water for two years for all 55 million people who lack safe water, family planning services for the estimated 20 million couples in need of such serivces, essential medicines for the nearly 13 million people without access to health care and basic education for the 12 million children out of primary school.[10]

And in such a situation, the trend of globalisation has provided a new context to these conflicts. This shift has meant greater power and autonomy with the market forces. The escalation of violent conflicts in a post-cold war globalised world, has brought to the surface that it is a continuation of dominant power philosophy in an aggravated form. The nation-state has surrendered to the market in the sphere of both the path and pace of development. In certain spheres some states having competitive advantage may benefit in terms of getting higher investment from multinationals and experience greater autonomy. But the backward states, even if they achieve constitutional autonomy, will see their backwardness multiplied in real terms as the market forces acquire greater autonomy to transcend non-friendly economies. The developing countries are being integrated into the new economic global order without having any autonomy to dissent. The economic integration with political marginalisation is the end result. These countries are being coerced to sign economic agreements. For instance, the WTO agreement has been arrived through 'consensus' rather using the well accepted democratic principle of one country–one vote. Consensus conceals coercion. It is in this context the Human Development Report recorded.

Small and poor countries generally participate little in global economic rule-making for a host of reasons, starting with the costs of participation and policy research. Just as nations require an inclusive democracy to guarantee respect for human rights, so the system of global governance needs to be transparent and fair, giving voice to small and poor countries and releasing them from their marginalisation from the benefits of the global economy and technology.[11]

Will the new reality of liberalisation of the economy with its emphasis on free market and scrapping of the protective regime grant autonomy to the states to reverse the process–the issue which granted the regime a popular mandate in the first place? The answer is obvious.

This shift has meant greater autonomy to the market forces. The real issue, therefore is "how the states can acquire autonomy to fix prices or nationalise foodgrain trade, from the market forces which are beyond their control?"[12]

Therefore, after signing of WTO agreement, will the countries be autonomous enough not to abide by the terms of the agreement which adversely affect their national interests? It has given rise to a paradox. The non-fulfilment of the national mandate, will result into deligitimisation of political system and shall provide fillip to intra-state conflicts such as fundamentalist movements. Whereas, the non-compliance of global mandate shall result into political isolation, and exposure to pressure both violent and 'peaceful' of the dominant global powers.

As mentioned above, in these post-colonial countries of South-Asia the organisation of societies around collectivities of caste, religion, ethnicity led to the explosion of identities without conditions for fulfilling the basic needs of these groups. The globalisation process empowered the market and weakened the nation state. The availability of resources for subsidies to finance social security and welfare programmes got further reduced. The political elites found illegitimate resources by opening up their economy to private sector and multinationals and used a part of this to dole out to their 'voters'.

> Political elites have often found the resources with which they 'finance' their political survival in economic exchanges with other groups of clients, in particular the slowly emerging class of industrial capitalists . . . Political 'corruption' led to economic corruption as each group of politicians organised their own network of resource collection and distribution.[13]

This increasing penetration of multinational has given further fillip to corrupt regimes like the conviction of Lockheed for making payments of $1.5 million to an Egyptian government official in 1995. The Bofors defense deal in India is well-known with respect to the kickbacks paid to high ranking public officials and politicians. The Human Development Report 2000 highlighted the role of global corporations and corrupt regimes in transferring resources from socially productive programmes to individual conspicuous consumption. 'Global corporations can have enormous impact on human right—in their employment practices, in their environmental impact, in their support for corrupt regimes or in their advocacy for policy changes.[14]

These tendencies results into channelising the capital into non-productive conspicuous consumption pattern which in turn affects the life chances of those who are living on the margins of society. The Bhopal gas disaster exposed the distortions like callousness of the market, inhuman face of multi-national corporations, corrupt system of governance. In this disaster a large number of people have died and many others are dying a slow death and still many are waiting for the justice to be done to them.

> The Bhopal gas was the climax of a hazardous system sponsored by a development paradigm that has been, even in its origins, profoundly anti-people and anti-nature . . . . The damage to persons, the corruption of politics and the degradation of nature, which until recently were only implicit in development can now be seen, touched and smelled.[15]

These developments have depicted the ugly face of development paradigm. This is being sustained by global authoritarianism. Consequently to realise 'other utopias' are negligible and even desire to speculate about 'other possibility' is being tamed. One is in agreement with Jan Oberg's observation that 'our best weapons' are better thoughts, ideas, ethics, compassion and networking and independent minds in an increasingly authoritarian era the slogan of which is that 'there are no alternatives'. There is a need to have a dialogue to create alternatives to cater to the needs of the poor.

As has been mentioned, conflict is a result of certain social conditions and is also inseparable from the existence and functioning of economic processes and political institutions.

The need is to evolve a collaborative international relationship between the states and within the states, among sub-systems and the community, particularly in post-colonial South Asian countries to resolve conflicts. The perspective needs to be interactive with the various components of the larger global world setting, while ensuring relative autonomy to various sub-systems within this. Therefore, the process of conflict resolution can be categorised into inter-state level in the global context and intra sub-system level in the local context. And strategies may be worked out to ensure the relative autonomy of each unit so that they are able to:

A. Identify their own conflicts according to their socio-cultural specific needs.
B. Work out resolution strategies maximising on existing authority system within the sub-system.

The emphasis of this approach is to sufficiently empower the parties in the conflict to identify and resolve these by themselves. This does not mean that the role of non-parties or observers in the conflict situation has no place in this scheme of things. On the contrary, their role is in correspondence with the international relationship which each layer has evolved within the larger global system. The conventional methods of conflict resolution may have to be amended to respond to the new set of issues posed by changes in socio-economic formations and developments in politics, culture and religion. And also to respond to the specificities of social institutions and norms like casteism, racism, religiosity and gender relations which have played a central role in shaping the conflict of divergent sorts.

The process of resolution of conflicts necessitates empowerment of the community and create conditions for democratisation of the global system of governance. To moderate the callousness of the market forces, the need is to strengthen regional institutions, for instance, SAARC in the case of South Asia. It has to be multi-

Issues *Solving Process*	*Achieving* *Conflict moderation*	*To be Achieved* *Conflict resolution*
1. Identifying alternatives	• Attempts towards strengthening SAARC • Attempts towards state autonomy • Towards empowerment of community organisation	• Achieving confederation of South-Asian countries • Achieving of state autonomy within national constitutional federalism • Decentralisation of power to grass-roots organisatons
2. Option Analysis Political–economic and cultural autonomy	Economic package	Structural transformation of economy, recognition of cultural and linguistic aspirations.
3. Redefining goals	• Peace • Social and religious harmony	Distributive justice
4. Activisation of decision-making process	• Democratisation of politics, i.e. holding of elections • Representation of cultural groups in decision-making bodies • Evolving institutional mechanisms for ensuring linguistic, religious and cultural rights of minorities	Secularisation of polity, i.e. effective people's participation in decision-making, democratisation of politics, economy and society.

staged process of conflict resolution with the active participation of the stakeholder at each corresponding layer to address the existing problematic of political marginalisation, economic exploitation and cultural hegemony.

NOTES AND REFERENCES

1. A classic example of structural conflict is the Indian caste system which regulates social life. The upper caste master demands 18 hours of daily working, sexual liaison with lower caste women etc. which is readily abided by the lower castes. This submission is normative and thus only refusal to accept this domination would result in visible conflict situation. The

superordinate and subordinate relationship between the two has been evolved over time and internalised. For instance, the labourer, due to his lower caste position, does not assert his right to use the village well, temple or even political franchise and accepts his treatment as an outcaste. In such a setting there is no conflict behaviour. This situation cannot be defined as free from conflict even though both the actors conform to rules and there is value consensus between them, in other words, conflict behaviour and attitude only constitutes the manifest evidence of the prevalence of conflict. Conditions of scarcity and incompatibility of interests are determined by social structures. Social structures may, and often do, favour interests of some against those of others.

2. India and Pakistan were found to be among the most corrupt nations in the world. In a study conducted by Gallup International (GIA), India was ranked 73rd and Pakistan ranked 88th from among 99 countries. The ranking was determined by the 'corruption' index' and 'bribe payers' perception index'. India had a score of 2.9 on a scale of ten to one, "There has been a marginal increase in the score, from 2.63 in 1996 to 2.9 now," it said. Pakistan was perceived as being more corrupt than India, though only marginally, ranking 88 with a score of 2.2.
   Indian Express, 26 October, 1999.
3. Newman, Graeme (ed.), (1999), *Global Report on Crime and Justice*, New York: Oxford University Press, p. 277.
4. Gur, Ted Robert and Harff, Barbara, (1994), *Ethnic Conflict in World Politics*, Boulder Westview Press, p. 11.
5. Wallensteen, Peter and Sollenberg, Margreta, (1998), *States in Armed Conflicts, 1998*, Report No. 54, Deptt. of Peace and Conflict Research.
6. Descending social groups or disadvantaged groups may deploy elements of the cultural repertoire or utilize cultural resources to mobilize and organise opposition and create a movement. The language of opposition may be more strongly cultural even though a motivation and cause of opposition is economic and social disadvantage.
   Moghadam Valentine M., (1994), Introduction: Women and Identity Politics in Theoretical and Comparative Perspective in Moghadam V. Ed. *Identity Politics and Women*, Boulder Westview Press, p. 8.
7. Patterson, V. Spike, (1990), 'Whose Rights? A Critique, *Alternatives* XV, pp. 303-4.
8. Burton, John, (1990), *Conflict Resolution and Prevention*, Macmillan, p. 42.
9. Human Development Report, (1994), New York: Oxford University Press, p. 7.
10. *Ibid.*, p. 54.
11. Human Development Report, (2000), New York: Oxford University Press, p. 10.
12. For instance, the trend of globalisation of the economy has provided a new context to the autonomy debate. The Shiromani Akali Dal (SAD) in Punjab in its 1973 autonomy resolution and later on in its 1985 memorandum to the Sarkaria Commission, set up to study centre-state relations, asked for apportionment of financial resources within the framework of command economy. In the 1973 resolution the Akali Dal demanded, "Complete

nationalisation of the trade in foodgrains and as such, shall endeavour to nationalise the wholesale trade in foodgrains through the establishment of state agencies." It further stated that 'the SAD shall try to fix the prices of the agricultural produce on the basis of the returns of middle class farmers. Such prices would be notified well before the sowing season and only the state governments would be empowered to fix such prices."

13. Khan, Mushtaq, H. (1998), Patron-Client Networks and Economic Effects of Corruption in Asia in Mark Robinson (ed.) *Corruption and Development*, London: Frank Cass, p. 28.
    To substantiate, India's capital flight to the United States during 1994 and 1995 was to the tune of four to eleven billion dollars. As the US accounts for nearly twenty per cent of India's exports as compared to thirty-five per cent to other hard currency areas, capital flight from India to those countries during these two years would work out to an additional seven to nineteen billion dollars on a pro-rata basis. *Times of India*, 30 January, 1997.
14. Human Development Report, 2000, Oxford University Press, p. 10.
15. Alvares Claude, (1994), *Science Development and Violence: The Revolt Against Modernity*, Delhi: Oxford University Press, p. 5.

17

Genesis of Crime and Corruption and their Impact on Development

GULAB MOHITE AND S.P. MALAPUR

An attempt is made in this paper to unearth the underlying forces behind crime and to find out whether there is any correlation between crime, corruption and the process of economic development of a country with specific reference to India. This paper is divided into three sections. Section I deals with the genesis of crime and corruption embedded in the organic process of social evolution. Section II tries to identify the causes of corruption and crime in the light of the 'rule of law' in contrast to arbitrariness and discretionary powers being misused by the public officials and servants. Competitive market mechanism is impersonal authority to establish a just society. It also draws attention to the correlation between crime and corrupt practices associated with the development process. Section III is concerned with the remedial measures.

I

INTRODUCTION

Crime and corruption have long history but the task is to unravel the nexus between crime, corruption and development. Certain revealing observations are made on the criminal-political nexus by a committee headed by N.N. Vohra, the then Home

Secretary. Following are some of the extracts from the Report:

"CBI has reported that all over India Crime Syndicates have become a law unto themselves. Even in the smaller towns and rural areas, muscle-men have become the order of the day. Hired assassins have become a part of these organisations. The nexus between the criminal gangs, police, bureaucracy and politicians has come out clearly in various parts of the country. The existing criminal justice system, which was essentially designed to deal with individual offences, crimes, is unable to deal with the activities of the Mafia; the provisions of law in regard to economic offences are weak; there are insurmountable legal difficulties in attaching/confiscation of the property acquired through Mafia activities."

The state of the nexus between crime, corruption and politics is best summed up by the observations of the DIB. The DIB has stated that there has been a rapid spread and growth of criminal gangs, armed senas, drug mafias, smuggling gangs, drug peddlers and economic lobbies in the country which have, over the years, developed an extensive network of contacts with the bureaucrats/government functionaries at the local levels, politicians, media persons and strategically located individuals in the non-state sector. Some of these syndicates also have international linkages, including the foreign intelligence agencies. The DIB has given the following examples:

(i) In certain states, like Bihar, Haryana and UP, these gangs enjoy the patronage of local level politicians, cutting across partylines and the protection of governmental functionaries. Some political leaders become the leaders of these gangs/armed senas and, over the years, get themselves elected to local bodies, State Assemblies and the National Parliament. Resultantly, such elements have acquired considerable political clout seriously jeopardising the smooth functioning of the administration and the safety of life and property of the common man, causing a sense of despair and alienation among the people.

(ii) The big smuggling syndicates, having international linkage, have spread into and infected the various economic and financial activities, including havala transactions, circulation of black money and operations of vicious parallel economy causing serious damage to the economic fibre of the country. These syndicates have acquired substantial financial and muscle power and social respectability and have successfully corrupted the government machinery at all levels and yield enough influence to make the task of investigating and prosecuting agencies extremely difficult: even the members of the judicial system have not escaped the embrace of the Mafia.

(iii) Certain elements of the Mafia have shifted to narcotics, drugs and weapon smuggling and established macro-terrorism networks, specially in the states of J & K, Punjab, Gujarat and Maharashtra. The cost of contesting elections has thrown the politicians into the lap of these elements and led to a grave compromise by officials of the preventive/detective systems. The virus has spread to almost all the centres in the country: the coastal and the border states have been particularly affected.

On the basis of the extensive experience gained by our various concerned intelligence, investigative and enforcement agencies, it is apparent that Crime Syndicates and Mafia Organisations have established themselves in various parts of the country. The various Crime Syndicates/Mafia Organisations have developed significant muscle and money power and established linkages with governmental functionaries, political leaders and others to be able to operate with impunity.

II

CAUSES OF CORRUPTION

Incentives for corrupt behaviour arise whenever government officials have more discretion and little or no accountability. Some corruptions arise from opportunities created by policy environment both at the bottom or the top of hierarchy. Commissions are frequently found at lower-level officials charged with collections of taxes, providing police protection, issuing permits or licences. When corruption is endemic, these officials may create additional red tape and delay to induce even higher extractions. Corruption also occurs at the highest levels of government in awarding of contracts, privatisation, in allocation of import quotas, regulation of natural monopolies, distribution systems due to distorted policies, e.g. black market exchange rate premium, lending and borrowing interest rates. Any policy that generates an artificial gap between demand and supply creates a profitable opportunity for greedy middlemen. Corruption is likely to be high where the government system does little to check bribes. When law-breakers believe that there is little chance of being caught or if caught the system can be corrupted or penalty or punishment is less than proportionate than the gain, corruption prospers.

For analytical purpose, causes can be classified into specific clusters:

(a) *Politics-related:* Election frauds, vote purchasing, patronage, sale of public offices, rigging ballot boxes, favouritism and wanton disregard for law and order.

(b) *Law-related:* Deliberate avoidance to enforce law; discretionary application of penal actions, harassment and intimidation, wilful failure to prosecute; treating differently based on wealth and power of criminals.

c) *Finance and Business-related:* Unequal assessment of taxes, licensing for consideration, land allotment by accepting bribes, giving government contract on financial considerations, purchases of supplies, closed bidding, indiscriminate lending by banks and financial institutions, etc.

The unaccounted money distorted the pattern of investment, not conducive to economic development. This led to unequal and iniquitous distribution of income and wealth among the community. Corruption manifested itself in the form of evasion of taxes, income tax, corporation tax, excise duty, sales tax, custom duty, etc. According to one estimate (Suraj B. Gupta), black money in the country is of the order of Rs. 1,49,300 crore for the year 1987-88.

Impact of Crime and Corruption on Development

The impact of the crime and corruption is likely to have

debilitating effect on the economic development. Following are some of the manifestations of crime and corruption:

(i) *Less than optimal use of resources*: An efficient allocation of resources is what is required for development. Any distortion or deviation results into wasteful use of resources. Scarce resources are employed in less socially useful and fruitful areas. For instance, unproductive profits create in consumption demand through which scarce foreign exchange is squandered for the import of conspicuous consumption items for the rich while essential capital goods for development are rationed.

(ii) *Adverse Impact on the Flow of Foreign Capital Particularly Foreign Direct Investment:* Corruption between political bosses and bureaucracy on the one hand and MNCs on the other lead to competitive corrupt methods to entice the granting authorities in recipient countries is a clear case of corruption. On the other hand, the corrupt practices and the high rents sought may force foreign investment to shy away from the country.

(iii) *Destabilising political situation*: MNCs can contribute massive political funds to parties favourable to them and their easy entry. The funds are being used to fight elections in a way to get those parties to win and gain power who are favourable to them. The victim is the democratic fabric of the country which may result in distorted development catering to the greed of the MNCs but not needs of the people.

(iv) *Distortion of Priorities*: Planned priorities get distorted if bribes and payoffs induce the diversion of real resource from socially high priority sector to low priority areas. Economic reform measures may not be able to achieve the desired results.

(v) *Adverse impact on law and order*: Corruption and crime create uncertainty, sense of helpless among people. Some people violate rules via crime and corruption. The perception of economic, social environment gets vitiated.

(vi) *Adverse impact on professional ethics and values*: Ethical values in all professions, business, at all level, get diluted due to crime and corruption in the society. Attitude towards work, efficiency level is affected adversely by prevalence of crime and corruption.

III

HOW TO REDUCE CORRUPTION?

Is it possible eliminate crime and corruption all together from all walks of life? The answer is negative because corrupt and criminal behaviour are tendencies of human beings. But the experience from elsewhere shows it can be reduced substantially. The task is Herculean but development ultimately could also be seen as a process of elimination of crime and corruption from the social fabric of a nation.

One of the basic requirements is the Establishment of Rule of Law. Controls, regulations, restrictions and licensing are the root causes of corruption. While it may not be in the social interest to eliminate these interventions altogether, transparency along with improved informed decision-making process may mitigate the problem. It is necessary to reduce and minimise the level of benefits arising out of the exercise of arbitrary powers vested in public servants and officials including the political bosses. If the rule of law is established and enforced, no individual is above the law of the land. If the government does not have the authority to restrict exports or imports or licence businesses, no one will pay the bribes. If subsidies are eliminated, the bribes that induce the authorities to grant subsidies which become the source of corruption will be eliminated. If price controls are lifted, market prices will reflect scarcity values, not bribes. If a parastral is a locus of corrupt pay-offs, privatising it will eliminate corruption. These changes should be effected in a manner that does not lead to market induced social costs which may deny certain welfare to the poorer sections.

Effective Enforcement of Law

Tough laws are necessary but not sufficient condition. There ought to be an effective machinery to enforce the laws. A strong independent judiciary can play this part. In India, the Supreme Court did push forward a corruption investigation that the government wanted to quash. If judiciary is to be effective, there are two prerequisites: (i) Judiciary must be paid very high salaries and future security. The working conditions and future economic security should be sufficiently attractive. (ii) The second condition is to insulate judiciary from executive authorities and day-to-day political pressures. Anti-corruption measures should be undertaken through appropriate machinery. Hong Kong experience is worth emulating. Simplification of tax laws to reduce bureaucratic discretion and having lower rates of tax are likely to result into better tax compliance. Less number of deductible items in taxation should be introduced.

Awareness about Benefits and Costs under Public Servants Control

Educating and creating public opinion against corruption will go a long way in fighting corruption. There are many officials who have immaculate record of unblemished and integrated character. They remain honest despite considerable temptations. The names of such people must be published through media so as to set exemplary behaviour. Efforts should be made to understand that the actual extent of corruption may not depend only on potential gains and risks but also on relative bargaining power of the players.

Minimizing Opportunities for Corrupt Practices

Competition ensures efficiency. Generally, any reform that increases competitiveness of the economy will reduce incentives for corrupt behaviour. Elimination of substitutes ushers in an element of monopoly power. Private monopolies are the result of government controls and regulations. Import/Export controls, barriers to entry tend to breed corruption. If price controls are removed, market prices will reflect scarcity values, not the payment of payoffs/bribes. Reducing official discretion through reforms are useful in containing corruption. However, reducing discretion does not mean removing regulatory measures. Welfare programmes with strong socio-economic justification need not be abandoned. Ambiguous laws generate uncertainties which in turn enhances the discriminating powers of the enforcing machinery. Complex laws subject to various interpretations are the breeding ground for confusion—a sure way for corrupt people to thrive. Hence, the need for simplification of laws and procedures. Deterrent punishment, vigilant body to monitor, citizens forums against corruption and administrative reforms involving greater competitive environment are some other measures needed for containing corruption.

REFERENCES

Ajit Kumar Sinha, "Organised Crime and Political Economy of Development—The Indian Panorama" (pp. 1 to 11) *The Indian Economic Journal,* Special Number, Vol. 47, No. 3, January-March, 1999-2000.

"A Global War Against Bribery", *Monthly Public Opinion Survey,* 1999 (pp. 30-32).

B.N. Uniyal, "Realising Power by misusing power, defying authority", *The Sunday Observer,* May 21-27, 2000, Mumbai.

Bibek Debroy, "The Roots of Corruption", Article courtesy Barons, Vol. 2, No. 4, http://www.mumbainet.com/magazine/roots of.htm

Dilip Raote, "Queuing up for corruption", *The Sunday Observer,* April 2-8, 2000, Mumbai.

Laurie, A. Rhodebeck (May 1993), pp. 342-64, *The Journal of Politics,* Vol. 55, No. 2, 1993, University of Texas Press.

N. Vittal (28.6.2000), "Towards Corruption Free - Services", *The Business Standard* (Daily, Mumbai.)

Ruddar Datt (1997), *Economic Reforms in India,* Chapter 22, pp. 303-9, A Critique (S. Chand and Company, New Delhi).

Robert Kittgaard, "International Co-operation Against Corruption", *Monthly Public Survey,* 1999. (pp. 10-15).

R.K. Raghavan (July 7, 2000,) "A Case Study on Crime", *Frontline.*

Sudesh Kumar Sharma (1978), (ed.) *Dynamics of Development—An International Perspective* (volume one), (Concept Pub. Co., New Delhi).

Transparency International, (1999), Annual Report, *Source*: Internet.

UNSDRI (May 1976), Econòmic Publication No. 15 (Rome), *Crisis and Crime,* UNSDRI (United Nations and Social Defence Research Institute).

World Bank (1997), *Annual World Bank Conference on Development Economics,* (ed.) Boris Ples Kovie and Joseph E. Stiglitz, pp. 35-180.

World Bank (1996), *World Development Report.*

World Bank (1997), *World Development Report* (Chapter 6, pp. 99-109), "Restraining Arbitrary State and Corruption".

18

Industrialisation, Environmental Pollution, Crime and Corruption: A Case Study

N.C. Ghosh

I

INTRODUCTION

Crime has been variously defined as 'antisocial act,' 'a failure or refusal to live up to the standard of conduct deemed binding by the rest of the community', and 'an act or omission, forbidden by law under pain of punishment'.[1] All these definitions emphasise on the attitude of society. Therefore, the concept of crime changes with the change of social structure. Specially industrial revolution has influenced to define the term crime in a new way. It is expected that due to the advent of modern technology in the 21st Century this definition will take a new shape. Corruption is a form of crime, has a circular causation, and the root of the both are money and power.

Crime causation theory is closely linked with anthropology, psychiatry, social psychology and sociology. The study of criminal acts and crime rates have been expressed in two principal forms. Firstly, criminologists have studied the processes by which persons become criminals and have developed theories. Secondly, criminologists have studied the relation of crime rates to variations in cultural and social organisation and have developed theories of crime.[2] Theories about the distribution of crime rates and theories about social systems are closely related to more general theories of social structure. William Healy's[3] multifactor approach is perhaps the most popular approach for integrating explanation of crime rates and explanation of individual criminology.

When the multifactor approach is used in the study of crime rates, the investigator merely lists conditions (factors) that are statistically associated, to a high or low degree, with crime. Generally speaking, the higher the degree of association, the more in the importance ascribed to a particular condition.

'Social Structure' theories of crime causation has been developed by Robert K. Merton.[4] Besides these theories Psychological theories, Psychiatric theories, Sociological theories, Limited theories are important.[5-8] In recent years environmental concepts have come up in a new form. No theory based on environmental aspects to determine causation of crime has yet been developed. The problem of heterogeneity has complicated the study of crime/corruption distribution function when the environmental factors are included in the investigation.

Here, the study is restricted to certain environmental aspects related to a thermal power station, a component of modern science and technology-based society, and how these influence crime and corruption in the area close to the thermal power station.[9]

II

BASIC PROBLEM

It is a well known fact that land is a natural resource. Man uses land and in so doing may deplete and eventually exhaust them. Also it is true that natural resources can sometimes be augmented (for example soil fertility can be improved, fisheries stocked can be increased in water bodies or changing soil strength may make it useful for building construction) but depletion is perhaps more common. So pessimistic propositions are: (i) The world is finite. This places a limit on resource supplies and hence on the level of output that can be sustained. (ii) Meadows[10] stated, nearly all . . . of mankind's current activities can be represented by exponential growth curves. The curves include the level of output. (iii) Growth in output is necessarily brought to halt when the supply limit is reached. (iv) This limit will be reached soon. (v) The effect of reaching this limit is likely to be disastrous. (vi) Deliberate attempt must be made to modify the tendency to exponential growth and to limit mankind's activities to the constraints imposed by finiteness of the world.

Most important factors in alleviating resource scarcity are: (a) Advances in existing resource efficiency, (b) Advances in transport, (c) New methods of economising on resource use, (d) Development of substitutes in resource use, and (e) More complex substitutions.

Optimists stress the role of price in triggering the various mechanism for alleviating resource scarcity. As resource becomes scare, its price should rise.[11]

Price of resource/commodity is considered as its value. Market value is defined as: The estimated amount for which an asset should exchange on the date of valuation between a willing buyer and a willing seller in an arm's length transaction after proper marketing wherein the parties had each acted knowledgeably prudently and without compulsion.[12] It is needless to mention that value is directly related with optimal resource.

Economic growth is normally defined in terms of G.N.P. Constraining the over-all change in some aggregative index such as G.N.P. to zero is neither desirable or feasible and so is Zero Economic Growth (Z.E.G.).[13]

Environmentalist have rightly stressed the interconnectedness of everything and the inadequacies of a partial approach. But the question is whether Zero Environmental Degradation (including resource depletion) [Z.E.D.] is possible. Daly[14-15] carefully stressed that Z.E.G. and Z.E.D. are long-term objectives and part of the wider objective of the stationary state. Continuous changes in the society is a physical contradiction of the stationary state concept. As Z.E.G. is not desirable, there is a sustainable growth in the power generation capacity either in developed or in developing countries. Z.E.D. may be achieved by environmental friendly measures.

Now-a-days special attention is given on various environmental factors and as a result in the land valuation this factor has also been incorporated. How environmental factors can influence land valuation surrounding a thermal plant are discussed here, keeping all the aspects stated above in mind. Also, the question of how changes in the valuation of land brings about changes in crime distribution surrounding thermal plants is discussed.

III

LAND VALUATION SURROUNDING A THERMAL POWER STATION

Like other places lands surrounding a thermal plant may be used for agricultural, fishery and residential purpose. Rules of valuation of land surrounding thermal plant depends on the utility and scarcity. Here these cases are discussed separately.

Pollution Hazard Surrounding Bandel Thermal Power Station (BTPS)

Like other thermal power stations B.T.P.S. is generating energy polluting environment in several ways. Here the pollutions are: (i) Air pollution, (ii) Water pollution, (iii) Land pollution, (iv) Sound pollution, and (v) Cultural pollution. Air pollution is due to enormous amount of coal particles, ash, and gaseous pollutants. For one mega watt of electricity, 0.58 tonnes coal is needed, i.e. B.T.P.S. needs 6682 tonnes coal per day. Coal is not free of dust particles and at least 35% to 46% of ash is produced from each tonne of coal. That means total amount of coal used in B.T.P.S. everyday is producing at least 2339 tonnes of ash; 80% of this ash, i.e. 1871 tonnes is fly ash and rest, i.e. 468 tonnes is bottom ash.

There are several hoppers in B.T.P.S. viz. mechanical dust collector hopper, air preheater hopper, economiser hopper, electrostatic precipitator hopper, and stack hopper. The maximum amount of ash that can be collected by these hoppers is 1335 tonnes per day; out of which 1050 tonnes of fly ash and 285 tonnes of bottom ash. It means a good amount of fly-ash per day is emitted through the chimney along with flue gas into the atmosphere.

Valuation of Agricultural Land

In a survey[16-17] surrounding Bandel Thermal Power Station it is seen that discharged liquid from the plant is affecting flora and fauna. Discharged fly ash from the plant is changing fertility of the agricultural land around it. Effect on microbs of the discharged liquid and fly-ash is not only serious but also of long term nature. This damaged land can be improved using chemical and biological techniques upto the exponential growth limit of the land, if it is cost effective. But Meadows curves[10] declining production rate for the land near the plant is not at all cost effective.

Random dumping of fly-ash surrounding the thermal plant is changing the character of agricultural land permanently as a result of which changes in land valuation occur. Due to availability of electricity and establishment of new township after installation of a power plant, urbanisation starts near the thermal plant, and as a consequence of this link land valuation changes. Undoubtedly this is agricultural land valuation. Therefore, environmental concepts changes there.

Valuation of the Area Used for Fisheries

Fishery stock can fluctuate widely and unpredictably due to both climate variations and inbuilt cyclical processes resembling models of the trade cycle. Stocks may also follow secular trends as environmental conditions alter. This makes optimal management of a fishery a very complex task. When environmental factors are constant, and adjustment from a disequilibrium position is smooth, a logistic growth process is generally assumed[18] as $n = as(\bar{s} - s)$, where $n = as$ is proportionate growth, $\bar{s}$ is natural equilibrium growth and s is stock. From the survey[16] noted above, it is revealed that liquid discharged from the thermal plant contains hot water and chemicals which deeply affect the aqua animal lives. Fish growth rate has been reduced and some species have already disappeared.

Random dumping of fly-ash is filling the wet-land continuously reducing the catchment areas. Due to these factors the logistic growth process of fish in the vicinity of the thermal plant changed and as a consequence of which value of the wetland there changed. The residential area of the poor fishermen is also changing in its character. Thus, for money environmental crime is increasing with the changes in the land valuation.

Foundation Design and Construction

It has already been noted that installation of thermal power station starts urbanisation. Waste-land, agricultural land then are converted to residential areas. Some wet-lands are also used for construction of buildings/house. Naturally, then value of land used for urbanisation takes new pattern. Mobility of land value is then not uniform and related with complex social parameters. In short, here I will confine myself to analyze those aspects related with foundation deigns and construction.

Foundation is an important element of building of all civil engineering structure. Every structure is founded in or on the surface of the earth. Therefore, it is necessary to know the bearing capacity of the soil, the pattern of stress distributions in the soil beneath the loaded area, the probable settlement of the foundation, effect of ground water and the effect of vibrations, etc.[19]

A soil mass is a three phase system consisting of solid particles, water and air. The void space between the soil grains is filled partly with water and partly with air. In dry soil mass the voids are filled with air only. In case of perfectly saturated soil, the voids are filled completely with water. In general, the soil mass has three constituents which do not occupy separate spaces but are blended together forming a complex material, the properties of which depend upon the relative percentages of these constituents, their arrangement and a variety of other factors.

1335 tonnes of ash is discharged by Bandel Thermal Power Station everyday. Firstly, the large quantities of ash discharged from the thermal plant are collected in two ash ponds and then private promoters are removing this from ash ponds for dumping it according to their own choice. In most cases they prefer to use this huge quantity of fly ash to fill-up ponds and wetlands. Some times, it is also used for making low land high. Due to urbanisation, scarcity of land is causing high demand for residential land and as a result filled-up ponds, wet-lands and low land are also in high demand. The valuation of land for residential purpose is influenced by the cost of foundation. In the solidified ash land, water content, void ratio, porosity and degree of saturation are not the same as normal soil. Elasticity and plasticity of ash land is less than that of normal soil. Capillary siphoning through ash-land sometimes increases collapse potential, specially if ash land is nearer to water storage or just beside the low land and if there is not strong concrete barrier between this type of land and ash-land. The coefficient of structural collapse of the ash-land becomes high if measure is taken to augment ash-land; it may not be cost effective in some cases. Changing soil strength of solidified ash land if high rise building is constructed then all risk factor stands as primarily it is seen from the textural classification of the soil that soils of different types beneath a structure may be cause of disaster due to their different degree of saturation. Further, different porosity factors of land under a structure usually create problems. If part of the said land is solidified ash-land this problem becomes acute as capillary siphoning takes important role: and this role becomes most disastrous if the building is nearer to a lake.

Considering these factors, value of solidified ash land changes with the location of land depending upon the augmentation cost, scarcity and some other factors.[24] Common people do not know all these technical matters. So usually, when they buy a piece of land, can not assess the real value of the land. Real-estate businessmen take advantage of buyers' ignorance. Purchaser of such land when he comes to understand the problems, tries to violate civic rules. Thus, crime increases with the increase of scarcity of land.

IV

CONCLUSION

Micro-level observations reveal following things:

(i) It is seen surrounding the BTPS different types of crimes relating to land deals have been on the increase during the last thirty years. People not aware of the land condition are cheated by the land brokers and consequently facing heavy loss. Land values are raised high by the activities of criminal real estate business men, who supress the information on high foundation costs.

(ii) Bandel Thermal Power Station used to pay good amount for removing ash from their ash-pond and it is expected that remover will dump it in proper places without creating any environmental problem and free of cost. But the reality is people, interested to change their land character, purchase ash through link-men from the ash collectors. A net-work for dumping ash from the BTPS has been developed by the crime offender surrounding the BTPS. No one can have even a single lorry of ash without the help of linkmen. But none thinks it as a crime.

(iii) Dumping of ash here and there create environmental hazards. People sometimes dislike it and object random dumping of ash. Due to public pressurisation sometimes administration tries to impose certain restrictions. These actions initiate various types of crime. Real estate businessmen tactfully involve concerned persons in crime racket. Persons of the public administration and local-self government become part of the corruption of land changing and trading. Power and money thus become the main aspects of the crime and corruption of such land transformations.

(vi) Industrialisation brings some cultural hazards degenerating environment. Criminal activities increase with the increase of industrialisation. In the BTPS area, antisocial groups are engaged in looting coal, oil and costly materials. This crime racket is most powerful and well connected with the corrupt officers of the administration.

(v) BTPS authorities are well aware of the hazards caused by the power plant. BTPS authorities are therefore deliberately misleading local people giving wrong information on environmental aspects. In the last earth summit held at Rio De Jenerio, Brazil has declared such activities as crime.

(vi) From police records it is revealed that murders, loots, etc. are the frequent occurrences surrounding thermal power station. But no single complaint on land-use pattern change, falsification of land values and creation of environmental pollution are shown in police records.

(vii) Shortcomings of this investigation is that no mathematical model of crime analysis depending on environmental factors has been developed. Different types of theories stated in the introduction may be recast with the induction of environmental factors. Also, new theory to measure causation effects of crime and corruption based on environmental aspects may be developed. A statistical approach may help to analyse crime distribution functions depending on environmental parameters.

NOTES AND REFERENCES

1. Encyclopaedia Britannica: London.
2. Encyclopaedia of Social Science: New York, USA.
3. Healy, W. (1915): *The Industrial Development: A text-book of Diagnosis and Prognosis for all Concerned in Understanding Offender.* Boston: Littles.
4. Merton, R.K. (1949): *Social Theory and Social Structure,* Rev. & ed, Glencse, Free Press, 1957.
5. Glaser, Daniel (1956): "Criminality Theories and Behavioral Images", *American Journal of Sociology,* 61, 58-151.
6. Sellin, T. (1932): *Culture, Conflict and Social Science,* Personal Council, New York.
7. Jones, H. (1950): *Crime and the Penal System: A Text Book of Criminology,* 2nd ed., London: University Tutorial Press, 1962.
8. Vold, G.B. (1958): *Theoretical Criminology,* New York, Oxford University Press.
9. R. Lecomber (1979): *The Economics of Natural Resources.* The Macmillan Press Ltd., London.
10. D.H. Meadows, *et al.* (1972): *The Limits to Growth,* Earth-land, London.
11. J. Barnett and C. Norse (1963): *Scarcity and Growth: The Economics of Natural Resource Availability,* Johns Hopkins University Press, Baltimore.
12. International Valuation Standards (1994), Volume 7.
13. E. Stiglitz (1975a): "Growth with Exhaustible Natural Resources: Efficient and Optimal Growth Paths", *Review of Economic Studies,* Symposium on Natural Resources.
14. E. Daly (1971): *Essays Towards a Steady-State Economy.* Curnavaca, Mexico Centrio Inticultural de Documentation.
15. E. Daly (1972): "In Defence Steady State Economy", *American Journal of Agricultural Economics,* Vol. 54.
16. N.C Ghosh (1993): "Hazards from a Thermal Plant", *N. Bull.* Calcutta Mathematical Society, Vol. 16, No. 3.
17. N.C. Ghosh (1999): "Environmental Analysis Surrounding a Thermal Plant", *Bull. Environmental Science,* Vol. 13.
18. C. Pontecorvo (1969): *Optimisation and Taxation in an Openaccess Resource: The Fishery,* Ed. M. Gaffney.
19. B.C. Punmia (1995): *Soil Mechanics and Foundations,* Laxmi Publication Pvt. Ltd., New Delhi.
20. A.W. Sciption (1951): *The Bearing Capacity of Clays,* Building Research Congress, Div. 1, London.
21. W.J. M. Rankine (1957): "On the Stability of Loose Earth", *Philosophical Trans. Royal Soc.* Vol. 147, London.

22. J. Resal (1910): *La Pousse Des Terres, Deu Xieme Postie Teorie des Terres Coherantes*, Paris, Beranger.
23. A.L. Bell (1915): "The lateral pressure and resistance of clay and the supporting power of clay foundations". *Proceedings Inst. Civil Engineers*, Vol. 199, London.
24. N.C. Ghosh (1994): "Environmental Land Valuation Surrounding a Thermal Plant based on Mathematical Views," Proc Workshop on Introduction of Environmental' Valuation by the Inst. of Indian Environmental Engineering.

*Annotated Bibliography on Corruption and Development**

Ades, Alberto and Rafael Di Tella, 1996, "Causes and Consequences of Corruption: A Review of Empirical Contributions." *IDS Bulletin: Liberalization and the New Corruption,* 27, 2 (April): 6-11.
This paper reviews the empirical literature on corruption to show how new data sets are contributing to robust studies and testing of hypotheses.

______, 1997, "National Champions and Corruption: Some Unpleasant Interventionist Arithmetic," *The Economic Journal* 107 (July): 1023-42.
The essay suggests that interventionist industrial policies to promote investment and research and development encourage corruption. Consequently, benefits from such investments are diminished by the corrupt practices. The authors caution that their sample is small and the conclusions, while robust, stem from a narrow data base.

Alam, M.S., 1990, "Some Economic Costs of Corruption," *The Journal of Development Studies,* 27, 1 (October): 89-97.
This article argues that bribery cannot improve a country's economic efficiency through the creation of auction-like conditions. It takes the position that the patrimonial character of the LDCs restricts access to bribery and reduces the possibilities of detection.

_____, 1995, "A Theory of Limits on Corruption and Some Applications," *Kyklos,* 48, (3): 419-35.
This essay asks why does corruption vary across government agencies in the same state, and sometimes, even within the same agency. It notes that most of the literature takes the perspective of winners in an emphasis on inducements and pressures for entry into corrupt exchanges. The author

* This bibliography is drawn from the Anti-Corruption Knowledge Centre of the World Bank.

advocates taking the perspective of the losers, the victims of corruption. Based on evidence from South Asia, the author concludes that corruption is a contest between two parties. Variation among and within governments depends on political, economic, legal and cultural factors in a given country.

Alam, M.S., 1996, "Corruption and Countervailing Actions in Pakistan, "Northeastern University, Department of Economics, Mimeo.
Corruption necessarily creates winners and losers. This paper examines corruption from the perspective of losers.

Anderson, Gary and Peter J. Boettke, 1997, "Soviet Venality: A Rent-Seeking Model of the Communist State," *Public Choice,* 93, 1-2 (October): 37-53.
This essay draws on analogy between the former Soviet Union's centrally-planned economy and the extractive policies of 17th century mercantilist states. Staff working on transition economies may find this article useful for understanding policies that informed the previous regime.

Andvig, Jens Christopher, 1991, "The Economics of Corruption: A Survey," *Studi economici* 46 (4-3).
This literature review concentrates primarily on the literature in economics. The author divides the literature into themes of situational analysis, public contracts, queues, status of agents, institutional explanations, cultural differences or norm-based explanations, specific models of multiple equilibrium models of corruption, the welfare economics of corruption, and empirical investigations of corruption.

Andvig, Jens Chr. and Karl Oven Moene, 1990, "How Corruption may Corrupt," *The Journal of Economic Behaviour and Organization* (13): 63-76.
This article presents an argument that the same socio-economic structures can result in different levels of corruption. The authors develop a model showing that multiple equilibria may emerge in similar circumstances. It may be useful for task manager to understand variable levels of corruption in different countries.

Bamrud, Joachim, 1996, "The Other Face of Business in Latin America," *Latin Trade* (September): 34-41.

Nice Magazine article on the costs of corruption to trade. Points to the impact that privatization and deregulation has on reducing corruption. Concludes with a reprint of the Caracas Convention.

Bardhan, Pranab, 1997, "Corruption and Development: A Review of Issues," *Journal of Economic Literature,* 35 (Sept.): 1320-1346, Available at the Joint Library.

This article is a highly useful and excellent review of the literature on corruption. It divides the literature among five general issues: corruption and efficiency, corruption and growth, national differences in corruption, policy issues in reducing corruption, and incentives for reducing corruption. Task managers will find this article to be an excellent introduction into a large and highly varied literature on the subject.

Bayart, Jean-Francois, 1997, "Le << capital social >> de Pl'État malfaiteur, our less ruses de l'intelligence politique," in *La criminalisation de Pl'Éat en Afrique,* 55-76. Edited by Jean-Francois Bayartm, Stephen Eills, and Béatrice Hibou. Paris: Édition Complexe.

This chapter presents a cultural-historic argument for the extent of corruption in African states.

Bayart, Jean-Francois, Stephen Ellis, and BÉatrice Hibou, 1997. "De Pl'État kleptocrate à Pl'État malfaitour?" in *La criminalisation de Pl'État en Afrique,* 17-54. Edited by Jean-François Bayart, Stephen Ellis, and Béatrice Hibou, Paris: Édition complexe.

This chapter argues that corruption is a malaise that currently afflicts the African state. Governments in Africa have ceased to operate as political entities and become willing participants in a wide range of corrupt and criminal activities. The chapter proposes six indicators of a policy of *criminalisation* among African states: an extension of the private use of violence to office holders, a small coterie of people around the core of power that benefits from the extension of violence, the exploitation of official positions to engage in international commerce, the presence of international crime networks, a cultural image that condones criminal activities, and an increasing importance of criminal activities for a country's economy. Based primarily on evidence from Zaire, (Congo), the essay concludes that Africa has become increasingly populated by criminal states.

Becker, Gary S., 1968, "Crime and Punishment: An Economic Approach. "*The Journal of Political Economy,* 76, 2 (March-April): 169-217.

The classic article analyzes that relationship between punishment and an individual's willingness to engage in an illegal act. It asks what is the optimal level of punishment to deter crime. The optimal level of punishment is largely a function of the cost of enforcement, investigation, and punishment. It concludes that the optimal levels of sanction depends upon the overall cost of enforcement.

Bénin, République du, 1996, Decret No. 96-579 de 19 décembre, Portant création, organisation, attributions et fonctionnement de la Cellule de la moralisation de la via publique.

Berkman, Steve, 1996, "The impact of Corruption on Technical Cooperation Projects in Africa," *The International Journal of Technical Cooperation,* 2, 2 (Winter): 67-82.

This article assesses the impact of corruption on the management of public institutions. The article provides a useful list of corrupt practices that a task manager might encounter in managing a project in Africa. It finishes with a set of proposed responses to corruption that will improve public sector management.

Bhagwati, Jagdish N., 1982, "Directly Unproductive, Profit-seeking (DUP) Activities, *Journal of Political Economy,* 90 (5): 983-1002.

This paper provides a taxonomy of DUP activities. These activities include the use of funds for lobbying for protection, market share, licenses, and monopolistic barriers to market. The basic characteristic is that DUP activities use funds for rent-seeking and bribery with an aim of making a profit.

Bialos, Jeffrey P. and Gregory Hussian, 1995, *The Foreign Corrupt Practices Act: Coping with Corruption in Russia and Other Transitional Economies,* Washington: Weil Gotshal and Manges.

This paper analyzes the impact of the FCPA on corruption in the Russia and transition economies. The conclusion is that the US government needs to take some special steps to improve the competitiveness of American firms in Russia and transition economies.

Bigsten, Arne and Karl Ove Moene, 1997, "Growth and Rent Dissipation: the Case of Kenya," *Journal of African Economies,* 5, 1 (June): 177-98.

Corruption in Kenya is closely linked to the government's lack of legitimacy. Ethnic competition and patron client relationships have undermined both political stability and policy-making. The government uses its resources to purchase support while increasing repression of its opponents. As a consequence, the public sector is overstaffed and corruption permeates its capacity to deliver services. Kenya has accordingly suffered an economic decline.

Blalock, Joyce, 1989, "The Importance of a Multidisciplinary Approach in Fighting Corruption," The Fourth International Anti-Corruption Conference Report, 121-25. [Place of publication?].

Bliss, Christopher and Rafael Di Tella, 1997, "Does Competition Kill Corruption?" *Journal of Political Economy,* 105, 51 (October): 1001-23.

This article is useful for staff who want to understand the relationship between corruption and competition. It offers an explanation of under what circumstances competition may limit the costs of corruption.

Botswana, Government of, 1994, Botswana Government Extraordinary Gazette "Corruption and Economic Crime Bill." Bill Number 8 (25 May).

This law creates Benin's anti-corruption agency.

Braguinsky, Serguey, 1996. "Corruption and Schumpeterian Growth in Different Economic Environments," *Contemporary Economic Policy,* 14 (July): 14-25.

The article argues that corruption in a competitive environment is likely to enable economic growth. However, corruption in a totalitarian environment is economically inefficient and leads to stagnation.

Busch, Gary K., 1992, "Crime and Corruption: One View of a Parallel System," Mimeo, Transparency International.

This paper looks at the internationalization of corruption and crime. It looks specifically at four fields: fraud in construction, maritime fraud, money laundering, and 'parlour-room crime' (fake antiquities, art, etc.). The paper might be useful for managers working in any of these fields.

Cadot, Olivier, 1987, "Corruption as a Gamble," *Journal of Public Economics*, 33, 2 (July): 223-44.

The essay presents a model of corruption using a game in which players include a government official, a license, and an individual submitting a request. The paper demonstrates that corruption may operate at multiple equilibria.

Caiden, Gerald E., 1993, "From the Specific to the General: Reflections on the Sudan," *Corruption and Reform*, 7 (3): 205-13.

This case study on Sudan argues that the Numayri Government fell because of its extraordinary levels of corruption. The argument has implications for considering opportunities of action in cases of government failures.

Compos, Jose Edgardo L., 1991, "The 'Political Economy of the Rent-Seeking Society' Revisited: Cronyism, Political Instability and Development." Paper prepared for presentation at the World Bank, September 27.

This paper distinguishes between competitive rent-seeking and cronyism. It argues that cronyism leads to a capture of monopolies by a favoured elite, which contributes to political instability. The paper is an excellent analysis of the political-economy of cronyism, an economically expensive form of rent-seeking found in many developing countries.

Cartier-Bresson, Jean, 1997, "Corruption Networks, Transaction Security and illegal Social Exchange," *Political Studies* (65): 463-76.

This article argues that most studies of corruption concentrate on occasional and unorganized behaviour. It analyzes instead networks of corrupt actors who interact in regular, organized corruption. The article concludes that the study of networks has more to offer for an understanding of corruption than the classic political economy approach.

_______, 1997, "The Economics of Corruption," *in Democracy and Corruption in Europe*, 148-65. Edited by Donatella Della Porta and Yves Mény, London: Pinter.

This article outlines a broad range of economic theories and shows how their precepts may enrich the study of corruption in democratic governments.

Charlick, Robert B., 1993, "Corruption in Political Transition: A Governance Perspective," *Corruption and Reform,* 7 (3): 177-87.

Corruption reflects deeper problems in effective governance. The author argues that the transitions in Africa provide a unique opportunity to bring about positive change in policy pluralism, political accountability, and information openness. Corruption is seen as a product of political competition and a drive among politicians to remain in office.

Cheung, Steven N.S., 1996, A Simplistic General Equilibrium Theory of Corruption," *Contemporary Economic Policy,* 14 (July): 1-5.

Focusing on transition economies, the article assumes that all government officials are self-maximizers who are receptive to opportunities for corruption. It notes that whereas competitive arrangements in the private sector limit venal behaviour, monopolies in the public sector create incentives for corruption. The article concludes that introducing competition into transition economies will reduce opportunities for corruption.

Choi, Myung Ju, 1991, "Rent-Seeking, Growth, and Distribution: An Alternative Approach." Mimeo, Oxford University, June.

Chossudovsky, Michel, 1996. "Comment les mafias gangrènent l'économie mondiale," *Le Monde Diplomatique* (December): 24-25.

This essay discusses how organized crime that has accompanied the expansion of a global economy.

Coolidge, Jacquiline and Susan Rose-Ackerman. 1997. "High-Level Rent-Seeking and Corruption in African Regimes," *World Bank Policy Research Working Paper,* 1780 (June).

This paper analyzes the negative impact that rent-seeking by high level government officials has on African economic growth. It distinguishes between benevolent autocrats and kleptocrats to determine which has a greater incentive to engage in corrupt practices. The authors note that a kleptocrat has a greater incentive to be corrupt because of the shorter time horizon. In conclusion, the Bank has an incentive to use caution in lending to governments with kleptocratic leaders.

Crotty, John, 1997, "Measures to Address Corruption Problems in Tax and Customs Administrations." Paper prepared for presentation at the 8th International Anti-Corruption Conference, Lima-Peru, September 7-11.

Provides the IMF's perspective on measures that might be undertaken to reduce corruption in tax and customs administration.

Das Gupta, Arindam and Dilip Mookherjee, 1996, "Tax Amnesties as Asset-Laundering Devices," *Journal of Law, Economics, and Organization,* 12, 2 (October): 408-31.

This article analyzes how tax amnesties increase government revenues and diminish the overall size of a country's informal sector earnings.

Defensor-Santiago, Miriam, 1989, 'Corruption Prevention Strategies in Developing Countries." The Fourth International Anti-Corruption Conference Report, 8-12. [Place of publication?].

Keynote address by the Secretary of Agrarian Reform, the Republic of the Philippines on the problems governments face to reduce corruption.

De Speville, Bertrand, 1997, "Combatting Corruption: Hong Kong's Battle and the ICAC." Paper prepared for the Latvia Workshop on Anti-Corruption, Riga, 12-13 February.

This outline of a paper for a conference presentation describes the Hong Kong ICAC.

_______, 1997, *Hong Kong: Policy Initiatives Against Corruption,* Paris: OECD Development Centre.

This paper provides a detailed analysis of the Independent Commission Against Corruption (ICAC) in Hong Kong. It begins with a discussion of the history behind the ICAC, its statutes, and effectiveness. Most importantly, the paper acknowledges the centrality of Hong Kong's multifaceted approach to combatting corruption: enforcement, education, prevention. The paper is useful for any manager advising a client government about the strengths of an anti-corruption agency.

_______, 1996, "The Experience of Hong Kong in Combating Corruption," in *Uganda International Conference on Good Governance in Africa: Empowering Civil Society in the Fight Against Corruption,* 159-66. Edited by Petter Langseth and Fiona Simpkins, Washington: The World Bank.

The paper gives a description of the Hong Kong, Independent Commission Against Corruption.

Doig, Alan, 1995, "Good Government and Sustainable Anti-Corruption Strategies: A Role for Independent Anti-Corruption Agencies?" *Public Administration and Development*, 15 (May): 151-65.

The essay presents a discussion of government, good governance, and anti-corruption agencies drawn largely from a 1993 British Council report. Drawing largely on political science literature from the 1970s, the author advocates the expansion of anti-corruption agencies based on the Hong Kong Independent Commission Against Corruption.

Evens, Peter B. and James E. Rauch, 1995, "Bureaucratic Structures and Economic Performance in Less Developed Countries." IRIS Working Paper No. 175 (August).

This study assesses the extent to which internal promotion and meritocratic recruitment improve the functioning of a bureaucracy. It concludes that a better performing public sector, with rational promotion and recruitment, has less corruption.

Finch, C. David, 1996, "Role of International Agencies in Fighting Corruption." Mimeo.

This paper presents a critical assessment of the impact of international agencies in combating corruption.

Fung, Daniel, 1997, "Anti-Corruption and Human Rights Protection: Hong Kong's Jurisprudential Experience." Paper prepared for presentation at the 8th International Anti-Corruption Conference, Lima-Peru, September 7-11.

This paper provides a description of the statutes underlying Hong Kong's ICAC.

Galtung, Fredrik, 1997, "Frameworks for Sustainable Anti-Corruption Control." Mimeo. Cambridge University, May.

The creation of a sustainable anti-corruption framework is a major challenge for developing countries. This paper suggests a framework based on fostering an awareness of a country's economic and political institutions.

Geddes, Barbara and Artur Ribeiro Beto, 1992, "Institutional Sources of Corruption in Brazil," *Third World Quarterly*, 13 (4): 641-61.

This article discusses the apparent increase of corruption that occurred in Brazil after its democratic transition under the Collar Administration. It identifies the paradoxical roots of corruption in changes in electoral rules and the constitution at a time when controls were being relaxed. Government officials were able to extract revenues for personal use because the rules over their actions were not enforced.

Gillespie, Kate and Gwenn Okruhlik, 1991, "The Political Dimensions of Corruption Cleanups: A framework for Analysis," *Comparative Politics* (October): 77-95.
This article provides a conceptual framework to analyze anti-corruption campaigns within governments and across states. It explores the political variables involved in anti-corruption campaigns and is useful for understating the politics of reducing official venality.

Global Coalition for Africa, 1997, *Corruption: The Botswana Experience*, Washington: Global Coalition for Africa.
This paper chronicles Botswana's reasons of corruption leading to the passage of the Corruption and Economic Crime Act and Directorate on Corruption and Economic Crime.

Glynn, Patrick, Stephen J. Kobrin, and Moisés Naím, 1997, "The Globalization of Corruption," in *Corruption and the Global Economy*, 7-27. Edited by Kimberly Ann Elliot, Washington: The Institute for International Economics.
This chapter argues that an international backlash against corruption has been manifest in the outcry among governments and international non-governmental organizations. The effort to extend the United States' Foreign Corrupt Practices Act internationally is evidence of this globalization of intolerance.

Gorta, Angela and Suzie Forell, 1994, *Unravelling Corruption: A Public Sector Perspective: Surveys of NSW Public Sector Employees' Understanding of Corruption and their Willingness to Take Action*, Sydney, Australia: Independent Commission Against Corruption (March).
The report summarizes the work of the Independent Commission Against Corruption in New South Wales, Australia. Researchers conducted a survey on the question "you can't call something corrupt if it is done for the right

reasons. Agree or disagree?" The report publishes the results of responses to the survey question.

Gould, David J. and Jose A. Amaro-Reyes, 1983, "The Effects of Corruption on Administrative Performance: Illustrations from Developing Countries," World Bank Staff Working Papers Number 580, Washington: The World Bank.
This working paper argues that conditions in the developing world make corruption a strong problem. It notes that rapid socio-economic change, strong kinship and ethnic ties, and new institutions combined with political softness, widespread inequalities, and a state lacking legitimacy are conducive to corruption. Considering that corruption has a deleterious impact on development, the paper concludes that a political and public climate that favours impartiality and clean government is necessary for a reduction in corrupt behaviour.

Harriss-White, Barbara and Gordon White, 1996, "Corruption, Liberalization, and Democracy," *IDS Bulletin: Liberalization and the New Corruption*, 27, 2 (April): 1-6.
This article analyzes the emergence of a new corruption of rapacious elites who engage in criminal behaviour free from constraints of cold war patrons. It notes the challenge that such a change presents to combating corruption.

Heidenheimer, Arnold J., Michnael Johnston, and Victor T. LeVine, eds., 1997 (Fourth edition), *Political Corruption: A Handbook*, New Brunswick, N.J., Transaction Publishers.
This book is a compilation of 56 of the classic studies of corruption drawn from academic journals and books. It is particularly useful for its interdisciplinary approach.

Heimann, Fritz F. 1997, "Combatting International Corruption: The Role of the Business Community," in *Corruption and the Global Economy*, 147-61. Edited by Kimberly Ann Elliott, Washington: Institute for International Economics.
The author, a founding member of TI, focuses his chapter on the U.S. Foreign Corrupt Practices Act (FCPA) and its impact on international business. Corruption, according to the author, must be attacked from both the demand side—officials who demand bribes—as well as the supply side—business people willing to pay bribes. Among the major organizations to combat corruption is the International Chamber of Commerce (ICC). The chapter advocates

extending the FCPA to other countries and thereby ending the tax subsidies that competing corporations enjoy.

International Monetary Fund, 1997, "IMF Adopts Guidelines Regarding Governance Issues," *IMF Survey* (August 5): 233-34.

This article lays out the governance guidelines for IMF staff.

________, 1997, "World Bank Development Strategy Targets Corruption, Environment, and Institution-Building," *IMF Survey* (May 26): 162-63.

An article that discusses the papers presented by Susan Rose-Ackerman and Michael Johnston at the Annual Bank Conference on Development Economics, 1997.

James, Wilmont, 1996, "Parliamentary Ethics and Government Corruption: Playing with Public Trust," *Public Opinion Service Reports,* 3 (February).

This paper presents survey results from South Africa on popular perceptions about corruption.

Johnson, Simon, Daniel Kaufmann, and Andrel Schleifer, 1997, "The Unofficial Economy in Transition," Paper prepared for presentation for the Brookings Panel on Economic Activity, Washington, September 4-5, 1997.

The unofficial economy has played a critical role in the transition of Eastern Europe and the former Soviet Union from socialism to capitalism. We provide a theory of the unofficial economy in transition. In this theory, unattractive combinations of taxes, regulations, and public goods supplied by the government can lead to the movement of economic activity to the unofficial sector and poor overall economic performance. The article shows that an understanding of the shift from official to unofficial economy is critical to understanding what has occurred in transition economies.

Johnston, Michael, 1997, "Public Officials, Private Interests, and Sustainable Democracy: When Politics and Corruption Meet," in *Corruption and the Global Economy*, 61-82. Edited by Kimberly Abb Elliot, Washington: The Institute for International Economics.

This chapter argues forcefully that any assessment of corruption must take a country's political dimensions into account. To make this argument, Johnston asserts that it is critical to understand who decides corrupt distributions about who gets what benefits from corruption. He concludes that to combat corruption and analysis of the distribution of benefits is necessary to formulate a feasible, multi-dimensional effort.

Johnston, Michael, 1997, *Political Corruption and Public Policy in America*, Monterey, CA: Brooks/Cole Publishing Company.
This book provides a number of useful definitions of corruption and explores how they relate to policy in the United States.

_______, 1996, "The Search for Definitions: The Vitality of Politics and the Issue of Corruption," *International Social Science Journal: Corruption in Western Democracies*, 149 (September): 321-36.
This article explores the multiple problems that confront efforts to define corruption in a meaningful fashion. It is useful for understanding the complexity of defining corrupt behaviour.

_______, 1997, "What Can Be Done About Entrenched Corruption?" Paper prepared for the Annual World Bank Conference on Development Economics, Washington, April 30—May 1.
Corruption is endogenous to a given country and is symptomatic of deeper conflicts. Entrenched political and bureaucratic corruption are in equilibria. The paper suggests that it is only possible to move from high to low corruption by encouraging competition and providing guarantees of civil liberties and economic rights.

_______, 1993, "'Micro' and 'Macro' Possibilities for Reform", *Corruption and Reform*, 7, (3): 189-204.
This chapter argues that democratic transitions revitalize civil society, which in turn, imposes greater accountability on a government by demanding less corruption. It concludes that improved public sector management is essential if a government wishes to reduce corruption.

Kaflholo, T.M. 1996, "Crime in Southern Africa: Toward the 2000". Paper presented at a regional workshop, Grand Palm Hotel, Gaberone (19 June).
This paper discusses the three-way strategies of the Botswana anti-corruption agency of education, investigation, and enforcement. It gives a highly optimistic assessment of progress against corruption in Botswana.

Kaufmann, Daniel, 1996, "Listening to Stakeholders Spell the C......Word: The 'Tackling-Corruption-is-Taboo' Myth meets some Evidence." Mimeo, Cambridge: Harvard Institute of International Development (September).

Based on survey work, this paper advocates that the Bank emphasize reducing corruption in its approach to lending.

_______, 1997. "Corruption: the Facts," *Foreign Policy,* 107 (Summer): 114-31.

This paper explains the costs of corruption to a government. The paper rejects arguments that corruption "greases" development, that reforms breed bribery, and the notion that corruption cannot be controlled. Having exposed the "myths" about corruption, the paper argues that reducing venal behaviour requires the involvement of civil society and a mix of programs including liberalization, deregulation, and tax, budget, institutional, civil service, and legal reforms.

Kaufmann, Daniel and Paul Siegelbaum, 1995, "Privatization and Corruption in Transition Economies." *Journal of International Affairs,* 50, 2 (Winter): 419-458.

Privatization was effectively forced upon the transition economies after the break-up of the Soviet Union. This paper presents an analysis of different privatization techniques and how those methods have affected the incidence of corruption. It concludes that despite the incidence of corruption that followed privatization, the policies were positive for the transition economies.

Khan, Mushtaq, 1996. "A Typology of Corrupt Practices in Developing Countries," *IDS Bulletin: Liberalization and the New Corruption,* 27, 2 (April: 12-21).

This article a behavioural definition of corruption. It then presents various typologies for corrupt behaviour.

_______, N.d., "Corruption in South Asia: Patterns of Development and Change," Mimeo. University of London, SOAS.

This paper argues that the capitalist classes in Pakistan, India, Malaysia, and Thailand have seized the state and uses corruption to extract capital from the workers and peasants and maintain a hold on power.

Klitgaard, Robert, 1996, "Cleaning Up and Invigorating the Civil Service." Background Paper prepared for the Civil Service

Reform Study, Mimeo, Washington: The World Bank (November).
The development agenda is moving from policy-based reform to institutional reform. The paper asserts that a reform of incentives and information, implicit in civil service reform, will decrease the incidence of corruption in developing economies.

Klitgaard, Robert, 1988, *Controlling Corruption*, Berkeley and Los Angeles: University of California Press.
This seminal book on the subject has shaped much of the thinking about corruption for students and practitioners since its publication. The book uses various case samples including the Philippines, Singapore, and Hong Kong. Among the lessons the book contributes to thinking about corruption is the notion that the costs of eliminating corruption are excessively high and an optimal level of control is possible. This book is a useful work for anyone wishing to understand the phenomenon of corruption and strategies to bring it under control.

________, 1996, "Roles for International Organizations in the Fight Against Corruption." Paper presented at the XIIIth International Congress of the International Society of Social Defense, Lecce, Italy, November 28-30.
The paper argues that international organizations may assist individual countries combat corruption by helping them draft changes in laws, share information and operational knowledge, and implement tactics to facilitate change.

________, 1997, "'Unanticipated Consequences' in Anti-Poverty Programs," *World Development*, 25, 12 (December): 1963-1972.
This article examines unanticipated effects of anti-poverty programs conducted by multilateral donors. It asserts that the unexpected effects may include a variety of distortions, including increased corruption. When an official acquires discretionary power over a good or service, corruption may result as a consequence of diminished accountability.

Kong, Tat Yan, 1996, "Corruption and its Institutional Foundations: The Experience of South Korea," *IDS Bulletin*, 27 (2): 48-55.
The South Korean economy has grown steadily despite fairly significant levels of political corruption. This paper argues

that this growth is a consequence of the institutional foundations of Korean growth. As in Japan, donations to political parties in exchange for business favours remains a major form of corruption in South Korea. This close relation between business and government is suggested, first, as a reason for corruption's resilience in South Korea; and second, as a predictor that corruption will continue despite Korea's move toward democracy and economic liberalization.

Kpundeh, Sahr John, 1997, "Corruption and the Fight Against it: The Case of Sierra Leone," *Fighting Corruption: A Model for Building National Integrity*. Edited by Rick Stapenhurst and Sahr Kpundeh, Washington: The World Bank, EDI Seminar Series.

This paper is a case study of corruption in Sierra Leone and the negative impact of corruption on governance.

_______, 1993, "Prospects in Contemporary Sierra Leone," *Corruption and Reform*, 7, (3): 237-47.

This article assesses the capacity of the Sierra Leonian government to reduce administrative corruption during a period of political liberalization. It highlights the impact of corruption on bringing about political economic reform. The article is useful for managers working in countries with a lot of corruption.

Krueger, Anne O., 1974, "The Political Economy of the Rent-Seeking Society," *The American Economic Review*, 64, 3 (June): 291-303.

This seminal article introduces the concept of rents that are present in government monopolies. Competitive rent-seeking is a factor in societies where governments control sectors of the economy. The articles analyzes the opportunities created through state-owned enterprises, quantitative restrictions, and tariffs that lead to rent-seeking.

Kurer, Oskar, 1993. "Clientelism, Corruption and the Allocation of Resources," *Public Choice*, 77, (20), 259-73.

This article shows the errors of what Kurer calls the revisionist approach to corruption. The revisionist approach—notably Leff, Nye and others—argues that corruption enhances market efficiency. The author argues convincingly that the revisionist approach is misleading and that corruption carries high costs, especially for developing economies.

Lambsdorff, Johann Graf, 1997, "Corruption in Comparative Perspective." Paper prepared for presentation at the 8th International Anti-Corruption Conference, Lima-Peru, September 7-11.

This paper aggregates the results of surveys for 102 countries to present a "poll of polls."

_______, 1997, "An Empirical Investigation of Bribery in International Trade." Mimeo, University of Gŏttingen, April.

This paper argues there exists a relationship between the extent of corruption in an importing country and the exporting country that complement each other. The relationship obtains because of the propensity of the exporter to offer bribes.

Langseth, Petter, Rick Stapenhurst, and Jeremy Pope, 1997, The Role of a National Integrity System in Fighting Corruption. EDI Working Paper 400/142, E1976, Washington: The World Bank.

This working paper explains the national integrity system approach pioneered by the Bank's Economic Development Institute and Transparency International.

Langseth, Petter and Rick Stapenhurst, 1997, National Integrity System: Country Studies, EDI Working Paper 400-144, E1978, Washington: The World Bank.

This working paper reports on the experiences with National Integrity Seminars in Tanzania and Uganda.

Larrain, Claudio Orrego, 1994, "Corruption y modernization del Estado," Mimeo, Banco Inter-Americano de Desarrollo (Agosto).

This paper analyzes the cost of corruption to democratizing Latin American regimes.

Leak, Tan Ah, 1996, "The Experience of Singapore in Combatting Corruption," in *Uganda International Conference on Good Governance in Africa: Empowering Civil Society in the Fight Against Corruption*, 151-58, Edited by Petter Langseth and Fiona Simpkins, Washington: The World Bank.

This paper presented at an EDI Conference in Uganda, describes Singapore's experience fighting corruption.

Lee, Pak K., 1997, "The Political Economy of State Enterprise Relations in China's Shaanxi Province," *Journal of Contemporary Asia*, 27 (3): 287-314.

This article examines the relations of China's state-owned enterprises and the government in Shaanxi province. It analyzes the creation of rents and the incidence of local state intervention in the market. The article is useful for understanding the creation of rents in China's state-owned enterprise sector.

Leiken, Robert S., 1996-97, "Controlling the Global Corruption Epidemic," *Foreign Policy*, 105 (Winter): 55-73.

A highly readable article. It argues that an explosion in the incidence of corruption has occurred worldwide. The reasons for this explosion are two: the Cold War's end led to higher disclosures of malfeasance and the spread of democracy.

Leung, C.M., 1989, "The Effect of Corruption on Economic Growth," The Fourth International Anti-Corruption Conference Report, 147-48. [Place of publication?].

This presentation describes corruption as a costly activity for any economy. It uses a discussion of the costs of corruption to highlight the important progress that Hong Kong has made in controlling venality in its public sector.

Lewis, Peter, 1996, "From Prebendalism to Predation: The Political Economy of Decline in Nigeria," *The Journal of Modern African Studies*, 34 (1): 79-103.

This essay traces the process of decline and then collapse of Nigeria's public sector after the 1984 coup. It shows how the disintegration of public sector management led to the emergence of a predatory state, the leaders of which extract resources for their personal gain.

Leys, Colin, 1965, "What is the Problem About Corruption?" *The Journal of Modern African Studies*, 3, (2): 215-30.

Among the earliest statements on corruption as an efficiency-enhancing market behaviour. The essay concludes that corruption is a positive developmental force by creating competition and market structures for private sector actors.

Little, Walter, 1996, "Corruption and Democracy in Latin America." *IDS Bulletin*, 27 (2): 64-70.

Reform movements in Latin America have increased considerably over the last decade. Dismissals of ministers in Mexico, judges in Venezuela, and two presidents have been forced from office. This essay analyzes how these events occurred. It concludes that the events resulted from a mix of policies that enabled reforms throughout Latin America.

Lodge, Tom, 1998, "Political Corruption in South Africa," *African Affairs*, 97 (387): 157-87.

This article disputes the public perception that the South African bureaucracy is largely corrupt. It finds that contrary to public opinion, corruption is more prevalent in the regional governments than the central administration. The article concludes that the extent of corruption in regional governments is a consequence of corrupt homeland civil services.

Lui, Francis T., 1996, "Three Aspects of Corruption," *Contemporary Economic Policy*, 14 (July): 26-29.

This article argues that corruption entails three aspects: first, it is rent-seeking that deviates from a competitive market; second, it is illegal; and third, corruption is a perversion of political power.

Malik, S.P., 1989, "An Anti-Corruption Strategy," The Fourth International Anti-Corruption Conference Report, 119-20. [Place of publication?].

An address by the executive director (Vigilance), Engineers India Limited on the impact of the Central Bureau of Investigation that came out of the Prevention of Corruption Act, 1988.

Manion, Melanie, 1996, "Corruption by Design: Bribery in Chinese Enterprise Licensing." *The Journal of Law, Economics & Organization*, 12, 1 (April): 167-95.

This article employs game theory to examine the payment of bribes to officials. It demonstrates how the information asymmetries lead to an official's ability to demand payment for services that are part of their positions. The article concludes that to move away from an equilibrium in which corruption is common required substantial institutional changes. The utility of this piece is that it provides a rigorous analysis of information availability and corruption.

Mauro, Paolo, 1995, "Corruption and Growth," *The Quarterly Journal of Economics*, 106, 2 (August): 681-711.

This important article analyses a data set, obtained from Business International, that shows that corruption, red tape, an inefficient judiciary and political instability lower investment and economic growth. It shows that a one-standard deviation improvement in bureaucratic efficiency contributed to an increase in investments. The article argues forcefully that reducing corruption and bureaucratic impediments has a direct impact on investment and economic growth.

_______, 1997, "The Effects of Corruption on Growth, Investment and Government Expenditure: A Cross-Country Analysis." In *Corruption and the Global Economy*, 88-107, Edited by Kimberly Ann Elliot, Washington: The Institute for International Economics.

This article identifies a number of causes and consequences of corruption through cross-country analysis. It presents new results of the impact of corruption that uses a larger data set than the author's previous *QJE* article. Results indicate that corruption lowers an overall investment and economic growth by altering the composition of government expenditures.

_______, 1997, "Why Worry About Corruption?" *Economic Issues*, 6, Washington: IMF.

This paper lists various causes of corruption including trade restrictions, subsidies, price controls, low civil service salaries, natural resource endowments, and sociological factors. The consequences include lower investment rates, loss of tax revenues, poor aid flows, and distortions in government expenditure and capacity to deliver services. It concludes that corruption negatively affects investment and growth.

Médard, J.F., 1986, "Public Corruption in Africa: A Comparative Perspective," *Corruption and Reform* (1): 115-31.

The author sees corruption as a defining characteristics of African governments. He defines corruption as the misuse of public office for personal gain. This definition then shapes an analysis of bribery and embezzlement that contribute to what the author calls a neo-patrimonial state. This article may interest task managers working in African countries in which corruption is systemic.

Mény, Yves, 1997, "'Fin de Siècle' Corruption: Change, Crisis and Shifting Values," *International Social Science Journal: Corruption in Western Democracies* 149 (September): 309-20.

Shifting values have elevated corruption as a critical problem for government. Perceptions of the costs of corruption hold that it has increased and an urgency has become apparent to control its incidence. Corruption reflects a crisis in the efficient functioning of the public sector and has become a priority for governments to control. Task managers and staff may find this a useful article to think about corruption conceptually and how it affects public sector efficiency.

Moody-Stuart, George, 1992, "Grand Corruption in Third World Development." Paper prepared for "Transparency International" Meeting, Latimer House, 24-25 July.

This paper lays out an analysis of the costs of corruption and suggests some practical remedies.

Mookherjee, Dillp and I.P.L. Png, 1995. "Corruptible Law Enforcers: How Should They Be Compensated?" *The Economic Journal,* 105 (January): 145-56.

This essay builds on the premise that any delegation of authority creates opportunities for corruption. Concentrating on individuals who are responsible for the enforcement of regulations, the authors explore the relationship between sanction and opportunity. The conclusion is that only large increase in penalty will effectively diminish corruption.

Moore, Mick, 1988, "Death Without Taxes". Paper presented at the Poverty Reduction and Economic Management Public Sector Seminar Series (March 13).

This paper discusses the extent to which governments of the world's poorest countries are becoming financially dependent on aid. Many obtain over half of their revenues from aid. These levels of aid undermine creating accountable governments.

Moore, Mick and John Toye, 1997, "Corruption and Taxation," Mimeo, June.

This paper situates corruption in larger processes of taxation. It notes that in a democracy, taxation needs to be essentially invisible, or at least as equitable as possible. Reducing corruption therefore benefits tax collection and the legitimacy of the state.

Morice, Alain, 1995, "Corruption, loi et société: Quelques propositions," *Revue tiers monde,* 36, 141 (March): 41-65.

This article takes an anthropological approach to analyze corruption as widely encompassing social phenomenon. It advocates a socio-anthropological approach to corruption and thereby provides a useful, non-economic perspective on the phenomenon.

Murphy, Kevin M., Andrei Schleifer, and Robert Vishny, 1993, "Why is Rent-Seeking So Costly to Growth," *The American Economic Review,* 83, 2 (May): 409-14.

This article argues that rent-seeking is harmful to growth for two reasons. First, rent-seeking tends naturally to have increasing returns. The effect is that high levels of rent-seeking are self-sustaining. Second, public rent-seeking is particularly harmful to innovation. The authors assert that innovation is a key element in economic growth and rent-seeking is therefore costly to growth.

Nasaha, Alfred P.W., 1996, "Anti-Corruption Legislation in Uganda and its Improvement." In *Integrity Workshop in Uganda II: Final Workshop Proceedings,* 64-86. Edited by Petter Lagseth and Fiona Simpkins, Washington: The World Bank.

This paper describes the anti-corruption legislation in Uganda.

Olivier de Sardan, J.P. 1996, "L 'économie morale de la corruption en Afrique," *Politique Africaine,* 63 (October): 97-118.

This article posits that corruption in Africa results from a cultural impulse to assist family members and build a moral economy.

Olowu, Dele, 1993, "Roots and Remedies of Governmental Corruption in Africa," *Corruption and Reform,* 7(3): 227-36.

The article argues that the causes of corruption in Africa may be attributed to the over-centralization of the state. A resulting pauperization of the public sector has resulted in endemic corruption. The chapter is useful for considering the political causes of corruption.

Olson, Mancur Jr., 1996, "Big Bills Left on the Sidewalk: Why Some Countries are Rich and Others Poor," *Journal of Economic Perspectives,* 10, 2 (Spring): 3-24.

This essay argues that economic performance is determined by the structure of incentives in a given society. It notes that national boundaries have a direct impact on different structures of incentives. The paper concludes that incentives vary from location to location and that collective action is oftentimes quite dissimilar from individual rationality.

Olson, Mancur Jr., 1993, "Dictatorship, Democracy, and Development," *The American Political Science Review,* 87, 3 (September): 567-76.

This essay examines the incentives of autocrats to extract as much revenue from their countries as possible within limits imposed by optimal taxation rates. A dictatorship may extract less from an economy than roving bandits because of his longer time horizon. The shorter the time horizon for a leader in office, the greater the incentive to plunder an economy. Implications of this argument are that dictatorships are economically inefficient over longer periods of time.

_________, 1996. "Why Poor Economic Policies Must Promote Corruption," *Rivista di Politica Economica,* 111, 3 (March): 9-51.

Olson argues that corruption may be understood best by looking at economic institutions and policy. Corruption is a response to legislation and regulations that are 'market contrary'. Evidence from Eastern Europe and the former Soviet Union support an argument that market contrary policies contributed to an extensive corruption.

Parfitt, Trevor W., "Corruption, Adjustment and the African Debt," *Corruption and Reform,* 6 (2): 25-44.

This article refutes the argument that endemic corruption is responsible for the African debt crisis. Argues that democratic reforms are necessary to effect change in the incidence in corruption.

Pieth, Mark, 1997, "Contribution of Industrialised Countries in the Prevention of Corruption: The Example of the OECD." Paper prepared for presentation at the 8th International Anti-Corruption Conference, Lima-Peru, September 7-11.

This paper outlines the OECD anti-bribery initiative, particularly tax deductions for bribes.

Posner, Richard A., 1975, "The Social Costs of Monopoly and Regulation, *Journal of Political Economy,* 83(4): 807-27.

This article argues that competition to attain a monopoly transforms monopoly profits into social costs. Costs associated with regulation may exceed the social costs of monopoly. This is an argument that supports notions of corruption as enhancing competition.

Przeworski, Adam and Fernando Limongi, 1993, "Political Regimes and Economic Growth," *Journal of Economic Perspectives*, 7, 3 (Summer): 51-69.

This article disputes the notion that democracies necessarily protect property rights. It is an example of a larger debate on the relationship between democratic governments and economic growth. It concludes that politics underlie the capacity of a government to enact reforms and contribute to economic growth.

Quah, John S.T., 1997, "Singapore's Experience in Curbing Corruption." In *Political Corruption: A Handbook*, 841-53. Edited by Arnold J. Heidenheimer, Michael Johnston, and Victor T. Le Vine, New Brunswick, NJ: Transaction Publishers, fourth edition.

This paper analyzes the anti-corruption campaign in Singapore. It chronicles the passage of the Prevention of Corruption Act (POCA) and the Corrupt Investigation Bureau. The author argues that Singapore has succeeded in reducing corruption because of the commitment of its political leadership, its comprehensive anti-corruption legislation, and the establishment of an incorrupt anti-corruption agency that investigates and enforces violations of the POCA.

Riley, Stephen P., 1993, "Post-Independence Anti-Corruption Strategies and Contemporary Effects of Democratization," *Corruption and Reform*, 7 (3): 249-61.

This article attacks the corruption as a consequence of African culture argument. Variations of this viewpoint are found in defense of gift-giving, reciprocity, or patron-client relations. The author rejects these arguments and focuses on political leadership as the primary force behind corruption. This article is useful for thinking about the political factors underlying corruption in Africa.

Root, Hilton, 1996, "Corruption in China: Has it Become Systemic?" *Asian Survey*, 36 (August): 741-57.

This article explores how *guanxi* relationships respond to information asymmetries and create incentives for venal commercial deals. It is useful for understanding the role of informal networks and corruption in China.

Rose-Ackerman, Susan, 1997, "Corruption and Development." Paper prepared for the Annual World Bank Conference on Development Economics, Washington, April 30-May 1.
Corruption occurs throughout the world but is of special concern in poor countries. Widespread corruption is a symptom that the state is functioning poorly, and ineffective states can retard and misdirect economic growth. The economic costs and causes of corruption are reflected in the empirical evidence and the theoretical literature. It is useful to distinguish between corruption that is concentrated at the top and centralized corruption involving many payers and recipients. The policy options are explored for developing countries with leaders who are committed to reform. Structural reform is often necessary in such areas as tax and customs collection, regulation of private business and development of state-sponsored infrastructure projects. Furthermore, basic government reform is often required to increase the transparency and accountability of the public sector and to facilitate the organization of independent oversight groups. Most developing countries must also face the difficult task of civil service reform and improvement of enforcement capabilities. The World Bank can assist in such anti-corruption efforts as part of its growing interest in the creation of institutional structures favourable to shared growth.

________, 1996, "Democracy and 'Grand' Corruption," *International Social Science Journal: Corruption In Western Democracies*, 149 (September): 365-80.
This article argues that corruption scandals are a sign that a people differentiate between the public and private realms of finance. Whereas in a democracy, the consumption of public revenues constitutes a corruption scandal, such a distinction is impossible in an autocracy in which the ruler has ownership over the state. The article concludes that democracy may limit corruption as politicians may fear losing office as a consequence of involvement in scandals.

________, 1996, "Corruption in Pakistan: Causes and Cures." Paper prepared for the Pakistan 2000 Report, May.
This paper analyzes the causes of corruption in Pakistan. Its evidence is drawn from survey work that demonstrates the

extent of private sector corruption is quite high in Pakistan. As a consequence, business in Pakistan is expensive and the government is not perceived as being legitimate. The paper concludes that although corruption cannot be eliminated in Pakistan, its incidence may be reduced enough to enable the economy to grow.

Rose-Ackerman, Susan, 1997, "The Political Economy of Corruption." In *Corruption and the Global Economy,* 31-60. Edited by Kimberly Ann Elliot, Washington: The Institute for International Economics.

Corruption is a dysfunctional outcome of the interaction between the public and private. It is a behaviour that often reflects the size of the state. Although corruption cannot feasibly be eliminated because that would be too expensive, it is possible to limit its extent and impact.

_________, 1996, "The Political Economy of Corruption: Causes and Consequences," *Viewpoint,* 74 (April).

This paper states that corruption occurs at the interface of the public and private sectors. It notes that bribes are paid to get government benefits or avoid costs. A resulting lack of efficiency imposes general costs. The article concludes that corruption is an impediment to growth and long-term economic performance.

_________, 1995, "The Political Economy of Corruption," Notes for World Bank Seminar. October 18.

This paper includes notes prepared for a presentation at a Bank conference in 1985.

_________, 1996, "Redesigning the State to Fight Corruption: Transparency, Competition, and Privatization," *Viewpoint,* 75 (April).

The level of corruption is often a function of the overall level of public benefits, the risk to officials who engage in venal behaviour, and the relative power of the two parties in a corrupt transaction. Civil service reforms, increased transparency, and the creation of an ombudsman or other anti-corruption agency assembled in an integrated approach are the most effective way to reduce corruption.

_________, 1996, "When is Corruption Harmful?" Background paper for the World Bank's 1997 World Development Report, *The State in a Changing World,* Washington: The World Bank (August).

An excellent literature review of the major issues on corruption.

Rose-Ackerman, Susan, 1995, "The Political Economy of Corruption," Notes for World Bank Seminar. October 18.

________, 1978, *The Political Economy of Corruption,* New York: Academic Press.

This is a seminal book on the political economy of corruption. Presents the idea that corruption exists at the interface of public and private sectors. The central argument is that corruption cannot be entirely eliminated, the cost of doing so would be excessively high. However, corruption may be reduced to a level that controls its costs and does not harm an economy. It is a statement that has influenced a significant number of subsequent studies on corruption and is therefore critical for anyone who wishes to understand the subject in any depth.

Rose Ackerman, Susan and Andrew, H.W. Stone, 1996, "The Costs of Corruption for Private Business: Evidence from World Bank Surveys." Mimeo, Washington: The World Bank, (July).

One way to discover how corruption affects private business is to survey managers concerning their relations with government. The authors summarize the results of two particularly useful surveys of private enterprise in Ukraine and Pakistan. They find that first, despite some differences in patterns between countries, the smallest firms pay proportionally more in bribes than larger firms, implying that bribery may be both a barrier to entry and a drag on growth of micro- and small enterprise. Second, bribes buy relief from a few basic things: most commonly, relief from potential tax or customs obligations, relief from the burden of complying with regulatory or administrative procedures and relief from uncertainty arising either from changing and unclear rules or from arbitrary, discretionary behaviour by bureaucrats. However, the relationship of bribes to the burden of taxes and regulation is starkly different between countries, suggesting that bribes buy different things in different places. In Pakistan, bribery is associated with a lesser perceived burden of taxes, while in Ukraine, the level of bribes and the burden of taxes are positively related. Third, bribes are higher in the commercial sector than in industry or services. This suggests two things— first, that extraction of rents or the complicitous sharing of the benefits of illegal behaviour is easier or more attractive in trade, and second, that like any "tax", a disproportionate burden on one type of activity will distort investment decisions (unless it is matched or exceeded by disproportionate benefits). Fourth, the variability of reported bribe payments across firms suggests that corruption increases economic uncertainty. Controlling for both size and activity categories of firms, bribe levels vary tremendously within groups of firms. This suggests that however much bribes may ameliorate harsh and unreasonable taxes and regulations, they are by no means uniform. Individual firms may perceive bribes as a way to deal with uncertainty, but the larger picture suggests bribery offers a poor substitute for a reformed, stable set of regulations that levels the playing field for all competitors and affords predictable costs of doing business.

Ruzindana, Alex, 1997a, "Building a National Integrity System in Uganda." In *Good Governance for Sustainable Development,* Final Workshop Proceedings, 13-14 March 1997, 1-5. Edited by Sahr J. Kpundeh and Petter Langseth, Washington: The World Bank.

This essay, written by the Inspector-General of Government responsible for anti-corruption in Uganda, argues that the key to an effective agency is strong leadership, political stability, and peace. It notes that the Ugandan IGG has employed a multi-faceted approach to combat corruption of education, prevention, and investigation and prosecution. The paper concludes that in the future, anti-corruption activities will move forward as a result of strong political leadership.

______, 1997b. "The Importance of Leadership in Fighting Corruption in Uganda." In *Corruption and the Global Economy,* 133-45. Edited by Kimberly Ann Elliott. Washington: Institute for International Economics.

Schleifer, Andrei and Robert W. Vishney, 1993. "Corruption," *The Quarterly Journal of Economics,* 58, 3 (August): 599-617.

The article focuses on the consequences of corruption for resource allocation. It argues that political structures and processes determine that extent of corruption in a given country. Unlike its sibling taxation, corruption is costly and therefore detrimental to a country's economic development. The paper draws important considerations of corruption as an activity that occurs under conditions of secrecy.

Schleifer, Andrei and Robert W. Vishney, 1992, "Pervasive Shortages Under Socialism," *RAND Journal of Economics,* 23, 2 (Summer): 237-46.
This article presents a useful analysis of centrally-planned economies where bureaucrats plan shortages to create opportunities for bribes. Bureaucrat's incentives are to produce less, cause shortages, and demand bribes for under-produced goods. Underpricing and shortages create rents that mangers consume. The implication is that bureaucrats and managers erect barriers through regulations and shortages that create opportunities for corruption.

Sherman, Tom, 1995, "Combating Money Laundering in the Asia Pacific Region," Research Institute for Asia and the Pacific Business Briefing, 27 September.
This paper discusses the increase in money laundering activities internationally with an emphasis on East Asia.

Standing Committee on International Legal Practice. 1996. "Report: Survey of Law on Bribery of Public Officials", Mimeo.

_______, 1996, Resolution of the Council on the International Bar Association." Mimeo.

Svenson, Jakob, 1997, Foreign Aid and Rent-Seeking." Mimeo, Washington: The World Bank (March).
This paper presents a game-theoretic model of public choice to show the relationship between widespread levels of corruption and rent-seeking.

Tanzania, The United Republic of, 1996, Presidential Commission of Inquiry Against Corruption, Report on the Commission on Corruption, Volumes 1 and 2. Dar es Salaam: November.
These two volumes, also know as the Warioba Report, describe the extent of corruption in Tanzania before 1996.

Tanzi, Vito, 1995, "Corruption, Governmental Activities, and Markets," *Finance and Development* (December): 24-26.
An argument that special measures must be taken for situations where existing moral and social codes require that one help family and friends. Civil servants will then be

expected to help their relations at significant cost to the government. Recommends a forced, periodic reassignment of civil servants to prevent favoritism to family members and friends.

Tanzi, Vito, 1996, "Money Laundering and the International Financial System." IMF Working Paper WP/96/55 (May).
This paper examines money laundering from a macro-economic and international perspective to argue that such actions have an impact on the international allocation of resources and the stability of international financial markets. It has implications for work on the globalization of financial markets and the world economy.

Triole, Jean, 1996, "A Theory of Collective Reputations (With Applications to the Persistence of Corruption and to Firm Quality)", *The Review of Economic Studies* (63): 1-22.
The paper posits that collective reputations are composites of individual reputations and may be modelled as such. Four assumptions underlie the essay: (a) the reputations of a group's members determine collective reputations; (b) collective reputations build on imperfect past observations; (c) past practices structure current behaviour; (d) new members mimic a group elders. The paper concludes that individual reputation stems from collective reputations that are based on past behaviours.

______, 1992, "Persistence of Corruption," Institute for Policy Reform Working Paper, 152 (October).
Triole argues that corruption persists over time as a consequence of historical patterns. He avoids the tautology that corruption persists because it was historically present by arguing that corruption ratchets up or down according to opportunities for collusion between bribes and bribe-takers.

Torres, Craing, Loel Millman, and Diane Soils, 1996, "Raul's World: Cash, Connections and Corruption?" *The Wall Street Journal,* August 7.
A *WSJ* story that chronicles the probe into the Raul Salinas and corruption in Mexico.

Tullock, Cordon, 1996, "Corruption Theory and Practice," *Contemporary Economic Policy,* 14 (July): 6-13.
This article presents an article that circumstance in which civil servants do not receive salaries and therefore offer a

fee-for-service arrangement, an economically efficient outcome may result.

United Nations Development Programme, 1997, *Corruption and Good Governance*. Discussion Paper 3. Management Development and Governance Division, New York: UNDP, July.

This study beings from an assumption that corruption is a symptom of something wrong in the management of the state. It presents options to combat corruption. When corruption is endemic, the study argues that piecemeal reforms are probably ineffective. It argues that a multifaceted approach, including the cooperation of the donor community, is essential for an effective anti-corruption program.

Van Rijckeghem and Beatrice Weder, 1997, "Corruption and the Rate of Temptation: Do Low Wages in the Civil Service Cause Corruption?" IMF Working Paper WP/97/73.

This paper develops and tests two efficiency wage models of corruption in the civil service. Under fair wage models, civil service wages are an important determinant of corruption. Under shirking models, the level of wages is of secondary importance, as potential bribes dwarf wage income. The empirical evidence points to a negative relationship between corruption and wages across developing countries.

Vincke, Francois, 1997, "The Business Community's Attitude towards Corruption: Special Focus on Private-to-Private Corruption." Paper prepared for presentation at the 8th International Anti-Corruption Conference, Lima-Peru, September 7-11.

This paper provides an analysis of private-to-private corruption in OECED countries.

Wade, Robert, 1984, "Irrigation Reform in Conditions of Populist Anarchy: An Indian Case," *Journal of Development Economics*, 14 (3): 285-303.

This essay addresses the persistence of corruption in irrigation administrations in India. Often repeated patterns of behaviour allow an effective resistance to reform efforts. The highly-political nature of corruption is demonstrated by the politics of personnel transfers out of a region of those who oppose corruption and the transfer in of sympathetic and venal replacements. The conclusion is that policy reform in how resources are allocated is the best means to decrease corruption.

Wade, Robert, 1982, "The System of Administrative and Political Corruption: Canal Irrigation in South India," *Journal of Development Studies*, 18 (3): 287-328.

Irrigation engineers are able to illicit significant revenues by controlling the distribution of water to users. Corruption is facilitated by personnel transfers for civil servants who work as engineers in irrigation projects. This process is a functional part of Indian politics.

Wallace, J. Clifford, 1998, "Resolving Judicial Corruption while Preserving Judicial Independence: Comparative Perspectives." *California Western International Law Journal*, 28, 2 (Spring): 341-51.

This paper analyzes the issues around combating corruption in the judiciary using evidence from Asia and the United States. It addresses specifically the tension implicit in the requirement that a judiciary be at once independent and accountable. The essay concludes that while accountability is crucial, judicial oversight must remain in the judiciary to avoid political investigations and removal of judges.

Waterbury, John, 1976, "Corruption, Political Stability and Development: Comparative Evidence from Egypt and Morocco," *Government and Opposition*, 11, 4 (Autumn): 426-43.

The article posits that corruption may contribute to economic, social and political stability according to whether it is endemic, planned, or developmental. It might be useful for managers working in countries with extremely high levels of corruption.

Wedeman, Andrew, 1997, "Looters, Rent-Scrapers, and Dividend-Collectors: The Political Economy of Corruption in Zaire, South Korea, and the Philippines," *The Journal of Developing Areas*, 31, 4 (Summer): 457-78.

This article tries to explain different patterns of corruption, that the author identifies as looting, scraping, and rent-collection, and development. The article is useful for thinking about the types of corruption that might be encountered in different circumstances.

Weinberg, Mark, 1989, "Prevention *versus* Prosecution in Dealing with Corruption," The Fourth International Anti-Corruption Conference Report, 110-14. [Place of Publication?]

Address by the OC Commonwealth Director of Public Prosecutions, Australia.

Werlin, Herbert H., 1996, "Treating Political illness: Using a Proactive Approach." Paper submitted to the World Bank World Development Report, Mimeo.

The paper argues that improving governance is critical to reducing corruption.

Wignjowijoto, Hartojo, 1996, "Floods and Corruption." Mimeo, Asian Pacific Economic Consultancy, Indonesia, February 11.

This paper argues that corruption has contributed to inefficient land use planning by the government of Indonesia with a result that floods have grown more and more common for at risk areas.

Index

Abedin, M. Zainul 190
Administrative Reforms 95
Agenda for Anti-Evasion and Anti-Corruption Strategy 103
Age of Reason 19
Alternative Part of Development 80
Angul-Talcher Area of Orissa 118
Announcing Anti-Corruption Campaign 22
Arthasastra 13
Arthasya Purusho Daaso 137
Asian Development Outlook, 2000 197

Bardhan 13
Basic Problem 221
Basu, Kaushik 46
Bension, L. 35
Bhumi Sena 79
Blair, Tony 58
Brahmarshi Sena 79
Bribe Payers Index for Selected Countries 91
Brief Historical Note 157
Business International Survey 14
Busse, Laurence 86

Causes and Consequences of Corruption 25
Causes of Corruption 91, 214
Central Vigilance Commission 21
Challenge to Development:
  Effect on Foreign Investment 76
  Investment Preferences in India 76
Choudhury, Amita Kumari 107
Choudhury, Faruq 196
Combating Corruption 44
Competitive-bribery State 26
Control of Corruption 30
Cooley, C.H. 162
Corruption and Development, Bangladesh Perspective 190
Corruption and Foreign Investment 27
Corruption Perceptions Index 40
Counter Measures 147
Crime against Women 129
  Crime and Per Capita Income 129
  Crime and Unemployment 130
  Crime Controlling Factors 130
  Crime and Police Infrastructure 130
  Crime and Public Expenditure 132
  Crime and Punishment 132-33
Crime and Corruption, Obstacles to Development 74
Crime and Punishment in Orissa 126
Crime, Corruption and Development in Indian Economy 97
Crime in India:
  Reported Crimes 74
Crime in Relation to Deprivation Indices 67
Crime Promoting Factors 128
Current Trends in Economic Crimes 140
  Loopholes in Economic Policies 140
  Corporate Crimes 142
  Emerging Trends 145

Daily Inqilab 195
Daly 107

Decentralisation of Power and Public Cooperation 96
Democratic Republican Party 20
Dennison 63
Destabilising Political Situation 216
Detection and Disposal of Forest Offences in Orissa, 1980-81 to 1989-90 117
Development Experiences 50
Differences in Levels of Corruption 14
Direct Taxes Enquiry Committee 54

East-India Company 84
Economic Analysis of Crime and Punishment 124
Economic and Traditional Offences in Mumbai 143
Economic Crime 137
Economic Implications of Environmental Crimes 107
Economic Reforms 95, 102
Economic Theory of Crime and Punishment . 108
Economics of Corruption and Development 24
Effects of Corruption 16
Electronic Funds Transfer 146
Environmental Crimes 113
Environmental Statutes 110
Evolution of Corruption 84
Expenditure on Crime Control Activities in Orissa 133
Extent of Corruption in different Countries 40

Factories Act, 1948 111
Feature of Economic Crimes 138
Financial Action Task Force 148
Foreign Corruption Practices Act 21
First Information Report 192

Gandhi, Ram 39
Gang War 175
Garibi Hatao 53
Gazanavi, Mahmud 54
Gender-Related Development Index 10
Genesis of Crime and Corruption and their Impact on Development 212
German Rocket Corporation 15
Ghosh, N.C. 220
Ghosh, Santanu 166
Globalisation of Economy and Conflicts in South Asia 200
Government Resolution, 1950 50
Gram Panchayat 79
Green Revolution 5
Gross Domestic Product 78
Growth of Police Infrastructure in Orissa 131
Growth Rate of Crime under Indian Penal Code 69

Historical Perspective 100
How to Reduce Corruption? 217
  Effective Enforcement of Law 217
  Awareness about Benefits and Costs under Public Servants Control 218
  Minimizing Opportunities for Corrupt Practices 218
Human Development Index for Indian States, 1995 10, 69
Human Development Report, 2000 10

IMF Survey, 1997 17
Impact of Crime and Corruption on Development 215
Impact of Development 196
Impact on National Economy 139
  Magnitude 139
  Enforcement Agencies in India 140
Import Export Act, 1947 141
Incidence of Crime in Orissa, 1983-1996 128
Indian Penal Code 64
Indian Tax Reform 54
Indian World War 1
Industrialisation and Environment in Orissa 111
Industrialisation, Environmental Pollution, Crime and Corruption 220

Interface of Corruption and Development in the Third World 82
Inter-Linkages between Tax Evasion and Corruption 99
Inter-state and Intra-state Armed Conflict, 1988-89 201
Investment Preferences of Big Business Times 77
Italian School of Criminology 108

Jain, Anil Kumar 98
Jenkins 109
Judicial Deterrence to Crime in Orissa 134
Juvenile Delinquency Cases in India 71

Kaur, Harvinder 63
Kleptocracy 25
Kiltgaard, Robert 98
Kumar, Pramod 63, 200
Kuper, A. 35
Kuper, J. 35

Lakshmanasamy, T. 24
Land Valuation Surrounding a Thermal Power Station:
  Bandel Thermal Power Station 223
  Valuation of Agricultural Land 223
  Valuation of the Area Used for Fisheries 24
  Foundation Design and Construction 225
Level of Corruption and Economic Growth in Selected Countries 89
Level of Corruption in Selected Countries of Asia 87
Levels of Crime Cross-Classified 68
Levi, Margarate 52
Lewis, C.S. 139
Lorik Sena 79

Mafia-Dominated State 26
Malapur, S.P. 212
Mansoor Mamoon 195
Mauro, Paoplo 38
Meaning of the Corruption 82
Measurement of Corruption 29
  Business International Index 29
  International Country Risk Guide Index 29
  Global Competitive Report Index 29
  Transparency International Index 29
Measures to Control Corruption 93
Merton, K. 221
Micro-Theoretic Issues in Generation of Crime 166
Mitra, Sandip 155
Model 64
Mohite, Gulab 212
Motor Vehicles Act, 1988 111
Mukherjee, Debes 35

Narasimha Rao Period, 1990 54
Narasimha Rao, P.V. 93
National Coal Development Corporation 158
National Thermal Power Corporation 113
Nature and Intensity of Corruption 192
  Police 192
  Judiciary 192
  Social Sector 193
  Municipal Services 193
  System Loss 194
  Trade Licence 194
  News Media 194
  Some other Reports on Corruption 194
Nehru, Jawaharlal 101
N.N. Vohra Committee 42
No Harassment Tax 101
Number of Armed Conflicts by Region, 1989-98 202

Oberg, Jan 207
Oliver Williamson 159
Orissa State Pollution Control Board 115

Panigrahy, S.K. 124

Patro, B. 124
Perraze, Carlos Andress 93
Pigou 110
Pillai, S. Iyyam 12
Population Cases in Orissa, 1986-87 to 1996-97 116
Population-Police Force Ratio 75
Post-Cold War 2
Pradhan, N.B. 124
Prakash, S. 63
Public Interest Litigation 60
Public Works Department 39

Ranveer Sena 79
Reforms in Police-Judicial System 95
Relationship among Crime, Corruption and Development 38
Rose-Ackerman 25

Sahoo, Nirmal Chandra 107
Schelling 156
Second Five Year Plan 51
Securities and Exchange Board of India 144
Sen, Amartya 36
Sen, Dipankar 155
Shah, Ghanashyam 36
Sharma, S.C. 82
Shastri, Lal Bahadur 101
Shavell 126
Sick Industrial Company Act 141
Singh, Binay Kumar 82
Singh, Inderjeet 63
Singh, R. 63
Singh, Satya Pal 137
Singh, Shyam Sunder 82
Sino-Indian Conflict 5
Social Physics 66
Socio-Economic and Political Dimensions of Corruption 12
Socio-Economic Aspects of Organised Crime 155
Socio-Economic Dynamics of Crime in India 63
South Asian Human Development Report 99
Special and Local Law 9
State-wise Distribution of Investment, 1998-99 78
Strategies for Coping with Environmental Crime 120
Structure of Incidence of Crime under Woman Penal Code 67
Summary Assessment Scheme 103
Suvidha Shulka 102
Swedish Economist 59

Talcher Thermal Power Station 112
Tax Evasion and Corruption 98
Tax Reforms Committee 102
Theobald 13
Theoretical Framework 124
Transparency International 40
Trend and Level of Corruption 15
Tsebelis 125

U.N. Conference on Human Environment, 1972 111
United Nations Drugs Control Programmes 146

Vision of Development 48
Vittal, N. 82
Vohra, N.N. 1, 212
Voluntary Disclosure of Income Scheme 141

What can be done in Near Future? 197
Why Corruption is More Apparent in UDCs? 15
Williams, Glanville 108
World Bank Study on Corruption, 1998 35
World Development Report, 1997 43

Zemin, Jiang 58
Zero Economic Growth 222